THE REAGAN REGULATORY STRATEGY

*A Conference Sponsored by
the Changing Domestic Priorities Project
of The Urban Institute*

THE REAGAN REGULATORY STRATEGY

An Assessment

Edited by
George C. Eads and Michael Fix

The Changing Domestic Priorities Series
John L. Palmer and Isabel V. Sawhill, Editors

THE URBAN INSTITUTE PRESS · WASHINGTON, D.C.

Copyright © 1984
THE URBAN INSTITUTE
2100 M Street, N.W.
Washington, D.C. 20037

Library of Congress Cataloging in Publication Data
Main entry under title:

The Reagan regulatory strategy.

(The Changing domestic priorities series)
 1. Trade regulation—United States—Addresses, essays, lectures. 2. United States—Politics and government—1981–   —Addresses, essays, lectures. I. Eads, George C., 1942–   . II. Fix, Michael. III. Series.
HD3616.U47R135   1984   338.973   84-20923
ISBN 0-87766-369-6 (cloth)
ISBN 9-87766-346-7 (pbk.)

Printed in the United States of America.

BOARD OF TRUSTEES
Carla A. Hills
 Chairman
Katharine Graham
 Vice Chairman
William Gorham
 President
Warren E. Buffett
John J. Byrne
Joseph A. Califano, Jr.
William T. Coleman, Jr.
John M. Deutch
Anthony Downs
Joel L. Fleishman
Philip M. Hawley
Aileen C. Hernandez
Ray L. Hunt
Robert S. McNamara
David O. Maxwell
Lois D. Rice
Elliot L. Richardson
George H. Weyerhaeuser
Mortimer B. Zuckerman

LIFE TRUSTEES
John H. Filer
Eugene G. Fubini
Vernon E. Jordan, Jr.
Edward H. Levi
Bayless A. Manning
Stanley Marcus
Arjay Miller
J. Irwin Miller
Franklin D. Murphy
Herbert E. Scarf
Charles L. Schultze
William W. Scranton
Cyrus R. Vance
James Vorenberg

 THE URBAN INSTITUTE is a nonprofit policy research and educational organization established in Washington, D.C., in 1968. Its staff investigates the social and economic problems confronting the nation and government policies and programs designed to alleviate such problems. The Institute disseminates significant findings of its research through the publications program of its Press. The Institute has two goals for work in each of its research areas: to help shape thinking about societal problems and efforts to solve them, and to improve government decisions and performance by providing better information and analytic tools.

Through work that ranges from broad conceptual studies to administrative and technical assistance, Institute researchers contribute to the stock of knowledge available to public officials and to private individuals and groups concerned with formulating and implementing more efficient and effective government policy.

Conclusions or opinions expressed in Institute publications are those of the authors and do not necessarily reflect the views of other staff members, officers or trustees of the Institute, advisory groups, or any organizations which provide financial support to the Institute.

THE CHANGING DOMESTIC PRIORITIES SERIES

Listed below are the titles available, or soon to be available, in the Changing Domestic Priorities Series

Books

THE REAGAN EXPERIMENT
   An Examination of Economic and Social Policies under the Reagan Administration (1982), John L. Palmer and Isabel V. Sawhill, editors
HOUSING ASSISTANCE FOR OLDER AMERICANS
   The Reagan Prescription (1982), James P. Zais, Raymond J. Struyk, and Thomas Thibodeau
MEDICAID IN THE REAGAN ERA
   Federal Policy and State Choices (1982), Randall R. Bovbjerg and John Holahan
WAGE INFLATION
   Prospects for Deceleration (1983), Wayne Vroman
OLDER AMERICANS IN THE REAGAN ERA
   Impacts of Federal Policy Changes (1983), James R. Storey
FEDERAL HOUSING POLICY AT PRESIDENT REAGAN'S MIDTERM
   (1983), Raymond J. Struyk, Neil Mayer, and John A. Tuccillo
STATE AND LOCAL FISCAL RELATIONS IN THE EARLY 1980s
   (1983), Steven D. Gold
THE DEFICIT DILEMMA
   Budget Policy in the Reagan Era (1983), Gregory B. Mills and John L. Palmer
HOUSING FINANCE
   A Changing System in the Reagan Era (1983), John A. Tuccillo with John L. Goodman, Jr.
PUBLIC OPINION DURING THE REAGAN ADMINISTRATION
   National Issues, Private Concerns (1983), John L. Goodman, Jr.
RELIEF OR REFORM?
   Reagan's Regulatory Dilemma (1984), George C. Eads and Michael Fix
THE REAGAN RECORD
   An Assessment of America's Changing Domestic Priorities (1984), John L. Palmer and Isabel V. Sawhill, editors (Ballinger Publishing Co.)

Conference Volumes

THE SOCIAL CONTRACT REVISITED
Aims and Outcomes of President Reagan's Social Welfare Policy (1984), edited by D. Lee Bawden
NATURAL RESOURCES AND THE ENVIRONMENT
The Reagan Approach (1984), edited by Paul R. Portney
FEDERAL BUDGET POLICY IN THE 1980s (1984), edited by Gregory B. Mills and John L. Palmer
THE REAGAN REGULATORY STRATEGY
An Assessment (1984), edited by George C. Eads and Michael Fix
THE LEGACY OF REAGANOMICS
Prospects for Long-term Growth (1984), edited by Charles R. Hulten and Isabel V. Sawhill
THE REAGAN PRESIDENCY AND THE GOVERNING OF AMERICA (1984), edited by Lester M. Salamon and Michael S. Lund

Advisory Board of the Changing Domestic Priorities Project

Martin Anderson, Hoover Institution
John Brademas, President, New York University
Hale Champion, Executive Dean, John F. Kennedy School of Government, Harvard University
Nathan Glazer, Professor of Education and Sociology, Harvard University ·
Aileen C. Hernandez, Partner, Aileen C. Hernandez Associates
Carla A. Hills, Partner, Latham, Watkins & Hills (Chairman)
Juanita M. Kreps, Economist and former Secretary of Commerce
Thomas G. Moore, Hoover Institution
Richard F. Muth, Professor of Economics, Stanford University
Eleanor Holmes Norton, Professor of Law, Georgetown University
Paul H. O'Neill, Senior Vice President—Planning and Finance, International Paper Company
Peter G. Peterson, Chairman, Peterson, Jacobs and Company
Henry B. Schacht, Chairman, Cummins Engine Co., Inc.
Robert M. Solow, Professor of Economics, Massachusetts Institute of Technology
Herbert Stein, Professor of Economics, University of Virginia; Senior Fellow, American Enterprise Institute
Arnold Weber, President, University of Colorado
Daniel Yankelovich, Chairman, Yankelovich, Skelly and White, Inc.

CONTENTS

Foreword — xi

Introduction / *George C. Eads and Michael Fix* — 1

REGULATORY REFORM UNDER THE REAGAN ADMINISTRATION / *Murray L. Weidenbaum* — 15

   Comments / *Robert W. Crandall* — 42
                Jerry J. Jasinowski — 45

THE REAGAN ADMINISTRATION'S REGULATORY RELIEF EFFORT: A MID-TERM ASSESSMENT / *Gregory B. Christainsen and Robert H. Haveman* — 49

   Comments / *Martin Neil Baily* — 81
                Isabel V. Sawhill — 84

REGULATORY RELIEF AND THE AUTOMOBILE INDUSTRY / *Robert A. Leone* — 87

   Comments / *E. Woodrow Eckard* — 106

FEDERALISM AND REGULATION / *Jerry L. Mashaw and Susan Rose-Ackerman* — 111

   Comments / *David Harrison, Jr.* — 146

TRANSFERRING REGULATORY AUTHORITY TO THE
STATES / *Michael Fix* — 153

    Comments / *James K. Hambright* — 180
    Jeffrey H. Joseph — 184

CONGRESS AND SOCIAL REGULATION IN THE REAGAN
ERA / *Christopher H. Foreman, Jr.* — 187

    Comments / *Patrick McLain* — 215
    Paul J. Quirk — 218

About the Authors — 223

Participants in the Conference — 227

FOREWORD

In late 1981 The Urban Institute initiated a three-year project—Changing Domestic Priorities—to examine the shifts in domestic policy occurring under the Reagan administration and the consequences of those shifts. This volume, a product of the Changing Domestic Priorities project, is one of six collections of analyses by leading scholars on subjects of considerable national interest in the 1980s. The other five volumes are focused upon budget policy, economic growth, governance, natural resources and the environment, and social welfare.

This volume is based on a set of papers presented at a conference assessing the Reagan administration's regulatory relief campaign. The conference—one of six sponsored by the project—was held at The Urban Institute in June 1983. At the time of the conference, the administration's regulatory effort appeared in disarray: Political controversy over the Environmental Protection Agency's and the Interior Department's policies had been in the nation's headlines through the early spring. Court challenges to regulatory action—many of them successful—were on the rise; little effort had been made to revise the key regulatory statutes, and, given the political climate of the day, any reform of these laws seemed out of reach.

It must be recalled that upon entering office the Reagan administration assigned regulatory relief a more prominent place in its economic program than had any other recent administration—a place rivaling that of tax, budgetary, and monetary policy. What had gone wrong and why? Looking beyond the days' headlines, what in fact had been accomplished? What were the prospects for future regulatory change and for the institutions that would shape and be shaped by it? These were some of the questions addressed at the conference.

The volume contains a number of important contributions to the regulatory policy literature. One of the book's most provocative essays is Murray Weidenbaum's candid account of the origin of the Reagan regulatory strategy, the intentions of its architects, its results, and immediate prospects.

One of the most forceful arguments behind regulatory relief was its importance in restoring productivity and economic growth. Gregory Christainsen and Robert Haveman have contributed an important paper that estimates the Reagan program's effects on productivity. The authors conclude that, even when administration savings estimates are taken largely at face value, regulatory relief generated only a marginal (.2 percentage point per year) improvement, which unless matched by equivalent additional cost savings, would dissipate within a few years.

Following Christainsen and Haveman's macroeconomic analysis, Robert Leone offers a "micro" assessment of regulatory relief's impact on the auto industry—one of the principal intended beneficiaries of administration-backed rule changes. Leone finds that massive cost cutting among the auto makers—not regulatory change—has been responsible for the surge in industry profits. Moreover, he notes that the administrative (vs. legislative) nature of the "auto package" left it vulnerable to the legal reversals it later suffered.

The two papers that follow analyze the administration's transfer of regulatory authority to the states. This transfer, which has been accomplished by both formal and informal delegations of federal authority, may eventually be judged as one of the most significant changes in regulatory policy effected by the administration. The paper by Michael Fix surveys what the administration did and did not do in this area and the variety of mechanisms available for devolving authority to the states. Jerry Mashaw and Susan Rose-Ackerman's paper provides a framework thinking about how regulatory authority should be assigned to different levels of government, and hence the criteria for evaluating the Reagan strategy. The authors conclude that the administration's ideological commitment to devolution may in the end fail to serve the goals of efficiency, democratic representation, and even of regulatory relief.

The book concludes with Christopher Foreman's essay examining the changing role of Congress in regulatory oversight, Congress's role in restraining and redirecting the Reagan regulatory relief effort, and Congress's resistance to enacting the Reagan program into law.

Besides the papers presented at the conference, the formal comments of each paper's discussants have been included in the text. The comments provide an interesting counterpoint to the positions taken by the papers and offer further insight into the character and the success of the Reagan program.

Foreword

The complete results of The Urban Institute's analysis of the Reagan administration's regulatory policies are contained in this book and in a companion volume written by George Eads and Michael Fix, *Relief or Reform? Reagan's Regulatory Dilemma*. In *Relief or Reform?*, Eads and Fix describe the principal strategies of the Reagan regulatory program, set it in historical context, and assess its success along economic and political lines.

The support of these efforts by the Ford Foundation and the John D. and Catherine T. MacArthur Foundation is gratefully acknowledged.

John L. Palmer
Isabel V. Sawhill
Editors
Changing Domestic Priorities Series

INTRODUCTION

George C. Eads and Michael Fix

In the spring and summer of 1983, the Reagan administration's regulatory relief program was in turmoil. Begun in early 1981 with great fanfare and high expectations, the program had, by its second year, fallen on hard times. Popular support had waned, Congress was growing increasingly hostile, and the courts had struck down a number of the administration's most publicized actions. These and other developments triggered a wave of resignations and removals among some of the president's most visible champions of regulatory relief.

In March 1983, the long-running drama involving the Environmental Protection Agency (EPA) and Congress came to a climax when the agency's administrator, Anne Burford, was forced to resign along with all but one of the twenty-one members of her management team. Rita Lavelle, the assistant administrator for toxic waste programs, was later convicted of perjury in connection with statements she had made to Congress concerning her knowledge of investigations involving her former employer, Aerojet General.

The administration's problems with Congress were not confined to EPA. Congress was also growing increasingly unhappy with the efforts of the Office of Management and Budget (OMB) to exert more control over the rule-making activities of executive branch agencies. OMB's new and expanded responsibilities had been set out in an executive order (12291) issued by President Reagan early in his administration. Congressional displeasure had initially taken the form of hostile oversight hearings, generally before Democratic-controlled committees or subcommittees of the House of Representatives. But as the outcry over the regulatory relief program grew louder, legislation had been introduced that would have severely limited OMB's ability to conduct "off the record" negotiations with agencies or to influence the content of final regulations.

Congressional, media, and popular resistance eventually began to influence agency policy. Internal debates over the appropriate direction of regulatory relief began to be reported. For example, regulations proposed by the Occupational Safety and Health Administration (OSHA), an agency that had frequently been the target of unfriendly congressional hearings, came under fire from OMB, which found that several of OSHA's proposed rules imposed excessive costs on industry. OMB's objections, however, were overridden in a number of closely watched policy showdowns. Outside observers speculated that OSHA's director, Thorne Auchter, wanted to avoid the political fate suffered by his counterpart at EPA, Anne Burford.

Administration worries over the viability of regulatory relief were not limited to the political arena. The courts—most notably the Supreme Court—were busy reviewing and, in some cases invalidating, heavily publicized administration regulatory actions. Successful legal challenges forced reversals of administration activities in areas ranging from auto safety to teenage birth control.

By the spring of 1983 the administration appeared to be growing increasingly aware of the political damage that a loosely managed and ideologically driven regulatory relief effort could cause. In April 1983, following the housecleaning at EPA, the controversial head of the National Highway Traffic Safety Administration (NHTSA), Raymond Peck, was removed by the Department of Transportation's newly appointed administrator, Elizabeth Dole. Peck had "engineered" the failed effort to roll back a number of auto safety regulations and his removal seemed to signal official disapproval of his confrontational style, if not a softening of administration opposition to the rules themselves.

Late in the summer of 1983, the most politically controversial regulatory appointee of all, Secretary of the Interior James Watt, resigned under pressure after making an imprudent off-the-cuff comment concerning the composition of a commission appointed to examine his coal-leasing policies. The comment focused attention on the probability that he and some of his policies could be significant political liabilities in the upcoming 1984 presidential election.

The regulatory relief program's shift from the status of a political asset to that of a political liability is perhaps best illustrated by the decision in August 1983 to terminate the showpiece of the administration's effort to increase White House control over regulation, the President's Task Force on Regulatory Relief. On August 11 this body, chaired by Vice President Bush, "declared victory" and went out of existence, claiming that its job was essentially finished. To support this claim, the task force issued a "going out of business" report in which it claimed credit for generating $150 billion in already realized and prospective regulatory cost "savings"—all without any reduction in regulatory benefits. Outside the administration, however, the credibility of this claim was generally questioned.

The conference whose papers are published in this volume was held at the height of this period of turmoil. The papers themselves have been revised since the conference (as have the discussants' remarks) to reflect events that took place subsequently. Yet they still reflect the pressures that the regulatory relief program was undergoing during that time. As Murray Weidenbaum notes in the introduction to his paper, by the early summer of 1983, enough time had passed to permit at least a preliminary assessment of the Reagan program. The papers in this volume provide both an assessment and guidance for the future to regulatory policymakers.

In choosing the topics on which to commission papers, we were guided by our ongoing research in which we were seeking to document the impact of the Reagan regulatory relief program on the economy—research that resulted in the publication of *Relief or Reform? Reagan's Regulatory Dilemma*. As our research progressed, it became apparent that it would be desirable to explore certain issues in considerably greater depth than we believed ourselves capable of doing alone. The reader of both this volume and our book will see that we made use of the conference results in our work, but it will also be clear that in many instances the papers in this volume go well beyond the boundaries of our own book. Thus the two are best seen as complementary.

Overview

This volume has been organized in three parts. The first broadly surveys and assesses the regulatory relief program as a whole. The second assesses the early economic impact of Ronald Reagan's regulatory relief efforts. The final part discusses shifts in regulatory roles instituted by and occurring in reaction to the Reagan administration's efforts.

A Survey of Regulatory Reform under the Reagan Administration

It was crucial to the kind of discussion we hoped to provoke at the conference (as well as to our own understanding) to know what the officials who had launched and guided the Reagan regulatory relief effort during its early days had expected from it. To provide this necessary perspective and to launch the conference, we could think of no one more appropriate than Murray Weidenbaum, who, when the program was inaugurated, had been chairman of President Reagan's Council of Economic Advisers. As Weidenbaum notes in his broad-ranging paper, he also was, to some degree, the intellectual "father" of the regulatory relief effort, having served as chairman of the task force formed in late 1980 to advise president-elect Reagan on how regulation should be handled by his administration. Weidenbaum's account of what advice was and was not taken, as well as what the program's successes and failures were, is fascinating.

Weidenbaum discusses the Reagan administration's regulatory relief program under four general topics: the program's changes in the organizational structure of regulatory oversight and their consequences; its record in achieving statutory reform and the reasons for it; the operation and consequences of the procedural changes imposed by executive order 12291; and the impact that the program may have had on the overall economic burden imposed by regulation.

As a preface, Weidenbaum outlines the report presented to Ronald Reagan in late 1980 by the transition-period task force Weidenbaum chaired. (This task force should not be confused with the President's Task Force on Regulatory Relief organized in February 1981.) Weidenbaum stresses that regulatory relief as envisaged by the transition task force was not a "Neanderthal plea" to ignore genuine social problems but rather a conscientious effort to better achieve regulatory goals and to reduce regulatory burdens. The task force's report emphasized the importance of appointing to agencies "people who are sympathetic with the important social objectives to be achieved." It also cautioned against relying excessively on administrative deregulation, urging instead the need to lay the groundwork for a major set of legislative initiatives designed to change the statutory basis for social regulation. These initiatives would have included legislation "requiring each agency to demonstrate at least a reasonable relationship between the costs imposed and the benefits produced before a new rule was issued."

The Reagan program as it was actually organized and implemented differed significantly from the recommendations made by Weidenbaum's task force. Weidenbaum clearly attributes some of the difficulties the program later suffered to these differences. Consider, for example, how the program was organized. Reagan swept away the plethora of organizations that Carter had created to "coordinate" regulation—the Regulatory Analysis Review Group, the Regulatory Council, and the Council on Wage and Price Stability. Instead, primary authority for regulatory review was lodged in OMB, with the President's Task Force on Regulatory Relief, chaired by the vice president, serving as a "court of regulatory appeals." Weidenbaum gives the administration high marks for moving rapidly and decisively to implement this reorganization, but he also notes certain disadvantages that resulted from it.

Although this reorganization is generally viewed as a centralization of White House authority over regulation, Weidenbaum considers the result to have been a reduction in the role played by senior White House officials—such as the chairman of the Council of Economic Advisers—in comparison with their role under the Ford and Carter administrations. Whatever the intention of the reorganization, in practice the White House oversight process became primarily reactive. Neither OMB nor the task force proved to have any real power to launch or sustain major regulatory initiatives. Weidenbaum also suggests that the eclipsing of the role of senior White House staff contributed to increased media attention given to agency heads such as Watt and Burford and to their identification in the public's mind with the administration's goals of regulatory relief.

Given the significance that Weidenbaum's transition task force attached to achieving legislative changes in the major regulatory statutes, it is not surprising that Weidenbaum characterizes the administration's legislative record in this area as "disappointing." He does note with satisfaction that, for the first time in many years, no new statutes expanding regulation were enacted. He also applauds legislative deregulation of intercity bus lines and financial institutions. But clearly he wishes more had been accomplished.

Weidenbaum attributes part of this general lack of accomplishment to a lack of leadership on both ends of Pennsylvania Avenue. But he believes the problem goes deeper: "The necessary foundation has not been laid in terms of public understanding and support for reducing the burdens of regulation."

In describing the procedural changes wrought by the Reagan administration, Weidenbaum first notes the role that executive order 12291 gave OMB as a regulatory gatekeeper. Because virtually all regulatory proposals pass OMB muster, it is hard to know how effective the OMB review process has been. He does cite—without comment on their quality—the estimates, published by the administration in August 1983, of cost and paperwork savings due to the operation of this process. Weidenbaum also surveys the administration's actions in granting trade relief to numerous domestic industries and cites two significant administrative actions—one by the Department of Labor and one by the Securities and Exchange Commission—that resulted in significantly increased regulatory burdens.

In discussing the difficulty he has in evaluating the economic impact of the regulatory relief program, Weidenbaum says that he would be surprised if the "multiplier" he developed years ago in an attempt to relate private regulatory costs and regulatory costs that appeared in the federal budget were today anything like what it was when it was first developed. (It was through the use of this multiplier that his famous estimate of regulation's $100 billion cost was derived.) Hence he cautions against attempting to infer reductions in regulatory burden from reductions in the budgets of regulatory agencies. However, he suggests that a properly updated multiplier might be so used.

Although Weidenbaum clearly supports many of the budget reductions at regulatory agencies, he notes that they might in certain cases be counterproductive. For example, excessive cuts in regulatory staffs unaccompanied by cuts in their statutory duties could actually increase the costs of regulation by increasing the time required for the issuing of environmental permits.

Weidenbaum concludes with a plea for patience on the part of people who expected the regulatory system to wither away once President Reagan assumed office, and with an attack on people (principally former regulators from past administrations) who have, in his view, unfairly whipped up public sentiment against regulatory reform of virtually any sort through charges that significant regulatory protections are being dismantled. He renews his call for a significant legislative program to eliminate some of social regulation's more unrealistic goals, but he does not underestimate the difficulty of achieving such a program, given the current climate of mistrust: As he states, "We will be lucky if, in January 1985, we will be back to where we were in January 1981 in terms of the public's attitude toward statutory reform and social regulation."

Economic Impacts

Estimating the Program's Impact on Productivity

The administration's primary rationale for the regulatory relief program was the favorable impact it would have on the performance of the economy. To assess the program's success in this regard, we commissioned Gregory Christainsen and Robert Haveman, who had previously investigated this subject, to attempt to measure the extent to which the program had improved measured productivity. Both we and they were aware of the formidable difficulties involved in such an effort, but their paper provides an important perspective on this critical question.

Christainsen and Haveman use two separate methodologies to estimate the impact on measured productivity of the volume of regulatory relief provided by the first eighteen months of the operation of the Reagan regulatory relief program. Their paper begins with a brief review of the theory of "supply side'' economics—the theory that inflation could be rapidly and painlessly licked by relying on policies designed to reduce business costs, stimulate investment, and improve productivity. They describe the role that a program of significant regulatory relief might play in such a process.

Christainsen and Haveman then review a number of previous studies (including several of their own) that have attempted to measure the relationship between the growth of regulation over the past decade or so and the decline in productivity. They conclude that as much as 15 to 20 percent of the slowdown could be attributed to regulation in general, with perhaps half of that attributable to environmental regulation. This estimate provides a baseline against which to evaluate the effects of the Reagan program.

The first methodology Christainsen and Haveman employed is the familiar "growth accounting" approach popularized by Denison. This approach translates reductions in regulatory expenditures by government and business into dollar-for-dollar savings in business costs. Accepting (but certainly not endorsing) the numbers published in the August 1982 report of the President's Task Force on Regulatory Relief, Christainsen and Haveman estimate that the Reagan program may have reduced business costs by between $7.2 and $9.9 billion annually during 1981 and 1982. Taking total business costs in 1980 as a baseline, this reduction translates into an average annual increase in productivity due to reduced regulatory burdens of between 0.15 and 0.29 percentage point. The authors note, however, that this represents a "one-shot" savings. If annual savings of similar magnitude were not to be realized in future years, this boost to productivity would dissipate over time.

The second methodology employed by Christainsen and Haveman is multiple regression. The authors develop an equation in which the dependent variable is labor productivity and the independent variables are various productivity-related factors, one of which is a measure of regulatory intensity. According to their estimates, a stable or decreasing level of regulatory intensity during 1980–1981 raised the growth rate of labor productivity by between 0 and 0.15 percentage point between 1981 and 1982.

The authors stress the need to interpret these results with great caution. They are especially aware that the numbers by which their growth accounting estimates were generated are controversial. They also are aware that the variable they used to measure regulatory intensity in their econometric model is crude. Despite these cautions, they conclude that the Reagan administration's "deregulatory activity" has increased the growth rate of measured productivity by about 0.1 percentage point above what it would have been had the 1980 level of regulatory intensity continued.

The Impact of Regulatory Relief on the Auto Industry

The regulatory relief program was not intended merely to improve the performance of the economy as a whole; it was "targeted" to give special relief to certain major industries, particularly the automobile industry. To explore how the program has influenced that industry's costs, its general economic health, and its approach to doing business (its "strategic focus"), we commissioned a paper by Robert Leone.

Leone begins by reviewing the auto industry's role in regulatory relief and its importance to the overall success of the administration's economic "game plan." Not only did the industry provide a convenient "target" for regulatory relief, but concentration on regulatory relief permitted the administration to be "doing something" to help this critical domestic industry while avoiding other economically or politically distasteful options such as overt trade restrictions, targeted tax benefits, or an explicit "automobile industrial policy" of the kind that had been called for by President Carter's outgoing secretary of transportation, Neil Goldschmidt.

Thus in April 1982 the Reagan administration, with considerable fanfare, announced its auto package—a program of thirty-four specific regulatory actions designed to reduce auto industry regulatory costs by $1.4 billion per year. As part of this announcement, the administration forecast what its economic program—of which regulatory relief was but one part—would do to aid auto industry sales, employment, and net operating income. Leone compares these forecasts with what actually occurred. The sales and employment goals did not come close to being met. Largely because of the depressed state of the economy, auto sales remained low through early 1983—long after the administration had forecast their strong recovery. Yet profits increased substantially. Why? The answer lies in the employment figures. Through massive cost cutting, automakers managed to significantly lower their break-even point, allowing them to produce cars with substantially decreased labor.

What role did regulatory relief play in all this? Some, to be sure, but Leone believes that its contribution was modest. Another contributing factor (although Leone does not attempt to quantify its impact) was the "voluntary" import restraints imposed by the Japanese.

What about the longer term? Did the Reagan regulatory relief program mark a watershed in the business-government relationship, enabling automakers and similar industrial managers to focus less on their dealings with government and more on the difficulties of designing and producing competitive products? Leone says no. As some members of the Reagan administration had foreseen, the program's almost total reliance on administrative actions, plus the incompetence of the administrators, left the "auto package" vulnerable to judicial reversal. Several major elements—the air-bag rescission being the most important example—have in fact been reversed. The administration's efforts to defuse public concern about its regulatory relief initiatives have caused the "regulatory pendulum" to begin to swing backward, with agencies such as the National Highway Traffic Safety Administration once again showing their "tough" side. Thus, the attention that the industry must devote to regulatory matters has not significantly diminished; dealing with regulation is still an important part of the industry's "strategic focus."

Regulatory Roles

One goal of the incoming administration was to reduce the discretion and authority available to mistrusted federal agencies. The strategy was implemented by two major power shifts: (1) the enhancement of state and local regulatory authority and (2) the creation of a more muscular executive oversight process than previously existed. The former raises fundamental questions of federalism. The latter sparked strong criticism from Congress and induced a greater level of congressional oversight. Administration efforts to dramatically reduce federal support for state environmental enforcement programs, coupled with widespread fears of interstate regulatory competition, suggested that deregulation and devolution might be linked phenomena.

Transferring Regulatory Authority to the States: The Reagan Record. The Reagan devolution strategies and the fundamental questions they raise regarding the allocation of regulatory responsibilities between the state and the federal governments are the subjects of two papers in this volume: Michael Fix's "Transferring Regulatory Authority to the States" and Jerry Mashaw and Susan Rose-Ackerman's "Federalism and Regulation."

The Fix paper surveys the various strategies employed by the administration to enhance state regulatory authority, looking primarily to the environmental area and actions taken within the context of partial preemption statutes. (These federal statutes assign states a potentially important administrative role once they adopt regulations that are acceptable to federal authorities and demonstrate that they have adequate enforcement capacity.)

The paper identifies a number of transfer strategies, including formal delegation of program authority to the states, adoption of generic regulations (such as EPA's "Bubble Policy"), reduced federal oversight of state program administration, and relaxation of federal standards that set the "floor" for state program rules. The paper assesses the merits of the administration's devolution strategy, emphasizing the fact that a transfer of authority was already contemplated by existing legislation and thus the strategy could be implemented comparatively easily and inconspicuously—a fact that may partially account for some of the strong results obtained. The author contends that the political characteristics of devolution make the reassertion of federal authority unlikely. Thus the Reagan administration's efforts in this area are likely to prove more enduring than other, more conspicuous actions taken in the name of regulatory relief.

Fix concludes, however, by noting that one reason for the effort's success was the extensive groundwork laid for devolution by prior administrations—groundwork that had developed support within regulated industries and among federal and state bureaucrats. Fix cautions, however, that the administration has appeared willing to depart from its stated goal of transferring regulatory authority to the states in certain instances when state activities conflict with the achievement of other administration goals or require "expensive" political sacrifices.

Transferring Regulatory Authority to the States: A Conceptual Framework. Jerry Mashaw and Susan Rose-Ackerman's paper develops a conceptual framework for allocating regulatory responsibility to differing levels of government in the federal system. They approach the question by setting out normative arguments for placing regulatory authority at the state rather than the federal level. To determine how these normative principles might play out in the political marketplace, they proceed to a positive (i.e., descriptive, rather than prescriptive) analysis of the interests of state and federal bureaucrats and politicians as well as national and local firms in the distribution of regulatory authority.*

Among the normative issues the authors contend must be addressed in designing appropriate regulatory roles are these:

- Developing policies to induce low-level governments to take account of the costs and benefits imposed on other political jurisdictions and, thus, to internalize externalities.

- Accounting for "prisoner's dilemmas," or situations in which one state's citizens try to benefit at the expense of the citizens of other states—setting off a "race to the bottom" as states compete for economic development using the lure of regulatory laxness.

---

*One economist distinguishes positive from normative statements in the following manner:
Positive statements concern what is, was, or will be. Normative statements concern what ought to be. Thus disagreements over positive statements are appropriately handled by an appeal to the facts. Disagreements over normative statements cannot be settled by an appeal to facts.

- Achieving scale economies in administering regulatory programs—particularly with regard to the development and transmission of information relevant to particular regulatory strategies.

- Maximizing the substantive benefits achievable in some instances by uniform national policies and in other instances by regulatory variety and interstate regulatory competition.

- Ensuring that principles of democratic responsiveness are advanced by promoting approaches tending to better insulate the regulatory process from interest-group capture.

The authors conclude their normative analysis by observing that the Reagan administration's "rhetorical commitment to states' rights and devolution has oversold states' rights as the desirable goal for regulatory legislation."

Mashaw and Rose-Ackerman then tackle the conflict between these normative claims and the interests of bureaucrats, politicians, firms, and other interest groups in dividing intergovernmental regulatory authority. The authors point out that the claims most frequently made for delegation—enhanced innovation, variety, democratic responsiveness, administrative efficiency, and scale economies—are not necessarily the goals of all devolution's advocates. For example, politicians and bureaucrats at both state and federal levels will be inclined to retain the credit and other benefits associated with regulatory interventions while attempting to shift program costs and burdens to other levels of government.

The authors find that an industry's position on federalizing regulatory authority will not always be consistent with that favored by the Reagan administration. Among other things, the authors find that an industry's preferences will depend on the industry's bargaining power at each level of government, the distribution of benefits from regulatory variety or uniformity, and the industry's regulatory costs compared with those of its competitors. According to the analysis, some firms will prefer federal preemption whereas other members of the same industry may favor state controls. Delegation in such instances may not necessarily lead to less stringent rules, as local firms may push for restrictive state regulations to reduce competition from their out-of-state competitors.

The authors conclude by arguing that an ideological commitment to devolution and states' rights may be misguided when viewed from the perspectives of efficiency, democratic representation, and even regulatory relief. They hold that shared regimes of authority—such as the incentive-based approach found in current partial preemption statutes—hold the greatest promise for striking a balance between uniformity and diversity, economy and equity.

Congress, Regulatory Reform, and Regulatory Relief. With some exceptions, many states fell in line behind the administration's preferred reallocation of regulatory authority and roles. The same cannot be said regarding the administration's ability to chart a course for Congress and regulatory relief. Indeed, as we have already noted, Congress was instrumental in spurring the administration's regulatory "mid-course correction" in 1983. That correction was brought about in large part by one of the most intense, publicized congressional oversight efforts in recent memory. Some observers considered this exercise to have been primarily a partisan affair conducted by a Democratic House; others considered it a classic example of the exercise of Congress's constitutionally mandated role to ensure the proper execution of the laws.

Not only did Congress reject several of the less politically popular elements of the regulatory relief campaign, but it also ignored the administration's half-hearted efforts to revise important social regulatory statutes. Thus, despite the fact that many of the statutes thought to be most in need of reform (the Clean Air and Water Acts, for example) were due for reauthorization as early as 1981, by 1983 no significant revisions had been achieved.

Throughout this period, Congress and the courts were reexamining and redefining the constraints and possibilities that should guide congressional interventions in the regulatory arena. In fact, Congress was in the middle of a debate over the content of a new, administratively focused regulatory reform bill at the same time that one of its favored instruments of regulatory review—the legislative veto—was being declared unconstitutional by the Supreme Court.

Christopher Foreman's paper takes a broad look at these developments, focusing on the capabilities and limitations of congressional oversight of regulation. Foreman begins with a taxonomy of the tools on which Congress has traditionally relied to control agency rule-making activity. He then discusses the limits imposed on congressional activity and the conventional critiques of Congress's oversight activities. He surveys current thinking on Congress's role in making appointments determining agency organization and location, settling appropriations, determining agency mission, and developing regulatory procedures. After noting the proliferation of committees and subcommittees with overlapping jurisdictions, Foreman argues that dispersed oversight can provide important information and lead to a healthy check against committee capture.

The author briefly reviews Congress's role during the first years of the Reagan administration—calling particular attention to Congress's unyielding opposition to change in many areas of social regulation and to the administration's half-hearted efforts to provide a workable legislative agenda.

Finally, Foreman considers the prospects for the reform of regulatory procedures and the development of substantive standards; he finds that Congress is far more inclined to the former than the latter. He explores the political acceptability of alternatives to the recently invalidated legislative veto (such as the joint resolution veto), as well as the acceptability of cost-benefit analysis, "sunset," and regulatory budget proposals.

He concludes with a series of policy recommendations based on his observation that in the future Congress will be determining how to manage an existing regulatory agenda, not how to expand its reach.

REGULATORY REFORM UNDER THE REAGAN ADMINISTRATION

Murray L. Weidenbaum

The middle of 1983 is not exactly a high-water mark in the movement to reform federal regulation of private economic activity. The Environmental Protection Agency (EPA) is just beginning to emerge from an unparalleled assault. The Occupational Safety and Health Administration (OSHA) and the National Highway Traffic Safety Administration (NHTSA) have seen some of their key initiatives overturned in the courts. The tempo of deregulation of surface transportation has wound down. Protectionism is on the rise, and industrial policy is no longer an obscene term in the business community.

Enough time has elapsed since January 1981 to enable us to take stock of the changes made by the Reagan administration—and there is still enough time until January 1985 to warrant some suggestions for the future. In effect, we are only a little late in presenting a mid-term report card.

Let me say at the outset that I do not equate regulatory reform with minimizing the costs of complying with regulation. Nor do I view the reform task as one of maximizing the burden of regulation or of attempting to use the regulatory process to punish business for its various sins of commission or omission.

Rather, I think of reform in terms of optimization, of moving toward more efficient regulatory activity (an approach that is guaranteed to upset our libertarian friends). If anything, adopting a less burdensome method of achieving regulatory goals is a way of enhancing support for this type of governmental activity, or at least of diffusing the opposition. But my motive is far less Machiavellian. Regulatory reform can help lead us to a more productive

---

The author benefited from comments by Kenneth Chilton, Robert Crandall, George Eads, Jerry Jasinowski, Thomas Moore, Ronald Penoyer, Kenneth Shepsle, and Barry Weingast.

economy, one whose industries are more competitive in world markets, and one that delivers a better living standard to its citizens.

A Base for Comparison

An an initial base of comparison, I would like to refer to the Report of the Task Force on Regulatory Reform, which I chaired in 1980. Ronald Reagan established the group during his presidential campaign, and we submitted our report to him shortly after the 1980 election. A public (sanitized) version of that report was published in the November/December issue of *Regulation*.[1] I will refer to portions of that public document.

The task force report urged a "new approach" to government regulation that would pursue two objectives simultaneously: (1) to better achieve regulatory goals while (2) reducing regulatory burdens. We provided some specific guidance to the new administration. The range of federal regulatory activities requires varied approaches to regulatory reform. In the case of economic regulation, we urged the dismantling of controls to enhance consumer welfare. In the case of social regulation, we advised seeking out the most effective and least burdensome methods of achieving the desired objectives. For some regulatory programs, such as efforts to reduce product hazards, we suggested that the provision of better information would enable consumers themselves to make more sensible trade-offs between safety and price than any government standards.

We pointed out that the selection of new appointees to regulatory agencies requires great care. We specifically urged that Reagan appoint "people who are sympathetic with the important social objectives to be achieved."

We also noted that the fundamental shortcomings of government regulation resulted more from statutory than from executive deficiencies. "There is an urgent need to change the fundamental regulatory statutes," the report stated. We proposed a one-year moratorium on new regulations, to provide a breathing spell in which to adjust to the rapid proliferation of regulatory rules and programs that were promulgated in the 1970s.

In addition, we advocated imposing a cost-benefit test requiring each agency to demonstrate a reasonable relationship between the costs imposed

---

1. Murray L. Weidenbaum, "Reforming Government Regulation," *Regulation* (November/December 1980), pp. 15–18. See also Murray L. Weidenbaum, *The Future of Business Regulation* (New York: Amacom), 1980.

and the benefits produced before a new rule is issued. Administratively, we recommended that the president abolish the Regulatory Council, which we described as a protective association for the regulators, who constituted its entire membership. We urged establishing a new White House office to spearhead the regulatory reform effort.

The article in *Regulation* noted, "These proposals . . . do not constitute a Neanderthal plea to ignore the real problems of pollution, discrimination, and so on. Precisely to the contrary, they are offered in the belief that every task government undertakes should be performed ably."[2]

This paper examines the extent to which these bold expectations for regulatory reform have been met during the past two and one-half years. Because the factors involved are not frequently subject to measurement, the findings are necessarily subjective, even impressionistic. We make this examination in terms of (1) the key organizational changes affecting regulatory policies and practices, (2) statutory changes to reduce the burden or improve the effectiveness of regulation, (3) procedural changes affecting the flow of regulation, and (4) changes in the burdens of federal regulation of private economic activity.

Organizational Changes

Very early in the Reagan administration, important changes were made in the organization for regulatory policy. To demonstrate clearly the importance of regulatory reform, the president appointed the vice-president to head a cabinet-level Task Force on Regulatory Relief. The task force was given the assignment of providing leadership to the administration's regulatory efforts and, in effect, to serve as a court of appeals for controversies emerging from the day-to-day review of proposed regulations by the Office of Management and Budget. In retrospect, use of the term *regulatory relief* (as with the term *deregulation* in an earlier administration) may have set the wrong tone for the effort. *Reform* may have predicated a more neutral approach to changes in the regulatory system.

President Reagan quickly abolished both the Regulatory Council and the Council on Wage and Price Stability (moving the regulatory review staff of the latter to the Office of Management and Budget (OMB)), and did not activate the Regulatory Analysis Review Group, which had been so prominent

---

2. Ibid., p. 18. See also "On Saving the Kingdom—Advice for the President-Elect from Eight Regulatory Experts," *Regulation* (November/December 1980), pp. 14–35.

in the Carter administration. In their stead, the president directed OMB to set up a detailed regulatory review function, which also built upon the authority provided in the Paperwork Control Act passed in 1980. In order to assure close coordination, the OMB official in charge of regulatory activities was also designated to serve as the executive director of the Task Force on Regulatory Relief. Executive Order 12291, signed by the president in February 1981, governs the regulatory relief effort of the administration.

These organizational changes provide, in effect, for a three-layered review of proposed rule making. Each agency or department having regulatory powers is responsible for conducting the basic regulatory review required by Executive Order 12291. OMB conducts the second level of review, focusing on the required analysis of benefits and costs. The vice-president's task force does the final review—unless the matter is appealed to the president. Clearly, the formal structure of regulatory review provides several checkpoints to ensure that regulatory activities are consistent with the administration's regulatory policies—subject, as always, to legislative restraints and individual discretion. These are points to which we shall now turn.

Personally, I give the administration high marks for quickly setting up an effective mechanism to spearhead and conduct regulatory reform on a continuing basis. (Obviously, my evaluation is biased insofar as my advice was taken.) However, in retrospect, I must acknowledge that the current approach lacks one advantage of the structure developed during the Carter and Ford administrations: In practice, there is little leadership for regulatory reform on the part of senior White House staff. This became apparent after the initial burst of regulatory reform initiatives (which were essentially adaptations of the transition task force's recommendations). The administration's Task Force on Regulatory Relief has responded primarily to the issues presented by the OMB review process. It has exerted little independent leadership in terms of initiating reviews of existing rules or identifying needed changes in basic regulatory statutes. The disbandment of the task force in August 1983 generated little public response. The major contributions that it was likely to make had been achieved or at least attempted.[3]

The impact of individual personalities is difficult to assay, but is too important to be ignored. The public attitude toward the Reagan administration's regulatory efforts was clearly not a response to the vice-president's task force. Rather, the public and, especially, the organized environmental groups were aroused by the strong language and public stands of Secretary of the Interior James Watt. EPA Administrator Anne Gorsuch evoked a similar

---

3. See *Statement by Vice-President George Bush*, August 11, 1983, p. 2.

public response. Moreover, her inability to provide effective leadership to the career staff of the agency prompted many to leak drafts of proposals for changes in the regulatory apparatus.

As a result, the entire spectrum of environmental organizations—including some that had maintained a relatively nonpolitical position over the years—became a solid phalanx of opposition to virtually every regulatory change proposed by the Reagan administration. Many of the environmental groups overreacted, perhaps a matter of keeping in step with the noisier elements of the environmental movement. In any event, a few key personalities among the Reagan appointees caused a great deal of tumult.

Statutory Changes

Turning to the changes in regulatory statutes since January 1981, here, I must report that the results have been disappointingly few. Significantly, the period from January 1981 to the present (almost three years) marks the longest time in several decades that the federal government has not embarked upon a major new regulatory program or established a new regulatory agency. But in terms of regulatory reform, nonevents also characterized efforts for improvement.

The flagship of environmental regulation, the Clean Air Act, contains a timetable providing for its renewal, and hence review, in 1981. To some extent, the administration was reluctant to propose substantial changes for fear that the Congress would be unsympathetic. The White House could not count on the strong Senate leadership that was evident in other areas of administration policy because the chairman of the Senate Environment and Public Works Committee was known to be very protective of the status quo. However, the major reason the administration was so extraordinarily timid in providing leadership was its desire to avoid raising controversial legislative questions that could impede the speedy enactment of its tax and budget initiatives. The administration, in practice, gave regulatory reform a low priority, a situation that continues to this day.

After reviewing the matter with the president in the Cabinet Council on Natural Resources and Environment, the EPA sent to Congress eleven general guidelines for reviewing the Clean Air Act, instead of proposing specific language changes as had been anticipated. Even the guidelines were diluted; they did not, for example, contain the cost-benefit requirement that Reagan had championed during the 1980 campaign. The EPA administrator contended that, given the expected difficulty of obtaining congressional approval for significant statutory changes, it would be wiser to attempt only to modify enforcement procedures. The unfortunate result of this policy is only too well known.

Passenger Bus Deregulation

In 1982, Congress advanced the cause of regulatory reform with a deregulatory initiative.[4] Following the pattern of earlier Congresses in deregulating the airline industry and reducing the scope of regulation in trucking and railroads, the ninety-seventh Congress in 1982 passed a statute substantially reducing regulation in the passenger bus industry. Although it was less comprehensive than the proposals considered in earlier Congresses, the Bus Regulatory Reform Act of 1982 (P.L. 97-861) eased conditions for market entry and preempted many state regulations that had restricted interstate operation of buses.

The new law authorizes the Interstate Commerce Commission (ICC) to issue a certificate for regular-route transportation if the applicant is "fit, willing, and able to provide" the service. Fitness refers only to adequate insurance and safety. The ICC may deny a certificate only if it finds that the authorization would not be consistent with the public interest. The burden of proof is on those objecting to the ICC's issuance of a certificate.

The 1982 law knocked down many of the previous obstacles to entry. For instance, the ICC may not use the "public interest" test to reject an applicant if (1) the proposed service is for a community not regularly served by passenger bus service, (2) the proposed service replaces discontinued air or rail transportation, or (3) the motor carrier serving the community has filed to decrease or discontinue service.

The new law also removed some operating restrictions. It allows carriers on interstate routes to serve intermediate points if this does not conflict with commuter bus operations. It permits, but does not require, round-trip operations where previously only one-way trips had been authorized. It also allows carriers to transport charter passengers intrastate in the same bus with noncharter passengers.

The bus act also established a zone within which fares may be raised or lowered without ICC approval. The zone of rate freedom will be increased gradually; prices will be totally deregulated in 1985 except for rates set collectively through rate bureaus. The ICC will still be permitted to suspend "predatory" special or charter rate proposals. Thus, bus regulation continues, as does progress toward deregulation.

---

4. Center for the Study of Government Regulation, *Major Regulatory Initiatives During 1982* (Washington, D.C.: American Enterprise Institute, 1982), pp. 86–95.

Financial Deregulation

Responding to the pressures on savings and loan associations and other financial institutions, Congress passed the Garn-St. Germain Depository Institutions Act of 1982, which provided a wide variety of new and expanded powers for banks and other depository institutions. The act directed the Deposit Institutions Deregulatory Committee (DIDC) to establish deposit accounts for financial institutions "directly equivalent to and competitive with money market and mutual funds." The new accounts carry no maximum interest rate and modest minimum balance requirements. The changes had virtually instantaneous effect. Since DIDC authorized the new type of account, the shift of deposits from money market mutual funds to commercial banks and savings institutions has been massive. The new law enables depository institutions to compete head-on with money market mutual funds.

The new law also accelerates the elimination of the interest rate differential favoring thrift institutions, thus helping to achieve the "level playing field" that commercial banks had been advocating. For a three-year period, the Garn-St. Germain Act authorizes interstate acquisitions of troubled financial institutions, including banks with assets of $500 million or more. The impending merger of SeaFirst into the Bank of America is the most dramatic example of the power of this new provision.

Using existing powers, the Federal Reserve Board and the Comptroller of the Currency in June 1983 began requiring that the seventeen largest banking organizations maintain capital equal to at least 15 percent of their assets. This action was taken in response to concerns about the potential impact of "soft" loans to developing nations on the financial condition of the major international banks.

The degree of competition among financial institutions is far greater today than it was two or three years ago. Some of the increased competition results from legislation passed in 1980 and prior years. The pace of change also results from technological advances and institutional innovation. But the political and economic climates have been important factors in encouraging more marketplace competition than in the past. A special panel of the Task Force on Regulatory Relief is actively considering further steps in the area of financial institutions.

Other Aspects of Deregulation

At the beginning of the Reagan administration, it seemed that progress made in prior administrations in reducing the extent of railroad regulation was being undone. The new chairman of the Interstate Commerce Commission tended to act as more of a conventional regulator than did his predecessor in the Carter administration. But the appointment of several reform-minded commissioners to the ICC has helped turn the tide. Some modest evidence is available on that score. For example, the number of contracts negotiated between rail carriers and shippers—a measure of the operating flexibility granted by the Staggers Rail Act of 1980—increased from 580 in fiscal year 1980 to 2,907 in fiscal 1982. In terms of output, railroads have increased their share of total freight traffic. They also have substantially increased their shipments of some commodities, such as fruits and vegetables, that previously were carried almost exclusively by trucks.[5] The next round of appointments to the commission may be vital.

The need for reforming the basic regulatory laws has been underscored by a flurry of court decisions that have struck down agency reforms on the grounds that they lacked a statutory basis. Administrative changes overturned by federal courts in the last two years include OSHA's cotton dust standards, EPA's bubble concept for the Clean Air Act, NHTSA's stance on passive restraints, and ICC's generosity on general commodity certificates.

All in all, those of us who support regulatory reform must look back with disappointment at the modest statutory changes enacted since January 1981. One can bemoan the lack of leadership on this score in either the executive or legislative branch, but the basic problem is that the necessary foundation has not been laid in terms of public understanding and support for reducing the burdens of regulation.

A senior officer of a major chemical company made a similar observation recently. William G. Simeral, executive vice-president of DuPont and outgoing chairman of the Chemical Manufacturers Association, stated in June 1983 that, "This fear of chemicals is the issue facing the chemical industry in its relationship with the Government and the public. . . ." He said that the chemical industry was not "poisoning America," but that the public did not share this belief.[6]

The media are generally unhelpful or at least extremely naive on this score. Try to change a comma in the Clean Air Act, and you lay yourself open to charges that you want to "gut" environmental protection. Perhaps some modern-day Shakespeare can write the script whereby a reform-minded economist convincingly declares, "If I am polluted, do I not cough?"

---

5. *Economic Report of the President, February 1983* (Washington, D.C.: Government Printing Office, 1983), p. 111.

6. Philip Shabecoff, "Chemical Industry Gets Warning on Public Fear," *New York Times*, June 10, 1983, p. 13.

Public opinion polls show growing support for the position of environmental activists. For example, an April 1983 poll by the *New York Times* and CBS News reported that 58 percent of the sample surveyed (up from 45 percent in September 1981) agreed with the following statement:

> Protecting the environment is so important that requirements and standards cannot be too high and continuing environmental improvements must be made regardless of cost.[7]

Of all the categories polled, the weakest support came from college graduates, of whom 46 percent supported the statement.

Looking toward the future, the results of a survey examining whom people trust to recommend regulatory changes are telling. In the case of the Clean Air Act, nearly three-fourths of the respondents said they trust "environmental groups" and "university professors." Nearly half trust the recommendations of the "news media," while only two-fifths have faith in the judgment of "business and industry."[8]

Procedural Changes

Reducing Regulatory Burdens

The Reagan administration's first important administrative act in the regulatory area was to put on hold the numerous so-called midnight regulations issued during the last month of the Carter administration. On January 29, 1981, President Reagan ordered the eleven major regulatory departments and agencies of the executive branch to postpone the effective dates of all regulations scheduled to take effect by March 20 and to refrain from issuing any final regulations until that date. In fact, 196 regulations were exempted from the freeze and became effective during the sixty-day period, while seventy-two regulations were further postponed or withdrawn by the agencies.

This was just a preliminary response to the tide of new regulations. A more lasting response came in February 1981, when President Reagan signed Executive Order 12291, titled "Federal Regulation," replacing an order issued by President Carter. The new policy statement created stronger White House oversight of regulatory activity and more stringent requirements for analyzing the benefits and costs of regulation.[9] It requires regulatory agencies under the president's jurisdiction to make their regulatory decisions according

---

7. "Attitudes on the Environment," *New York Times*, April 17, 1983, p. 17.
8. "Opinion Roundup," *Public Opinion* (February/March 1982), p. 37.
9. Center for Study of Government Regulation, *Major Regulatory Initiatives*, pp. 63–64.

to cost-benefit and cost-effectiveness criteria, to the extent permitted by law. (Independent regulatory commissions were not included.)

All proposed and final regulations must be submitted to OMB for review at least sixty days prior to publication in the *Federal Register*. OMB may ask for further information and consultations before a rule is published, but its concurrence is not required. Under E.O. 12291, regulatory agencies must determine which of their new regulations are "major" and must submit Regulatory Impact Analyses to OMB along with these proposals. An economic impact of $100 million a year is the designated threshold, although many exceptions and additions are provided for.

OMB's guidelines for preparing Regulatory Impact Analyses do not require a dollar estimate of all regulatory efforts, but the agencies are urged to identify all effects and to quantify them where possible. The guidelines also suggest that alternative approaches should be discussed and the benefits and costs of each estimated as far as possible. They recommend a discount rate of 10 percent for analyzing future benefits and costs.

It is difficult to gauge the quality of the OMB review effort. Some critics urge more public reporting of the key actions that OMB takes in its review of agency regulatory proposals. Others suggest strengthening the analytical capabilities in the regulatory agencies themselves—a sound approach, to be sure. I am concerned that the staff leadership in OMB is no longer at the associate director level and that regulatory review issues rarely get the attention of senior members of the administration. The termination of the Task Force on Regulatory Relief heightens these concerns.

Most draft regulatory proposals pass OMB muster. As of December 31, 1982, OMB found 4,660 of the 5,436 submissions (86 percent) consistent with Executive Order 12291. Another 410 (8 percent) were approved with minor changes; only 101 regulations (2 percent) were rejected, while 81 (1 percent) were withdrawn. The remaining 184 (3 percent) were technically exempt from the order and were submitted for informational purposes or involved emergency, statutory, or judicial deadlines. Of the 5,436 regulations reviewed by OMB, only 89 were considered "major." Regulatory impact analyses were prepared for those which were not exempted from the requirement by OMB.[10]

At first blush, it would seem that the OMB review is not normally a major obstacle to a regulatory agency desiring to issue new rulings. However, one would imagine the agencies now draft their proposals with an eye to obtaining OMB clearance. The small number of OMB rejections may also

---

10. Presidential Task Force on Regulatory Relief, *Reagan Administration Regulatory Achievements*, August 11, 1983, tables 1 and 2.

mean that OMB is concentrating on a few key regulatory issues and, thus, quickly approves minor and routine rule changes. One indication of this is the estimates of compliance cost reduction in the private sector.

In its final report on August 11, 1983, the Task Force on Regulatory Relief estimated that the review process and agency activity had by that date resulted in $9 to $11 billion savings in one-time investment costs, and $10 billion in annual recurring costs (see table 1). These numbers exclude the incremental interest to depositors resulting from the actions taken under the Garn-St. Germain Act.[11] Many of the regulatory changes affected the automobile industry; this reflected the desire of the Reagan administration to respond to the difficulties facing that industry and its belief that regulatory relief was a more constructive response than the statutory quotas being advocated in Congress in 1981.

In addition to the direct savings, the administration estimates that it has cut 300 million hours of paperwork annually (including regulatory and other federal requirements).

One specific administrative action should be noted. In January 1981, President Reagan used the authority provided in the Energy Policy and Conservation Act of 1975 to order the immediate decontrol of crude oil and refined petroleum products. In the absence of presidential action, these controls would have expired on September 30, 1981.

TABLE 1

ESTIMATED COST SAVINGS OF MAJOR REGULATORY REFORMS
COMPLETED, JANUARY 1981–AUGUST 1983
(In millions of dollars)

	Investment or One-Time	Annually Recurring
Architectural and Transportation Barriers		
Compliance Board		
Minimum Guidelines	—	250
Department of Agriculture		
Mechanically Processed (Species)		
Product	—	500
National School Lunch Program	—	117
WIC Program Recordkeeping	—	30
Special Milk Program Paperwork	—	28
Model Food Stamp Form	—	5

---

11. Ibid., table 4. The interest "savings" were excluded by the author on conceptual grounds.

TABLE 1 (*continued*)

ESTIMATED COST SAVINGS OF MAJOR REGULATORY REFORMS
COMPLETED, JANUARY 1981–AUGUST 1983
(In millions of dollars)

	Investment or One-Time	Annually Recurring
U.S. Army Corps of Engineers		
Section 404 of the Clean Water Act	—	1,000
Department of Education		
Bilingual Education Regulations	900–2,950	70–155
Education Consolidation and Improvement Act	—	2
Department of Energy		
Residential Conservation Service Program	—	100–150
Coal Conversion	—	100
Appliance Efficiency Standards	—	30–60
Building Compliance Form	—	20
Department of Health and Human Services		
Medicare-Medicaid Form	—	100
Regulations Implementing Block Grants	—	52
Patient Package Inserts	—	20
Department of Housing and Urban Development		
Direct Endorsement	—	11–15
Environmental Policies	—	5
Community Development	—	3
Modernization of Public Housing Projects	—	2
Department of the Interior		
Phase I Reform Effort	—	10
Federal Coal Management	—	3
Department of Labor		
Equal Pension Benefits for Men and Women	—	1,500
Prevailing Wage (Davis-Bacon)	—	585
Suspension of Pension Benefit Restrictions	—	200–300

TABLE 1 (*continued*)

	Investment or One-Time	Annually Recurring
OSHA Hearing Conservation Rules	—	81
ESA Salary Tests for Overtime	—	55
Occupational Exposure to Lead	—	50
OSHA Respirator Fit Testing for Lead	—	6
Department of Transportation		
Passive Restraints—Rescission	400	1,000
Passive Restraints—Delay	135	—
Highway 402 Program Paperwork	—	680
Bumper Standard	—	300
Driver's Log	—	164
Low Tire Pressure Warning	—	130
Railroad Power Brake Rules	—	100
Multipiece Rims	300	75
Field of Direct View—Cars	160	25
Marine Vessel Construction Standards	368	17
Speedometers and Odometers	—	12
Blue Signal Protection and Hours of Service	—	12
Uniform Tire Quality Grading Standards	—	10
Theft Protection	—	10
Marine Vessel Documentation	—	5
Pipeline Retention of Radiographic Film	—	3
Hydraulic Brakes	—	2
Limited Quantity Radioactive Materials	—	1
Plastic Pipeline Mechanical Joint Couplings	—	1
Section 504 of the Rehabilitation Act	2,200	—
Tank Truck Specification Relief	80	—
Coast Guard Complementary Navigation Systems	24	—
Department of Treasury		
IRS Simplified Tax Forms	—	650
Alcoholic Beverages Paperwork	—	5
ERISA Form 5500 and 5500C Paperwork	—	2

TABLE 1 (continued)

ESTIMATED COST SAVINGS OF MAJOR REGULATORY REFORMS
COMPLETED, JANUARY 1981–AUGUST 1983
(In millions of dollars)

	Investment or One-Time	Annually Recurring
Equal Employment Opportunity Commission		
EEO-1 Paperwork	—	3
EEO-4 Paperwork	—	2
EEO-5 Paperwork	—	2
Environmental Protection Agency		
On-Board Technology for Control of HC Emissions	103	240
1984 High Altitude Requirement	—	200
Diesel Particulate Emission Averaging	—	50–111
BCT Effluent Guidelines	1,100	80
Truck-Mounted Solid Waste Compactors	—	33
Iron and Steel Effluent Guidelines	580	30
Dual Definition of Source	1,300	—
Emissions Trading Policy	1,000	—
Noise Emission Limits for Trucks	130	—
Standards for Paint Shops	75	—
General Motors Offset Remedy for NOx	38	—
Acceptable Quality Level for Assembly Line Testing of Trucks	31	—
Steel Stretch-Out Agreements	10	—
Selective Enforcement Audit for Heavy Truck Engines	9	—
Motor Vehicle Certification	5	—
Assembly Line Test Orders	1	—
Self-Certification for Vehicles Sold at High Altitudes	1	—
Federal Communications Commission		
Maritime Radio Station Logs	—	21
Ham Radio Operator Logs	—	3
Mobile Radio Service Paperwork	—	1
Federal Energy Regulatory Commission		
Power Plants Paperwork	—	1
National Credit Union Administration		
Recordkeeping Requirements	—	670

TABLE 1 (*continued*)

	Investment or One-Time	Annually Recurring
Securities and Exchange Commission		
Integration Program	—	350
Regulation D	—	50
Office of Management and Budget		
Circular A-95	—	50
TOTAL	8,950–11,000	9,925–10,255

SOURCE: Presidential Task Force on Regulatory Relief, *Reagan Administration Regulatory Achievements*, August 11, 1983.

I am purposely ignoring the reduction in the number of new rules in the pages of the *Federal Register*. Those numbers may be indicative of the new approach, but they remind me of the bureaucratic response to President Eisenhower's preference for one-page memos: smaller margins, larger paper, and finer print. Nevertheless, the momentum of regulatory growth clearly has slowed down since January 1981, especially via administrative processes.

Increasing Regulatory Activity

Not all administrative actions taken since January 1981 have been aimed at reducing the burden of regulation. Quite a few have gone the other way, especially in the field of foreign trade. For example, after discussions with U.S. government representatives, Japan "voluntarily" agreed to limit its exports of automobiles to the United States to 1.68 million a year for three successive years. The decision was made to forestall legislative proposals to establish statutory'import quotas. Here, as in so many other cases, the administration has been far less protectionist than Congress, and has strongly opposed a congressional proposal that would require designated amounts of "domestic content" in most domestically manufactured automobiles.

In May 1982, President Reagan imposed emergency sugar import quotas in order to maintain the high domestic subsidy price. In October 1982, the president announced an agreement with the European Economic Community to limit European steel exports to the United States. In return, American steel companies dropped forty-two complaints charging European companies with selling subsidized steel or dumping steel in the United States below actual production costs. The self-imposed European quotas forestalled U.S. Commerce Department action to impose duties of up to 26 percent on imports of steel from Western Europe. Such tariffs, however, would have represented less interference with the marketplace than the quotas that were agreed upon.

Also in 1982, the president tightened the sanctions originally placed in 1981 on American companies participating in the Soviet Natural Gas Pipeline. The 1982 extension applied to European subsidies of U.S. firms and foreign firms operating under U.S. licensing agreements. After many complaints from domestic firms and foreign governments, the president lifted the pipeline sanctions in November 1982.[12]

In June 1983, the president raised tariffs and set import quotas on a variety of foreign-made stainless-steel products. He acted in response to a complaint from U.S. steel producers and a recommendation from the International Trade Commission. The tariff increase will be phased out over a four-year period, while the quotas will remain in effect for three years.

Not all of the increase in regulation occurred in the foreign trade area. In May 1983, the Task Force on Regulatory Relief overruled OMB and gave the Labor Department permission to continue requiring engineering controls to reduce textile workers' exposure to cotton dust. OMB had contended that workers could be adequately protected by respirators at far less cost.[13] Earlier, the president had allowed the Orderly Marketing Agreement (informal import quotas) on nonrubber footwear to expire.

In August 1983, the Securities and Exchange Commission ordered bank holding companies to increase the amount of information they must disclose about their foreign lending and about potentially risky domestic loans. The increased disclosure requirements were a response to the rising concerns about "soft" bank lending to Third World countries such as Mexico.[14]

Changes in the Economic Burden of Regulation

To my knowledge, no recent study of the total burden of federal regulation is available to examine the changing economic costs of regulation resulting from the actions of the Reagan administration. The oft-quoted work

---

12. Murray L. Weidenbaum with Michael C. Munger and Ronald J. Penoyer, *Toward A More Open Trade Policy* (St. Louis: Washington University, Center for the Study of American Business, 1983), chapter 1.
13. Joann S. Lublin, "OSHA Upholds Exposure Rules for Cotton Dust," *Wall Street Journal*, May 20, 1983, p. 4.
14. "Bank Concerns Must Increase Lending Data," *Wall Street Journal*, August 12, 1983, p. 3.

Murray L. Weidenbaum   31

of the Center for the Study of American Business was based on data for 1976. For a few years after that, I made rough estimates on the assumption that the "multiplier" connecting direct federal outlays and the resultant compliance costs was constant. I believe that such estimates were appropriate at a time when regulatory budgets and staffs, regulatory statutes, and new regulations were proliferating. The rise in federal regulatory budgets was then closely associated with the rising burdens of government regulation.

But given the many changes made in the budgets of the regulatory agencies in the last two years, I would be surprised if the "multiplier" is the same today as it was in 1976. In any event, neither the many users nor critics of the existing data have attempted to update the results. Given the amount of work involved in the earlier study, perhaps that is not too surprising.

Some indication of the changing burden of federal regulation may be gleaned from the budgetary data and the related estimates of federal regulatory personnel. On the basis of the federal budget submitted to Congress in January 1983, it appears that reductions in total regulatory spending made in fiscal year 1982 (a 3 percent cut) are being followed by far more modest increases than those seen during the 1970s. That, at least, is what the nominal data show. In real terms, when the numbers are adjusted to eliminate the effect of inflation, we see reductions in regulatory spending every year since 1980, aggregating to a 14 percent decrease in the real level of federal regulatory outlays over the five-year period from 1980 to 1984. Table 2 contains the highlights of these trends.[15]

Similarly, staffing at the major regulatory agencies dropped considerably in 1981 and 1982, and is projected to fall even further through 1984 (see table 3).

Cutbacks in Regulatory Spending

In 1970 the federal government spent a relatively modest $800 million to administer the regulatory activities of the forty-two major agencies that were then operating. By 1975 that amount had risen by 300 percent, to over $3 billion. By 1980 regulatory outlays had risen even further, to nearly $6 billion. Total spending by the major agencies grew more than sixfold during these eleven years—a period during which outlays for the Defense

---

15. For details, see Murray L. Weidenbaum and Ronald J. Penoyer, *The Next Step in Regulatory Reform: Updating the Statutes* (St. Louis: Washington University, Center for the Study of American Business, 1983), pp. 33–43. For background, see Murray L. Weidenbaum, *Business, Government, and the Public*, 2d ed. (Englewood Cliffs, N.J.: Prentice-Hall, 1981).

TABLE 2

BUDGET EXPENDITURES ON FEDERAL REGULATORY ACTIVITIES
(Fiscal years, millions of dollars)

Area of Regulation	1970	1975	1980	1970 to 1980 (% Change)	1981	1982	1983 (Estimated)	1984	1980 to 1984 (% Change)
Social Regulation									
Consumer Safety and Health	326	1,279	2,279	599	2,476	2,363	2,462	2,465	8
Job Safety and Other Working Conditions	62	379	734	1,084	775	758	803	832	13
Environment and Energy	85	967	1,926	2,166	2,122	2,048	2,023	2,032	6
Total, Social Regulation	473	2,625	4,939	944	5,373	5,169	5,288	5,329	8
Economic Regulation									
Finance and Banking	106	186	290	174	352	371	410	428	48
Industry-Specific Regulation	125	222	366	193	403	369	341	344	−6
General Business	96	169	309	222	325	341	384	394	28
Total, Economic Regulation	327	577	965	195	1,080	1,081	1,135	1,166	21
Total, Social and Economic Regulation	800	3,202	5,904	638	6,453	6,250	6,423	6,495	10
Year-To-Year Nominal Percentage Change		300	84		9	−3	3	1	
GNP Deflator		9.6	9.8		9.4	6.0	5.2	5.2	
GNP Deflator Index	100	139.2	197.6		216.2	229.1	241.1	253.6	
Total in 1970 Dollars	800	2,300	2,988	274	2,985	2,728	2,664	2,561	−14
Year-to-Year Real Percentage Change		187	30		−0.1	−8.6	−2.3	−3.9	

SOURCE: Center for the Study of American Business, Washington University.

TABLE 3

STAFFING FOR FEDERAL REGULATORY ACTIVITIES
(Fiscal years, permanent full-time positions)

Area of Regulation	1970	1975	1980	1970 to 1980 (% Change)	1981	1982	1983 (Estimated)	1984	1980 to 1984 (% Change)
Social Regulation									
Consumer Safety and Health	5,786	28,333	33,599	481	32,481	29,071	27,929	27,864	−17
Job Safety and Other Working Conditions	3,921	11,893	14,952	281	14,910	13,633	13,205	13,196	−12
Environment and Energy	NA	11,872	17,838	—	16,252	14,882	14,357	13,778	−23
Total, Social Regulation	9,707	52,098	66,389	584	63,643	57,586	55,491	54,838	−17
Economic Regulation									
Finance and Banking	6,203	7,413	9,305	50	8,933	8,850	8,831	8,797	−5
Industry-Specific Regulation	5,874	7,215	7,352	25	6,953	6,394	6,215	5,965	−19
General Business	5,877	7,280	7,449	27	7,137	6,915	6,880	6,789	−9
Total, Economic Regulation	17,954	21,908	24,106	34	23,023	22,159	21,926	21,551	−11
Total, Social and Economic Regulation	27,661	74,006	90,495	227	86,666	79,745	77,417	76,389	−16
Year-To-Year Nominal Percentage Change		168	22		−4	−8	−3	−1	

SOURCE: Center for the Study of American Business, Washington University.
NA = not available.

Department and total annual Social Security benefit payments rose by only 74 percent and 278 percent, respectively. In constant dollars, adjusted for inflation, the growth rate was also dramatic: Regulatory budgets grew by 274 percent in real terms from 1970 to 1980, reaching nearly $3 billion in 1970 dollars.

The long-term trend of rising federal outlays for regulation was reversed in fiscal years 1981 and 1982. In its first year, the Reagan administration made modest changes in the regulatory outlays slated by the Carter administration. The $6.5 billion total represented a 9 percent increase over 1980 (rather than a projected 10 percent) and roughly equaled that year's rate of inflation. In real terms, 1981 regulatory spending was just about at the level of the previous year.

In fiscal 1982, the drop in regulatory budgets was clear-cut and unprecedented in recent experience. In current dollars, regulatory spending decreased 3 percent, to $6 billion; in constant dollars it fell almost 9 percent. This turn toward austerity in the management of the federal government's regulatory agencies had not occurred in any of the previous twelve years (which is as far back as the Center for the Study of American Business has been compiling these data). The Consumer Product Safety Commission (CPSC) experienced the largest budget cuts, proportionally, of any regulatory agency. CPSC eliminated eight regional offices and three testing laboratories.

Estimates for regulatory spending in fiscal 1983 and 1984 show further declines in constant-dollar outlays. As indicated in table 2, total budgets are projected to drop 2 percent in 1983 (in 1970 dollars) and another 4 percent in fiscal 1984. In current-dollar terms, regulatory spending is projected to rise 3 percent and 1 percent in these years, respectively. In the five-year period from 1980 through 1984, the estimated administrative cost of regulation is projected to rise 10 percent, not accounting for inflation, to almost $6.5 billion. In constant dollars, however, the decrease will amount to 14 percent. Impending congressional action on EPA's budget is likely to reduce the aggregate cuts in regulatory agency budgets.

The Decline in Regulatory Staffing

The most dramatic reversal of the regulatory trends of the 1970s is shown in table 3. It can be seen that the federal regulatory workforce peaked at 90,000 in 1980. The number of people working in full-time, permanent positions in the major agencies is projected to continue to decline by 16 percent through 1984, when it will reach a total of 76,000. If these estimates hold true, there will be one-sixth fewer federal regulators in 1984 than in 1980—a five-year reduction of about 16 percent.

This decline in manpower contrasts sharply with increases during the 1970s. From 1970 to 1975, staffing at the major agencies increased 168 percent, growing from more than 27,600 positions to more than 74,000. Further increases in the next five years brought total staffing to an all-time high of 90,500 in 1980.

In 1981, the Reagan administration halted the growth of the regulatory workforce. Personnel dropped by 4 percent in that year and by an additional 8 percent in fiscal 1982. Further reductions in force of 3 percent in 1983 and 1 percent in 1984 are expected to bring staffing at the major agencies down to about the number of people employed in 1975.

Of the forty-four agencies for which regulatory personnel levels can be determined, only a handful plan increases. Overall, staffing in areas of social regulation is expected to decline by one-sixth from 1980 to 1984. Only four social regulatory agencies plan modest increases: the Nuclear Regulatory Commission, the Animal and Plant Health Inspection Service in the Department of Agriculture, the National Labor Relations Board, and the Inspector for the Alaska Natural Gas Transportation System. The largest reductions are projected for the various agricultural inspection services (3,600 fewer employees), the Bureau of Alcohol, Tobacco, and Firearms (approximately 1,000 fewer employees), the Occupational Safety and Health Administration (a reduction in force of 660), the Economic Regulatory Administration in the Department of Energy (about 1,900 fewer positions), and the Environmental Protection Agency (about 2,000 fewer employees). As noted previously, the Congress is making some upward revisions in the case of EPA.

Economic regulation is expected to experience total personnel cuts of roughly one-tenth during the period 1980 to 1984. Only one agency, the Patent and Trademark Office in the Department of Commerce, will increase employment—by 550 employees, or 20 percent higher than its 1980 staffing level. The largest personnel reduction, in percentage terms, will be made in the soon-to-be-abolished Civil Aeronautics Board, where staffing will be cut in half. The Interstate Commerce Commission will have the largest reduction in force, however. It will reduce its staffing by 740 employees, to one-third its 1980 level. The Securities and Exchange Commission will reduce its employment by nearly one-fifth.

The Outlook for Regulatory Growth

The Reagan administration's efforts to reduce the size and costs of the federal government's regulatory establishment are not a substitute for making substantive changes in the statutes that empower the agencies or in the rules that the agencies issue. Nevertheless, cutbacks in budgets and personnel can have important effects—and can also lead to important backlash effects.

The larger issue in this regard, however, is the ability of regulatory agencies to perform their functions in an effective manner. Merely funding and staffing an agency do not ensure that it will perform its functions well or that the intended objectives will be achieved. Likewise, cutting a regulatory agency's budget does not necessarily reduce the burdens it imposes on the private sector. In fact, some budget cuts could have the reverse effect—for example, by creating delays in issuing permits needed to authorize new construction.

For the time being, budgetary moderation and a small measure of austerity characterize the activities of most federal regulatory agencies. The slowdown in the growth of federal regulatory agencies which began in the late 1970s has been continued in the early 1980s.

As one astute observer has noted, the many specific changes introduced by the Reagan administration have significantly altered the tone of business-government relations: "A relatively adversary relationship has been replaced by a far more cooperative one. . . . For the first time in more than a decade, companies have begun to scale back their Washington lobbying efforts."[16]

Conclusions and Recommendations

Actions on the regulatory reform front during the past two and one-half years have simultaneously failed to meet the high hopes of regulatory reform enthusiasts and the fears of the defenders of the existing body of federal regulation. The regulatory system is far from consisting solely of rulings that generate more benefits than costs, nor is it about to wither away. The similarities between the regulatory system of mid-1983 and that of early 1981 are far greater than the differences.

Yet the spokesmen of the counterattack against regulatory reform provide a very different viewpoint. I provide an excerpt of a recent article by Michael Pertschuk, former chairman and now a member of the Federal Trade Commission:

> A goodly number of Mr. Reagan's regulators have now spent two years dismantling the very regulations that in prior incarnations as corporate lawyers and lobbyists they had opposed.

---

16. David Vogel, "Reagan and Regulation: Whence and Whither?" *New Management* (Spring 1983), p. 37.

... Their deregulatory plans are fueled by an admixture of free-market ideology and corporate sycophancy. Consumers are merely bugs on the windshield.[17]

Such vituperative attacks on motives rather than on substance may ultimately improve the prospects for regulatory reform. I am reminded of the old maxim: "If the law is against you, argue the facts; if the facts are against you, argue the law; if they are both against you, bang on the table."

This surely is not the time to rest on laurels. Only a fraction of the regulatory reforms envisioned at the beginning of 1981 have been accomplished. Most of the progress has been made in the form of administrative changes, especially in establishing a comprehensive and fairly effective system for reviewing pending rule making. The incorporation of formal cost-benefit analysis in that review process constitutes a major advance. Cost-benefit analysis is a developing mechanism, especially as it is applied to regulation. Additional improvements in administrative procedures are both desirable and possible.

Nevertheless, the major obstacles to further substantial improvement in the regulatory process clearly cannot be eliminated by executive action. The basic statutes governing all regulatory activities are full of rigid requirements and limitations that can only be changed by act of Congress.

Recent experience shows that the fundamental shortcomings of government regulation result from statutory deficiencies more than from administrative ones. As pointed out previously, the courts have struck down many specific changes on the grounds that the proposals were inconsistent with the statutes under which the regulatory agencies operate.

Many existing laws mandate unrealistic goals or unreasonable methods for social regulation and need to be revised. Such onerous regulations range from the "zero discharge" goal of the Clean Water Act to the "zero risk" provision of the Delaney Amendment of the Food, Drug and Cosmetic Act. Recent experiences in the environmental area demonstrate the need for regulators to conform to existing statutes, whatever their shortcomings may be. But that experience also underscores the need to update statutory requirements.

I do not underestimate the importance of improving administrative review of existing, as well as proposed, regulations. Nor do I ignore the counterpressures from those who constantly seek to enlarge the federal presence in economic decision making.[18] Nevertheless, the time is ripe for meeting those

---

17. Michael Pertschuk, "The Case for Consumerism," *New York Times Magazine*, May 29, 1983, p. 26.
18. "A Bipartisan Swing Back to More Regulation," *Business Week*, May 30, 1983, pp. 74–75.

pressures head-on by developing the groundwork for a new phase of regulatory reform: the review and revision of the substantive laws governing the regulatory process. I fear that the ensuing debate will be reported in the national media mainly via sensational charges and countercharges that obscure the underlying issues, and possibly result in a deterioration of the status quo. Preparing a solid foundation of information and analysis will indeed be a challenge. Regaining public support for improving the performance of the nation's regulatory apparatus is vital.

At the organizational level, the entire regulatory reform effort needs renewed leadership. The administration should assign a full-time, senior staff member to regulatory oversight if continued progress is to be made. Regulatory reform is too important to be assigned as a part-time responsibility to senior officials with many other responsibilities, as is the case since the termination of Vice-President Bush's task force. Nor should the task be delegated to middle management levels, which would clearly signal a lowered priority.

William Ruckelshaus, once again the head of EPA, sounds a cautionary note. He contends that the current climate in Congress is not favorable for considering changes in environmental legislation. The problem, as he put it, is that "Congress doesn't trust the agency to do what it's mandated to do" and, thus, is not willing to look favorably on legislative changes proposed by the White House, regardless of their merits.[19] Ruckelshaus's advice deserves special weight. We will be lucky if by January 1985 we are back where we were in January 1981 in terms of the public's attitude toward statutory reform and social regulation.

Perhaps it would be sensible to focus initially on a few key regulatory areas where serious professional analysis provides a strong foundation for statutory revision. The Food and Drug Administration comes to mind as a good example. Various academic studies have demonstrated the high costs and, more particularly, the adverse effects on consumers of the "drug lag."[20] In another area, the complexity of automobile regulation provides opportunity for reviewing and rationalizing the sometimes conflicting requirements of energy, safety, and environmental regulations.[21]

More fundamentally, Ruckelshaus's statement, as well as recent events at EPA, underscores the importance of carefully selecting appointees to reg-

---

19. Andy Pasztor, "EPA Chief Says Tougher Pollution Laws are Possible, Concedes White House Erred," *Wall Street Journal*, June 21, 1983, p. 2.

20. Henry G. Grabowski and John M. Vernon, *The Regulation of Pharmaceuticals* (Washington, D.C.: American Enterprise Institute, 1983), pp. 29–48.

21. Lawrence J. White, *The Regulation of Air Pollutant Emissions from Motor Vehicles* (Washington, D.C.: American Enterprise Institute, 1982), pp. 92–110.

ulatory agencies. The experiences of several administrations in recent years demonstrate the need to select people who take a balanced approach to the benefits and burdens of regulation. Appointing uncritical enthusiasts for expansion of government regulation produces a regulatory climate characterized by excessive burdens and cavalier disregard of economic impacts. Similarly, regulators who lack sympathy for the programs they administer—or who, through lack of sensitivity, project such a negative viewpoint—are counterproductive. As we have seen vividly in the last two years, such appointees can set back the prospects for regulatory reform substantially. The lack of progress on the Clean Air Act is the most striking case in point. Some may argue that the Reagan administration has forestalled a new burst of regulatory activism. On the other hand, its actions may be leading inadvertently to a round of expanding governmental intervention.

As our task force urged in 1980, worthwhile regulatory activities should be managed by people who are both sympathetic to the important social objectives to be achieved and who are equally concerned with minimizing the burdens they impose on individual citizens as taxpayers and as consumers. The leadership of the regulatory agencies must understand that good policy making means a careful balancing of a variety of important considerations—such as clean air *and* high employment, healthier working conditions *and* greater productivity.

It is often difficult for political appointees to take over the leadership of the regulatory agencies, particularly in the case of relatively new agencies where many employees were recruited during a very different policy environment. For example, a group of ex-regulators from the Carter administration boast that they will use networks of civil servants at their former agencies to oppose the Reagan administration's regulatory relief efforts. "These people will tip off the former administrators," says Robert Nelson, research director of the self-styled Regulatory Audit Group. "Yes, . . . the network exists," confirms group member Joan Claybrook, former head of the National Highway Traffic Safety Administration.[22] Managing a regulatory agency under such circumstances is quite a challenge. Public understanding is helpful, and a stronger statutory foundation for more balanced regulation becomes essential.

Most importantly, Congress needs to demonstrate a sense of balance when it writes the basic regulatory laws. The task of updating regulatory statutes is not easy. The types of changes that should be made depend on the nature of existing regulation, the specific regulatory mechanisms currently in

---

22. "The Moles of NHTSA," *Fortune*, April 18, 1983, p. 40.

use, and the shortcomings, if any, in the unregulated private economy. A simple or uniform response is not appropriate. Each regulatory law should be examined individually, carefully, and dispassionately.

Although they were generally ignored, the final report of Vice-President Bush's task force contained ten guidelines for regulatory policy. The guidelines were prepared with the regulatory agencies in mind, but Congress could well benefit from many of these concepts if and when it takes up the task of reviewing the statutory basis for regulation (see table 4).[23]

George Steiner, an experienced observer of business-government relations in the United States, has provided what may prove to be a realistic appraisal of what can be expected in the near term:

> The most optimistic assessment of success for the Reagan Administration's regulatory reform efforts will not spell more than a marginal diminution of the massive pile of present-day regulation. Nor will regulatory reform blunt the strong pressures for more government regulation of business. The best that can be hoped for is a slowing down of the trend of growing government regulations and a reduction in specific unwise, unjust, and unnecessary regulations.[24]

Steiner's relative pessimism results from his expectation that the numbers and strength of special interest groups will continue to grow. He concludes that most of these groups will be no more compromising in the future than they are at present.[25] Nevertheless, in contrast to its rapid growth and expansion in the recent past, federal regulatory activity has taken a more modest path in the Reagan administration. In part, it built on the earlier work begun in both the Ford and Carter administrations. When the current emotional clamor—especially surrounding EPA—has been dissipated, the Reagan administration or its successor may be able to provide new leadership for another round of regulatory reform. Such new leadership should learn from the successes and failures of its predecessors. Nevertheless, it may face an uphill battle. The high levels of enthusiasm and interest in regulatory reform that were so evident in early 1981 will be difficult to revive.

In developing public support for regulatory reform, we must distinguish between reducing the burdens on business and adopting more efficient and more effective modes of regulation. As long as regulatory changes are seen as primarily a problem for business, there will be limited public support for reform. The public believes that business executives are paid to deal with difficult problems, including those that arise in complying with regulation. Moreover, as David Vogel has noted, the business community itself does not necessarily welcome sweeping changes in the basic structure of government

---

23. Presidential Task Force, *Reagan Regulatory Achievements*, p. 19.
24. George A. Steiner, *The New CEO* (New York: Macmillan, 1982), pp. 13, 105.
25. Ibid., p. 105.

TABLE 4
Regulatory Policy Guidelines

1. Regulations should be issued only on evidence that their potential benefits exceed their potential costs. Regulatory objectives, and the methods for achieving these objectives, should be chosen to maximize the net benefits to society.
2. Regulation of prices and production in competitive markets should be avoided. Entry into private markets should be regulated only where necessary to protect health or safety or to manage public resources efficiently.
3. Federal regulations should not prescribe uniform quality standards for private goods or services, except where these products are needlessly unsafe or product variations are wasteful, and voluntary private standards have failed to correct the problem.
4. Regulations that seek to reduce health or safety risks should be based upon scientific risk-assessment procedures, and should address risks that are real and significant rather than hypothetical or remote.
5. Health, safety, and environmental regulations should address ends rather than means.
6. Licensing and permitting decisions and reviews of new products should be made swiftly and should be based on standards that are clearly defined in advance.
7. Qualifications for receiving government licenses should be the minimum necessary. Where there are more qualified applicants than available licenses, the licenses should be allocated by auction or random lottery rather than by administrative procedures.
8. Where regulations create private rights or obligations, unrestricted exchange of these rights or obligations should be encouraged.
9. Federal regulations should not preempt state laws or regulations, except to guarantee rights of national citizenship or to avoid significant burdens on interstate commerce.
10. Regulations establishing terms or conditions of federal grants, contracts, or financial assistance should be limited to the minimum necessary to achieving the purposes for which the funds were authorized and appropriated.

Source: Presidential Task Force on Regulatory Relief.

regulation, a structure that many firms have learned to adjust to and to integrate into their long-term planning.[26]

Regulatory reform is fundamentally a consumer issue. Consumers bear the burden of the costs of compliance and have the key stake in another round of regulatory reform.

---

26. Vogel, "Reagan and Regulation," p. 40.

COMMENTS

Robert W. Crandall

Murray Weidenbaum has set out on a difficult task: the evaluation of the first two years of the Reagan regulatory program—a program that he helped to design. Despite his close involvement with the program, Weidenbaum admits quite frankly that regulatory reform has not proceeded as rapidly as he would have liked. In part, this lack of progress is due to tactical errors made by the Reagan administration, but there are numerous other reasons. An unsympathetic Congress, an unhelpful press, and naive public support for the status quo are also to blame.

Weidenbaum reviews the recommendations made by a Reagan campaign task force on regulation which he chaired. These included strong appointments, a commitment to economic deregulation, forceful White House review of social regulations, and changes in fundamental environmental, health, and safety statutes. Weidenbaum confesses that after two years the administration can only claim success in establishing White House reviews, obtaining some minor statutory changes, and slashing agency operating budgets. Appointments, reform of the environmental, health, and safety statutes, and even economic deregulation have been major disappointments.

Weidenbaum contends that the appointments of James Watt and Anne Gorsuch created such widespread public reaction against the Reagan administration that meaningful progress in reforming environmental policy became impossible. He admits, however, that the decision to label the entire regulatory reform program as "regulatory relief" was also responsible for much of the new administration's difficulty in this area. The program appeared to be designed to save business firms compliance costs at the risk of increasing the public's exposure to unwanted health and safety risks. Had the administration been less eager to stress the reduction of regulatory burdens and more willing to emphasize the positive benefits of meaningful reform, it might have fared better in the court of public opinion.

Weidenbaum focuses most of his attention on the OMB review effort and the trend in regulatory agency budgets. He does not compare this effort with those of preceding administrations, nor did he convince me that Reagan's regulatory review process is much more effective than the Carter process. The totting up of total savings from "completed regulatory reforms" by the Bush task force is cited as evidence of progress, but I doubt the accuracy of this summation. Some of these reforms, such as the "emissions trading policy," cannot be attributed to the Reagan administration at all; others, such as those involving passive restraints, have not occurred. Moreover, one suspects that these crude estimates of cost savings are biased upward in many cases.

More important, I had hoped that Weidenbaum would reflect on how a regulatory review process might be structured to achieve the best results. Can such a process work when the number of regulations is very large? Will the agencies not find ways to defeat the process by submitting artificially stringent proposals from which they can retreat strategically? When should the review process begin? Should it be established at OMB, or should it be closed even to the president?

Weidenbaum's paper gives the impression that regulatory review and budget reductions have succeeded in slowing the regulatory process. To Weidenbaum, this represents progress although he admits the possibility that reductions in staff and budgets could increase the burden of regulatory delays. Until Congress reduces the scope of the agencies' regulatory authority and the necessity for detailed standard setting, one has to question whether smaller is better. If budget and staffing reductions induce changes in regulatory statutes, perhaps the Reagan "regulatory relief" program will eventually bear fruit. Unfortunately, Weidenbaum tells us, there is little momentum in Congress to reform the basic statutes that govern health, safety, and environmental regulation.

How then do we get meaningful reform? How can Congress be moved to change the regulatory statutes to admit sensible trade-offs and truly effective policies? I suggest that we need much more evidence on the effectiveness and efficiency of existing policies and the extent of regulatory failure. The Reagan administration has provided no such analyses, nor has it encouraged the agencies to indulge in introspective exercises. We appear to be missing a major opportunity for developing the empirical record that might facilitate legislative changes in the years or decades ahead. Without such evidence, environmental policy will still be made on the basis of emotional responses to the most recent health scare. OSHA will continue to regulate safety while delaying the difficult health-related decisions. Automobile safety regulation will remain an enormously costly legal and political football. Merely slowing the rate of new regulation is not enough to constitute a successful program of regulatory reform. I think that Weidenbaum would agree with this assessment, but he seems unwilling to suggest a way out of the current stalemate.

COMMENTS

Jerry J. Jasinowski

Murray Weidenbaum's paper provides a useful assessment of the Reagan administration's regulatory reform program. It avoids hyperbole, while correctly identifying many of the improvements made in the organizational and procedural review process compared to what existed in the Carter administration. And it honestly acknowledges the poor performance of the administration in significantly changing the underlying statutes.

The most significant question, in my opinion, is why the administration's record is so deficient in the area of substantive reform of underlying statutes. The short answer is the traditional political shortcoming of generating expectations far in excess of any reasonable assessment of the situation. The administration simply promised far more regulatory reform than it could hope to deliver. And the business community, for its part, was only too happy to accept the rhetoric at face value.

In more detail, I see four reasons for the expectation-reality gap in the area of substantive reform. First, the administration's inflated expectations fueled a growing sentiment for cutting regulatory interference at the national level. The administration's regulatory reform program also got caught up in the general supply-side rhetoric that characterized its first year in office. For example, at one point the unrealistic suggestion was made—and reported by the media—that much of the responsibility for the Clean Air Act be turned back to the states.

Second, the administration was not sufficiently committed to regulatory reform in terms of using its political clout to win major legislative battles. When senior members of the White House staff were asked when there would be a big push in a specific area of regulatory legislation, the reply was invariably, "After we finish the tax and budget issues." The tax and budget agenda never ended, and the administration never seemed to learn how to walk and chew gum at the same time.

Third, political and technical novices were given responsibility for some of the regulatory reform initiatives. The Clean Air Act again serves as an example. How could the administration have believed that a statement of principles would be a successful legislative vehicle for such a controversial issue? The technical and political expertise to get the job done on Capitol Hill was simply lacking.

Fourth, the public increasingly perceived that the Reagan administration did not care very fervently about the environment. This perception was generated in part by a hostile environmental movement and unbalanced press coverage, but the administration's probusiness rhetoric aggravated the perception that it was not sufficiently concerned about the environment. And, of course, the EPA developments made it extremely difficult to argue that such deficiencies were not present.

Whatever the deficiencies of the administration in this area, the Congress continues to be an enormous part of the problem with respect to moving regulatory reform forward. Whether because of the hopelessly complicated nature of the laws, or Congress's overly sensitive attention to the electorate, or its tendency for "policy entrepreneurism"—the constant search for new ways in which members can look good on the environment—Congress is a major part of the problem. We need to address ways in which the incentives and the structures in Congress can be changed to accommodate regulatory reform in addition to whatever criticism we make of the Reagan administration in the area of substantive legislative reform.

Let me now turn from legislative reform to my second point, which is the organizational and procedural changes that have occurred thus far in the Reagan administration. I concur with Murray Weidenbaum that the administration made major progress in its quest for regulatory reform by centralizing the process, strengthening the review procedures, and encouraging tougher analysis. Let me make five points here.

Executive Order 12291 was an exceptionally good framework built on the authority provided by the Paperwork Act passed under President Carter and continuing many of the elements of reform advocated by students of regulatory reform for some time. But it went much further and had a sharper focus.

Second, abolishing the Regulatory Council, which had consistently impeded major regulatory reform efforts in the Carter administration, and replacing it with OMB oversight under the vice-president, provided the means to get some overall control over the regulatory process and to place it on a footing that was comparable to budget policy.

Third, increasing the analytical requirements of the agencies, particularly with respect to more stringent cost-benefit requirements at the agency level, improved the quality of information sent to OMB and reviewed by the vice-president's Task Force on Regulatory Relief.

Fourth, slowing down the proliferation of new regulations, either because they were moving too rapidly, or because they were among the so-called midnight regulations approved in the final stages of the Carter administration, provided an opportunity for more reasonable review. As Weidenbaum pointed out, OMB approved most of the new regulations. Only 91 out of 2,715 were disapproved or sent back for further review.

Fifth, the Reagan initiatives resulted in major cost savings. You can argue about the numbers, but whether you accept the $9 billion estimate or the $6 billion figure, the progress was meaningful.

For these reasons, I would give high marks to the Reagan administration's procedural reform effort. I am aware of the arguments made against this reform—that it is too centralized and does not provide adequate review procedures. But I hope we would not back away from the advantages that accrued under OMB. I think we need to improve the agencies' analyses still more and further strengthen the review procedures, but to go back to the earlier decentralized regulatory environment would be a big mistake.

I would like more information in three areas. First, how do we make greater progress in substantive regulatory reform? Second, what do the budget cuts really mean? I am convinced that a substantial number of agencies were not harmed, but I think that others were. Weidenbaum does not provide a good sense of how the budget cuts have affected regulatory enforcement. Third, what qualities should good regulatory appointees possess? Weidenbaum does not sufficiently elaborate on this crucial question.

In conclusion, the Reagan administration took a major step forward in its improved review of federal regulations. Unfortunately, it has not moved on to the second stage of regulatory reform involving substantive legislative changes. I have outlined several reasons for this shortcoming, which cannot simply be attributed to lack of public support. I think, among other things, it is the result of a lack of administration commitment to substantive reform.

To move forward means moving toward a substantive legislative review, addressing the overall relationship of the legislative review to the procedural changes, and finally—and I think this is important—maintaining sufficient credibility and trust so that continued progress can be made. The Reagan administration needs to reestablish its credibility so that regulatory reform can go forward.

THE REAGAN ADMINISTRATION'S REGULATORY RELIEF EFFORT: A MID-TERM ASSESSMENT

Gregory B. Christainsen and Robert H. Haveman

When the Reagan administration assumed office in January 1981, it inherited an unattractive portfolio of serious macroeconomic problems. As measured by the consumer price index, the rate of inflation had been 12.4 percent during the previous year. Since 1973, the average annual rate of growth in nonfarm business productivity had been only 0.5 percent. The unemployment rate was 7.4 percent.

The incoming administration believed it was not mere coincidence that the nation's macroeconomic performance had worsened at the same time that the scope and volume of public regulations had increased. Considering first just the direct costs of federal regulatory activities, the expenses of regulatory agencies amounted to $2.3 billion in fiscal 1973 and had increased to $6.1 billion by fiscal 1980, an increase of more than 50 percent in constant dollars. Many believed the indirect burden imposed on the private sector by federal regulations in terms of compliance costs to be several times larger than the direct costs. Thus the new administration made deregulation an integral part of its supply-side policies.

This paper examines the impact of public regulation (and deregulation) on the nation's rate of productivity growth in the context of *supply-side* economics. Although conventional policies of monetary and fiscal restraint (*demand-side* economics) may bring about a reduction in the nation's inflation rate, they may also, for a time, cause a reduction in the nation's real output of goods and services. Unless these policies are complemented by measures that will bolster real aggregate supply, a decline in material living standards will result during the disinflation process. This paper addresses the issue of whether the impact of a general program of deregulation on the rate of productivity growth is likely to involve a significant increase in the nation's aggregate supply of goods and services.

The first section compares supply-side economics with more conventional approaches to the nation's macroeconomic problems. This discussion emphasizes the importance of productivity growth—and what determines it. The second section describes the nation's productivity performance.

The third section briefly reviews the research that has attempted to estimate the magnitude of the regulatory impact. We note that most of the attempts to assess the impact of regulation on productivity growth have been confined to regulations intended to protect the natural environment. We then offer a summary appraisal of the impact of regulation on productivity growth.

The fourth section discusses the deregulatory efforts of the Reagan administration and assesses their likely impact on productivity growth. In particular, we describe the activities of the Presidential Task Force on Regulatory Relief. This task force estimated the cost savings resulting from its deregulatory initiatives; using these estimates, we then employ a growth-accounting procedure to estimate the impact of these initiatives on productivity growth. We estimate the productivity benefits associated with deregulation efforts in each major regulatory agency, in addition to estimating the impact of deregulation efforts in general.

An alternative approach for assessing the impact of regulation and deregulation is to undertake new econometric estimates that include data from the deregulation efforts in 1981 and 1982, as well as data from prior years. We develop measures of the "intensity" of regulatory activities, and use these measures in time-series regressions designed to assess the relationship between regulatory efforts and productivity growth.

The paper concludes by assessing the overall relationship between regulation (and deregulation) and productivity growth, and the implications of this relationship for supply-side economics.

The Nature of Supply-Side Economics

In January 1981, public opinion polls proclaimed inflation to be the nation's "number one problem." The Reagan administration proposed to address the inflation problem through policy measures collectively known as supply-side economics. This section of the paper discusses the nature of supply-side economics and the issue it raises with respect to government regulation.

Standard economic theory postulates that rising prices are due to an increase in the demand for goods and services relative to the supply of goods and services. Government policies to reduce the nation's inflation rate must therefore bring about either a deceleration in the aggregate demand for output or an acceleration in the aggregate supply of output. Conventional policies of monetary and fiscal restraint (demand-side economics) might therefore help reduce the rate of inflation, but they might also, for a time, cause a decline in material living standards, as shown below.

According to standard theory, monetary and fiscal restraints cause the economy's aggregate demand curve to shift leftward of its position in the absence of restraint. Figure 1 represents this shift by the movement of the y^d curve, which shows the quantity of real output (y) demanded at the various possible price levels (P).

Looking at the equilibrium values of the price level and real output—as determined by the intersection of the aggregate demand curve (y^d) and a curve representing aggregate supply (y^s)—one sees that monetary and fiscal restraints result not only in lower prices ($P_1 < P_0$), but also in a reduction of real output ($y_1 < y_0$), implying lower living standards.[1]

A macroeconomic view that gained much popularity during the 1970s maintains, however, that if monetary and fiscal restraints persist, the reduced output will be a transitory phenomenon. According to this view, suppliers of output will realize that the general level of prices is lower than they had anticipated. This means the nominal price that they receive for their output has a higher real value than it would have had. Thus, they will supply more output at any given price level than they would have done otherwise. In figure 2, this situation is represented by a rightward shift of the aggregate supply curve (y^s). Thus, real output may end up at the same level that would have existed in the absence of monetary and fiscal restraints ($y_2 = y_0$), while prices end up significantly lower ($P_2 < P_1 < P_0$).

Before price perceptions change, however, there is a transition period during which aggregate demand restraint causes erosion of living standards. Policymakers have continually sought measures that would bypass such a period. Figure 2 shows that if one could cause a strong rightward shift in the aggregate supply curve from the very outset, one could, in principle, bring about price restraint without causing a reduction in real output.

---

1. This, of course, requires that the aggregate supply curve has a positive slope, as drawn. The standard argument is that, in the short run—holding workers' price-level expectations constant—a change in prices will, given nominal wages, have a negative effect on real wages and thus a positive effect on the quantity of labor demanded and the quantity of output supplied.

FIGURE 1

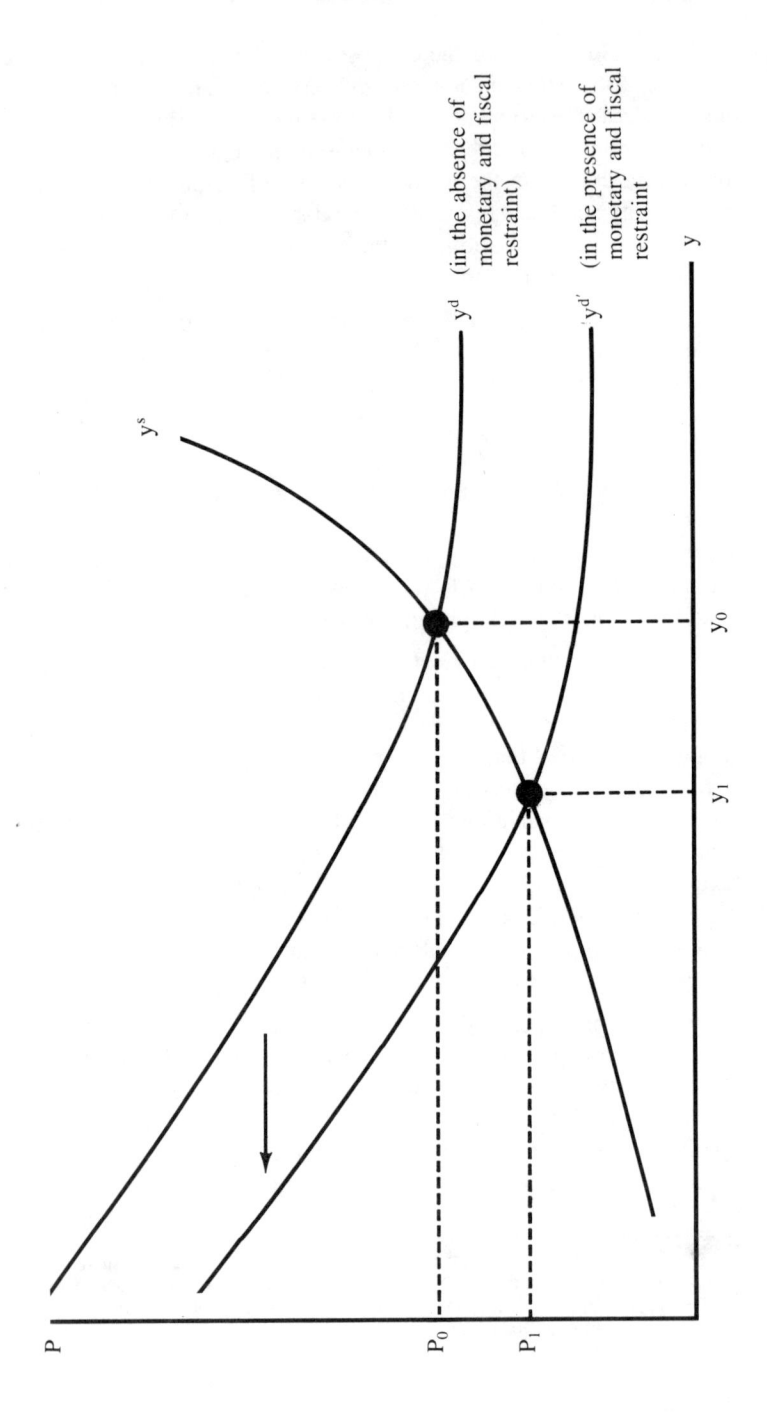

FIGURE 2

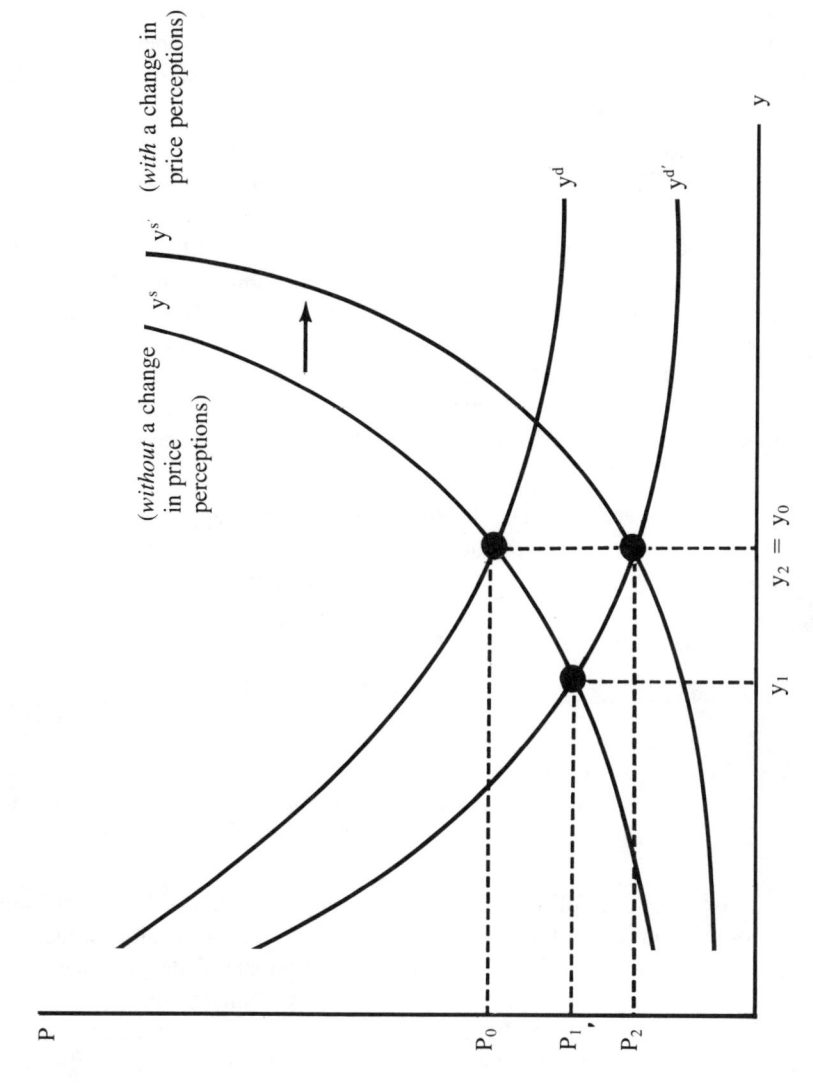

Economists have proposed a variety of measures to augment the aggregate supply of output. One common proposal suggests that the adjustment of price perceptions be speeded by an incomes policy (wage and price controls), wherein the government actively intervenes in the price-setting process. Another proposal is to subsidize employers or give them tax credits for additions to their work forces. Alternatively, subsidies might be granted for retraining or relocating workers who might have otherwise become unemployed. Likewise, subsidies might be granted for relocating capital that might have otherwise been unemployed.

The Reagan administration rejected the idea of actively intervening in the price-setting process; and while it has entertained proposals for employment subsidies and retraining and relocation assistance, these have not been prominent in its policy portfolio. Instead, the administration proposed to augment real output by supply-side measures including: (1) reducing marginal tax rates on personal and business income, (2) reforming or reducing the scope of income transfer programs, and (3) embarking on a general program of regulatory relief and reform. The administration argued that, combined with a program of gradual monetary restraint, such measures could bring about a reduction in the inflation rate without an extended period of declining real output—that is, without a prolonged recession.

To be successful, any measure for increasing aggregate supply must increase productivity or the quantity of inputs used in production. This can be seen simply by looking at the following identity:

$$y = \frac{y}{TFI} \times TFI,$$ where TFI is total factor input. Output per unit of total factor input is referred to as total factor productivity.

Alternatively, one can write:

$$y = \frac{y}{l} \times l,$$ where l is units of labor input; $\frac{y}{l}$ refers to labor productivity.

Whether one defines productivity as output per unit of total factor input or output per unit of labor input, the Reagan administration argued that (1) productivity growth had experienced a pronounced deceleration during the 1970s, (2) government regulation played a significant role in this deceleration, and (3) a general program of deregulation was an essential part of a set of policies designed to increase productivity and the aggregate supply of output. We now turn to an examination of these claims.

Productivity Growth from 1965 to 1980: Facts and Conjectures

By any measure, productivity growth in the United States has sharply declined since the mid-1960s. From 1947 to 1966, output per person-hour in the private sector grew at an average annual rate of 3.44 percent. During this period, except for cyclical deviations from the trend rate of growth, the series was a relatively smooth one. Beginning in 1966 or 1967, however, a break appears in the time trend. From 1966 to 1973, private-sector output per person-hour grew at an average annual rate of 2.15 percent, a decline of almost 1.3 percentage points from the earlier period. In 1973, a further break occurred; from 1973 to 1978, the annual growth rate of private-sector output registered only 1.15 percent—only one-third of the rate recorded for the immediate postwar period and a further decline of a full percentage point from the 1966–1973 period.

Beginning in 1979, the productivity series moved little if any. In both 1979 and 1980, the private-sector index declined by nearly 1 percent. Productivity grew by more than 1 percent in 1981, but it grew less than 0.5 percent in 1982. In 1982, the private-sector productivity index stood only one percentage point above its level in 1977; the productivity index for the nonfarm private sector stood exactly at its 1977 level. Whether this pattern reflects a third structural break in the series or simply the effect of cyclical factors reflected in the recession of that period is not clear at this point. Table 1 summarizes the postwar pattern of growth in aggregate productivity in the United States.

Numerous reasons have been put forward to explain the deceleration in aggregate productivity growth from 1965 to 1980. We shall discuss a few of these factors.

Two major sectoral shifts in the composition of output have occurred in recent decades, both of which have contributed to the productivity slowdown. The first shift has been from the low-productivity farm sector to the nonfarm sector. Second, within the nonfarm sector, output has shifted away from higher-productivity manufacturing industries toward lower-productivity service industries.

Most of the shift from farm to nonfarm output occurred before 1966; since 1967, very little additional movement has taken place. Hence, one of the major sources of productivity growth in the two decades after the war no longer existed in the 1970s.

The second shift—from production of manufactured goods to services—also contributed to the slowdown in the nonfarm business sector. The relative

TABLE 1

POSTWAR ANNUAL PRODUCTIVITY GROWTH RATES IN THE UNITED STATES, VARIOUS MEASURES OF PRODUCTIVITY
(In percentages)

	Output per Person-Hour, Private Sector	Output per Person-Hour, Nonfarm Private Sector	Nonresidential Business Income per Person Employed	Total Factor Productivity in Domestic Private Business
1947–1966	3.44	2.83	2.9	2.9[a]
1966–1973	2.15	1.87	1.3	1.4[b]
1973–1978	1.15	1.02	−0.1	NA
1979	−0.9	−1.3	NA	NA
1980	−0.7	−0.9	NA	NA
1981	1.8	1.4	NA	NA
1982	−0.4	0.2	NA	NA

SOURCES: Figures for output per person-hour in the private sector and in the nonfarm private sector were taken from the *Economic Report of the President* (Washington, D.C.: GPO, 1983). Figures for nonresidential business income per person employed were taken from E. Denison, *Accounting for Slower Economic Growth* (Washington, D.C.: Brookings Institution, 1979). Figures for total factor productivity in domestic private business were taken from J. Kendrick's testimony, 1978 in U.S. Congress, Joint Economic Committee, *Special Study on Economic Change*, 1978 Hearings, part 2, pp. 616–636.
a. For years 1948–1966.
b. For years 1966–1976.
NA = Not available.

share of manufacturing in total employment has declined steadily for more than two decades. Because the opportunities for introducing mass production techniques or achieving economies of scale are relatively limited in the service sector, productivity is below that in manufacturing and has tended to grow more slowly as well. As a result, the shift away from manufacturing and toward services has tended to reduce overall growth in productivity.

Advances in knowledge can enhance productivity in either of two ways. They can directly enhance the quality of inputs (e.g., better-educated workers) or they can enable producers to combine existing inputs more efficiently. As a percentage of gross national product (GNP), spending for research and development (R&D) reached a peak of 3 percent in the mid-1960s. After 1966, however, R&D spending underwent a slow decline and, in 1980, accounted for only about 2 percent of GNP.

Since 1966, the size of the labor force and labor force participation rates have increased sharply, especially among women and teenagers. Because these groups have modest amounts of work experience and job training, they have lower levels of productivity than their more experienced counterparts. This expansion in the less skilled portion of the labor force is likely to have reduced the average growth rate of labor productivity.

The level of investment in the economy and, in turn, the ratio of capital to labor are also important in achieving increases in productivity. At the same time that the labor force in the United States increased its growth rate, the country's capital stock grew at a somewhat reduced rate. Net of depreciation, capital per employed person rose at an average annual rate of about 2.0 percent from 1948 to 1969, whereas between 1969 and 1980, the annual rate of growth fell to about 1.2 percent.

For many years, the United States enjoyed the availability of cheap energy. The Organization of Petroleum Exporting Countries (OPEC) cartel increased the world price of crude oil first in 1973 and then again in 1979 after the Iranian revolution. These oil price shocks undoubtedly affected productivity and economic performance in a number of industrialized Western nations. Changes in relative prices occur daily without tremendous strain to the economic system, but the magnitude of the energy price changes in 1973 and 1979, combined with the complementary nature of energy and capital, was a serious blow. The sharp hike in energy prices increased the obsolescence of much of the capital already invested. Plants and equipment intended to be used for several more years suddenly became less profitable to employ. Moreover, businesses faced adjustment costs in learning how to operate in the face of increased energy prices and in making necessary changes in the structure of production.

By definition, government regulations are interventions into market processes. They alter the utility and profit-maximizing decisions of individual decision makers. In a smoothly functioning market economy, such interventions cause deviations in private-sector production levels. If output composition is held constant, this deviation means that additional inputs are required to reach any given level of output. Under these conditions, increases in government regulation are associated with larger deviations from the potential level of private output and, hence, reduced rates of growth of output per unit of input. In other words, increased regulation causes decreases in growth of productivity.

Over the past several years, government regulations have required increasing amounts of labor and capital to be devoted to pollution abatement. While such mandated investments may generate substantial benefits, their contribution to the output of marketable goods and services is minimal. In the mid-1970s, capital spending stood at about 9.5 percent of GNP. This figure drops to 8.6 percent if one assumes that the investments mandated by government regulations were nonproductive. If adapting to these regulations causes inputs to be employed that make little contribution to measured output, then measured productivity suffers on this account.

Several other factors have been cited as possible causes of the slowdown in productivity growth: disincentive effects of income taxes and transfers, disruption of expectations brought about by rapidly changing rates of inflation, negative attitudes toward work, and the deterioration of management capabilities. In general, investigations to date have been unable to measure accurately these factors or to identify the magnitude of their role in the slowdown of productivity growth.

Regulations and Productivity Growth in the 1960s and 1970s: Estimates of Impact

The intensity of public regulation of the private sector increased rapidly in the 1960s and 1970s. The list of areas in which the government intervened during this period is extensive: air and water pollution control, control of toxic wastes, occupational health and safety, consumer product safety, and food and drug safety are but the primary ones. Yet measuring the intensity of public regulation is difficult.

The Census Bureau, the Bureau of Economic Analysis of the Department of Commerce, and McGraw-Hill all collect reports from companies on the costs of complying with pollution control and worker safety regulations.[2] Given the reporting incentives in these government requests, the reported compliance costs are likely to be biased upward. Moreover, these series fail to accurately reflect a wide variety of other cost-related factors associated with regulations.[3]

We define *regulatory intensity* as the extent to which government regulatory activity distorts optimal private-sector decisions that would maximize the measured rate of productivity growth. We have constructed three alternative indices of regulatory intensity for the postwar period. The first is based on an estimate of the cumulative number of major pieces of regulatory leg-

---

2. See *Investment in Employee Safety and Health* (Annual McGraw-Hill Survey); U.S. Department of Commerce, Bureau of Economic Analysis, *Capital Expenditures for Pollution Abatement* (published annually in *Survey of Current Business*); and U.S. Department of Commerce, Bureau of the Census, *Pollution Abatement Cost and Expenditures*, annual issues.

3. An excellent discussion of these measurement problems is found in R. Crandall, "Regulation and Productivity Growth," Reprint no. 375 (Washington, D.C.: Brookings Institution, 1981). He crudely estimates that the BEA data are upward biased by 14–20 percent.

islation in effect during any of the years in question (R_1).[4] The second index is based on the volume of real federal expenditures on regulatory activities for the years in question (R_2), while the third is based on the number of full-time federal personnel engaged in regulatory activities (R_3).[5] For the present study, time-series for R_1, R_2, and R_3 have been constructed for the economy as a whole from 1947 to 1982.[6] Though they are crude proxies for regulatory intensity, we believe these indices provide a reasonable characterization of postwar trends in the regulation of the U.S. economy—indeed, the only characterization available at reasonable cost. These indices do not, however, reflect state and local government regulations or international trade restrictions.

Each of the R indices shows only a gradual increase in regulatory intensity until the mid-1960s. Then all three measures accelerate, with R_2 increasing the most rapidly and R_1 accelerating the least. All of the measures show a further acceleration during the early 1970s, though the acceleration is again least pronounced in the case of R_1. Setting each index equal to 100 in 1947, R_1 attained a level of 288.1 for the economy as a whole in 1980, while R_2 and R_3 reached 898.6 and 710.6, respectively, in the same year. Although there are exceptions, the indices generally imply a monotonic increase in regulatory intensity during the 1947–1980 period, with a decrease in the R_2 and R_3 indices beginning in 1981.

Assuming that a two-year lag is appropriate for measuring the impact of R_1 on economic performance, while the appropriate lags for R_2 and R_3 are

---

4. This series was calculated from data presented in Center for the Study of American Business, *Directory of Federal Regulatory Agencies* (St. Louis: Washington University, 1980, 1981). Regulatory acts such as the Occupational Safety and Health Act, of course, add to the value taken on by the index. Deregulatory acts, such as the Airline Deregulation Act of 1978, subtract from the value taken on by the index.

5. R_2 and R_3 were estimated from agency data published in the Budget of the United States Government. For large, diverse agencies such as the Environmental Protection Agency, data on regulatory functions are separable from other agency functions. For smaller regulatory agencies, we have used expenditure and staffing data for the agency as a whole.

Prior to 1976, calendar-year estimates were obtained by averaging the two fiscal years overlapping the calendar year in question. From 1977 on, calendar-year estimates were obtained by a weighted average—(calendar year = ¾ of associated fiscal year plus ¼ of next fiscal year)—reflecting the movement of the beginning of the fiscal year to October 1. For 1976 itself, calendar year = ½ of associated fiscal year plus value of "transition quarter," plus ¼ of next fiscal year, in the case of R_2. For R_3 in 1976, calendar year = ½ of associated fiscal year plus ¼ of "transition quarter," plus ¼ of next fiscal year.

6. In G. Christainsen and R. Haveman, "Public Regulations and the Slowdown in Productivity Growth," *American Economic Review* (May 1981), pp. 320–325, these indices were constructed for the economy's manufacturing sector.

one year, the intensity of regulatory activity can be roughly divided into five periods. These are indicated in table 2.[7]

The correlation between regulatory intensity during the periods shown in table 2 and the trends in productivity growth indicated in table 1 is noteworthy. This simple statistical relationship—combined with the substantive reasons that public regulations are likely to inhibit measured economic performance—has led analysts to undertake a variety of studies designed to measure the strength of the tie. While the analysts have adopted widely varying procedures in these studies—and the magnitude of the estimated impacts varies widely—they have uniformly established that public regulatory activities affect measured economic performance.

At an aggregate level, Christainsen and Haveman obtained a "first-cut" estimate of the contribution of federal regulations to the productivity slowdown in the manufacturing sector by using a straightforward, production-function-based, time-series regression model.[8] The model they employed presumes that relative factor price changes move the economy along the production frontier while time-related movements caused by business cycle shocks, technical progress, or changes in regulatory intensity cause the function to shift.

The concept of regulatory intensity used is based on adjusted values of the R_1, R_2, and R_3 measures described above, so as to reflect the intensity of

TABLE 2

REGULATORY INTENSITY AS MEASURED BY R_1, R_2, AND R_3, 1947–1982

Degree of Impact	Years During Which Impact Was Felt	R_1 Growth Rate, Two-Year Lag (Percent Change)	R_2 Growth Rate, One-Year Lag (Percent Change)	R_3 Growth Rate, One-Year Lag (Percent Change)
Mild regulatory impact	1947–1966	2.08	3.52	3.10
Increasing regulatory impact	1966–1971	3.98	10.53	5.16
Peak regulatory impact	1971–1975	8.54	19.57	18.56
Decelerating regulatory impact	1975–1981	4.25	4.13	3.55
Regulatory impact stable or decreasing	1981–1982	0	−6.19	−5.13

---

7. If lagged, the simple correlation coefficients among R_1, R_2, and R_3 are: 0.986 (R_1, R_2); 0.978 (R_1, R_3); 0.996 (R_2, R_3).

8. G. Christainsen and R. Haveman, "Public Regulations and the Slowdown in Productivity Growth," *American Economic Review* (May 1981), pp. 320–325.

regulation in the manufacturing sector. Table 3 shows the authors' estimates of the contribution of public regulations to the slowdown in productivity growth. From 1958 to 1965, the average annual impact was from zero to −0.1 percentage point; from 1965 to 1973, it was from −0.1 to −0.3 percentage point; from 1973 to 1977, it was from −0.2 to −0.3 percentage point. These figures suggest that the aggregate of federal regulations were responsible for 12 to 21 percent of the slowdown in the growth of labor productivity in U.S. manufacturing for the 1973–1977 period compared with the 1958–1965 period.[9] A reduction in the ratio of nonlabor to labor inputs accounted for about 15 percent of the slowdown. The contribution of the average cyclical impact accounted for zero to 15 percent of the slowdown.

Although aggregate federal regulatory activity increased in the 1960s and 1970s, the primary rule-making actions were designed to improve air and water quality. Environmental regulations mandated both "technology forcing" and waste treatment expenditures by private industry in an effort to meet ambient air and water quality standards. In addition, public expenditures for the construction of municipal waste treatment plants required either additional tax revenues or reductions in other public expenditures (both of which impact on measured productivity). The emergence of environmental regulatory policy during the 1960s and 1970s caused researchers to focus on these as the primary source of the adverse effect of regulations on productivity growth. Some of

TABLE 3

CONTRIBUTIONS TO THE RATE OF GROWTH OF LABOR PRODUCTIVITY IN U.S. MANUFACTURING, 1958–1977

	Contribution During		
Source	1958–1965	1965–1973	1973–1977
Regulatory intensity	0 to −0.1	−0.1 to −0.3	−0.2 to −0.3
Time trend	0.9 to 1.0	0.9 to 1.0	0.9 to 1.0
Cyclical adjustment	0 to 0.1	0	0 to −0.1
Unexplained	0.4 to 0.5	−0.1 to −0.2	−0.3 to −0.4
Growth in total factor productivity	1.4	0.6	0.3
Ratio of nonlabor to labor inputs	1.6	1.9	1.4
Average growth rate of labor productivity	3.0	2.5	1.7

---

9. See Christainsen and Haveman, "Public Regulations and the Slowdown in Productivity Growth," for the details of this calculation.

these studies have adopted a comprehensive accounting framework requiring that the sum of the contributions of all factors explaining productivity growth not exceed 100 percent. Others rely on time-series analyses of aggregate economic variables, while other studies measure the effects of environmental regulations on the performance of affected industries. Still others employ a comprehensive macroeconometric modeling framework.

Consider, first, the growth accounting studies, of which those by Denison are the most notable examples.[10] In his framework, output in the nonresidential business sector valued at factor cost including profits (i.e., national income originating in this sector) serves as the numerator in the productivity index. The input denominator is a combined measure of labor, capital, and land, in which relative earnings are used to weight the inputs, again consistent with the national product accounts usage. To evaluate the impact of environmental regulations on the productivity index, Denison estimates the incremental costs of production made necessary by environmental regulations. These costs as a percentage of total factor cost are then used as an estimate of the percentage reduction in output per unit of input (productivity) attributable to regulation. This procedure, in effect, assumes that the factor inputs required by environmental policy would, in the absence of these regulations, be used in the production of measured output. Using these definitions, Denison constructs an index indicating the impact of post-1967 regulations on productivity growth. From 1967 to 1969 the average annual impact was −0.05 percentage point; from 1969 to 1973, it was −0.1 percentage point; between 1973 and 1975, the effect peaked at −0.22 percentage point; and between 1975 and 1978, it decreased to −0.08 percentage point.[11]

The time-series approach is exemplified in a study by Siegel.[12] In a very real sense, this approach can also be viewed as an "accounting" or allocation

---

10. E. Denison, "Effects of Selected Changes in the Institutional and Human Environment Upon Output Per Unit of Input," *Survey of Current Business* (January 1978), pp. 21–44; E. Denison, "Pollution Abatement Programs: Estimates of Their Effect Upon Output Per Unit of Input, 1975–1978," *Survey of Current Business* (August 1979), pp. 58–59; and E. Denison, *Accounting for Slower Economic Growth* (Washington, D.C.: Brookings Institution, 1979).

11. One of the striking aspects of the Denison study is the huge residual factor labeled "advances in knowledge and not elsewhere classified" with which he is left. The factor accounts for over half of the total 1948–1969 productivity growth. For 1969–1973, the residual figure of 1.6 percentage points per year equals the measured rate of productivity growth for that period. For 1973–1976, the residual factor suddenly drops to 0.7 percentage point per year, but this is greater in absolute value than the rate of −0.5 percentage point at which productivity changed during these years. Although Denison argues plausibly that advances in knowledge may have contributed less to recent growth, his study does not explain such a sudden decline in this residual category in recent years.

12. R. Siegel, "Why Has Productivity Slowed Down?" *Data Resources U.S. Review*, (March 1979), pp. 1.59–1.65.

approach. The goal is to identify statistically those variables that explain changes in the productivity index—and any statistically significant breaks in the trend of productivity growth—and to allocate observed changes among these variables. In her analysis, Siegel found demographic factors to be a consistent contributor to the slowdown; but beginning in 1973, changes in the relative price of energy were the single most important factor. Pollution abatement expenditures were a significant negative factor in the post-1967 slowdown and contributed to the falloff in productivity growth until 1975.

Table 4 summarizes the results of all of the allocation studies we have been able to identify. Each of these studies seeks to account for the difference in productivity growth from a period before the 1970s to one during the 1970s. The varying periods of comparison and varying definitions of productivity account for differences in the percentage points of the decrease in productivity growth that are being allocated (see the top row). Across all the studies, twenty-one separate determinants of productivity growth are identified.

In the allocation studies that identified cyclical and work-stoppage effects, these determinants generally played a noticeable role. The largest role was assigned by Kendrick, who estimated that cyclical changes accounted for 40 percent of the change he was analyzing (-0.6 percentage point out of 1.5 percentage points). However, this estimate is biased upward by the fact that the study's end point was 1976, a year of very low resource utilization. Most of the studies assigned a somewhat more significant role to shifts in the sectoral composition of output (e.g., from manufacturing to service and from farm to nonfarm) or the age-sex composition of the labor force. These factors accounted for 11 to 40 percent of the change, with the bulk of the estimates in the 20 to 30 percent range. The range of estimated effects due to changes in the capital stock is large. One of the analysts (Kendrick) assigns it a zero role, three assign it a 10 to 15 percent role, and two of the analysts (Siegel and Evans) attribute about one-third of the total decline to a decrease in the productivity contribution of the capital stock. Most of the researchers did not explicitly consider the role of energy prices, wrapping it into their residual category or implicitly assuming that its effect on productivity occurs via the capital stock variable. Siegel, however, did consider energy prices separately and assigned them 39 percent of the total decrease. For environmental and other regulations, the changes range from 0.1 to 0.4 percentage point. In no case are pollution abatement regulations assigned more than 20 percent of the responsibilty for the decrease in productivity growth. The typical estimate of the role of environmental regulations is in the range of 5 to 15 percent.

In addition to the allocation studies described in table 4, a variety of other industry-based cross-sectional and macroeconomic simulation studies have been used to investigate the causes of the post-1965 slowdown in productivity growth.

TABLE 4

FACTORS ACCOUNTING FOR THE RECENT DECLINE IN PRODUCTIVITY GROWTH: VARIOUS ESTIMATES

Factor	Denison[a]	Denison[b]	Kendrick[c]	Siegel[d]	Kutscher et al.[e]	Mark[e]	Evans[f]	Clark[g]	Norsworthy et al.[h]	Thurow[i]
Estimated decline explained (=100%)	3.1[j]	1.1	1.5	1.8	1.2	1.5	1.5	1.9	2.1	2.1
Percentage of decline explained by:										
Labor market tightness			} 40	−11						
Cyclical and work stoppage effects	−7	40		22				11		14
Shifts:										
From manufacturing to service	} 13	10	7	0	} 0/8	−7/7				5
From farm to nonfarm		} 30	7		25	20			10	14
Out of self-employment	−13	−20								
Labor force:										
Hours worked	10	10			} −17/25[k]	13/20	33			
Composition	3	30	20	−11				−5	0	5
Education	−13	−20	−13							
Nonlabor inputs:										
Nonresidential structures and equipment	3	10		} 33	} 0/8	} 13	} 33	} 16/63	} 33	} 20
Inventories	3	0	7							
Other capital	0	10	13							
Land	7	0					20			
Economies of scale				39						} 20
Energy prices	} 13	} 20		0	} 8/17				5	
Government policies:										
Pollution abatement										10/14
Other regulation										
Government services			7							

Expectations			22	
Knowledge:				
Formal advances	⎫		10	⎫
Informal advances	⎬ 68	−20	0	⎬ 13 10 0
Diffusion	⎭		10	⎭
Residual Factors[1]		−7	17/50 40/60 32/84 4̄3̄ 8/12

SOURCES: E. Denison, *Accounting for Slower Economic Growth* (Washington, D.C.: The Brookings Institution, 1979); J. Kendrick, testimony before Congressional Joint Economic Committee, *Special Study on Economic Change: Hearings before Joint Economic Committee, Congress of the United States*, Part II (Washington, D.C.: Government Printing Office, 1978), pp. 616–636; R. Siegel, "Why Has Productivity Slowed Down?" *Data Resources, U.S. Review*, March 1979, pp. 1.59–1.65; R. Kutscher, J. Mark, and J. R. Norsworthy, "The Productivity Slowdown and the Outlook to 1985," *Monthly Labor Review*, May 1977, pp. 3–8; J. Mark, testimony before Congressional Joint Economic Committee, *Special Study on Economic Change*, pp. 476–486; M. Evans, testimony before Congressional Joint Economic Committee, *Special Study on Economic Change*, pp. 596–615; P. Clark, "Capital Formation and the Recent Productivity Slowdown," *Journal of Finance*, June 1978, pp. 965–975; J. R. Norsworthy, M. Harper, and R. Kunze, "The Slowdown in Productivity Growth: Analysis of Some Contributing Factors," *Brookings Papers on Economic Activity*, 2, 1979, pp. 387–421; L. Thurow, "The Productivity Problem," *Technology Review*, Nov./Dec. 1980, pp. 40–51.

NOTE: Components may not always add to 100 because of rounding errors. Positive (negative) numbers represent contributions (offsets) to productivity decline.

a. Compares nonresidential business income per employed person in the 1973–1976 period vs. the 1948–1969 period.
b. Compares nonresidential business income per employed person in the 1968–1973 period vs. the 1948–1969 period.
c. Compares private-sector output per total factor input in 1966–1973 vs. 1948–1966. Kendrick also considered "health and vitality," and found it to have no effect.
d. Compares private nonfarm output per person-hour in 1973–1978 vs. 1955–1965. Siegel also considered "taxes," and found them to have no effect.
e. Compares private output per person-hour in 1966–1977 vs. 1947–1966.
f. Compares private nonfarm output per person-hour in 1968–1977 vs. 1947–1968.
g. Compares private nonfarm output per person-hour in 1973:II–1976:IV vs. 1955:IV–1965:IV.
h. Compares private output per person-hour in 1973–1978 vs. 1948–1965.
i. Compares private output per person-hour in 1972–1978 vs. 1948–1965.
j. Productivity growth rate over recent time spans minus the productivity growth rate over earlier time spans, as indicated in notes a–i.
k. Numbers separated by a slash represent estimated ranges.
l. The portion of the decline in productivity growth not accounted for by the authors was assigned in the "residual factors" category. In the case of Thurow, most of the residual is explained by declining productivity growth in the construction industry.

Two of these studies deserve to be noted. Crandall employs an industry-based, cross-sectional regression model to analyze the potential role of environmental regulation variables on productivity growth.[13] Crandall's analyses are consistent with other studies suggesting a nontrivial role for environmental regulations in the recent productivity slowdown. When allowance is made for measurement and econometric problems in his results, however, he would appear to assign no larger a role to environmental controls than does Denison. Clearly, his estimates are consistent with those in table 4.

A final approach is that taken by the major macroeconometric models. These models typically assume that pollution control investments displace ordinary investments in plant and equipment on a dollar-for-dollar basis. The models then compare the base trend of the economy without the pollution control expenditures to the size and structure of the economy with these induced expenditures.

Data Resources Inc. undertook a recent analysis from this perspective.[14] For the 1970–1986 period, it estimated that environmental regulations would cause the growth rate of labor productivity to average only 0.1 percentage point a year below the growth rate that would have occurred in their absence.

Taking into account all of these studies,[15] no real consensus emerges on the relative magnitude of the contribution of the various factors cited. The changing demographic composition of the labor force and hours worked, together with sectoral shifts in the composition of output, receive substantial weight in most estimates, accounting for between 20 and 30 percent of the observed slowdown. The slowdown in the rate of capital investment—resulting in a declining capital-to-labor ratio, and a capital stock embodying a

---

13. R. Crandall, "Is Environmental Policy Responsible for Declining Productivity Growth?" Paper prepared for the Annual Meeting of Society of Government Economists, Atlanta, 1979; and R. Crandall, "Pollution Controls and Productivity Growth in Basic Industries," in T. Cowing and R. Stevenson, eds., *Productivity Measurements in Regulated Industries* (New York: Academic Press, 1980).

14. Data Resources Inc., "The Macroeconomic Impact of Federal Pollution Control Programs," Report submitted to the U.S. Environmental Protection Agency and the U.S. Council on Environmental Quality, 1979, 1981.

15. The results of all of these studies must be interpreted with caution. First, nearly all of them have taken, as the direct economic impact of regulations, estimates of the expenditures that these regulations have required. As we have emphasized, however, these data have serious weaknesses. It is, for example, difficult to claim that these estimates across industries are likely to give a correct ordering of impact among them, let alone provide reasonable point estimates of resource requirements.

Second, none of these studies has done justice to the role of regulations in creating an uncertain environment for business activity. The potential debilitating effect on investment and location decisions of regulations whose application and enforcement is problematic and unknown to the regulatee has not been accounted for. Similarly, while regulations may have caused serious delays and stretch-outs in investment plans, delays that have the inevitable effect of extending the use of outmoded facilities and retarding technical change and economic growth, these effects have not been modeled and estimated.

technology that increasingly deviates from what is possible—should be credited with 20 to 30 percent of the slowdown. The third important factor appears to be cyclical effects; during much of the period from the late 1960s through the 1970s the economy has shown many characteristics of a quasi-permanent recession, with persistent high unemployment and low utilization of the capital stock. These factors, together with weather and work stoppages, account for another 10 to 20 percent of the productivity slowdown.

If this characterization is correct, between 10 and 45 percent of the slowdown is allocable to the large number of other determinants, of which governmental regulations are one. It seems clear that public regulations cannot escape some of the blame for the productivity slowdown. However, little evidence exists to suggest that as much as 25 percent of the slowdown can be attributed to them. A reasonable estimate might attribute 15 to 20 percent of the slowdown in productivity growth to regulations in general, with perhaps one-half of this impact attributable to environmental regulations.

The Deregulatory Efforts of the Reagan Administration and Their Impact on Productivity Growth

The Reagan administration's first *Economic Report* suggested that increased federal regulation during the 1970s was partly responsible for the reduction in productivity growth that occurred during that period.[16] It noted that the average annual growth rate of private nonfarm labor productivity slowed from 2.6 percent during 1960–1965 to 0.7 percent from 1974–1979. At the same time, the growth rate of regulation (measured by the number of pages in the *Federal Register*) increased from 7.6 percent to 13.9 percent.

In an attempt to improve productivity growth, the Reagan administration embarked on a drive to deregulate the economy. To spearhead the effort, the president appointed a Task Force on Regulatory Relief, chaired by Vice President George Bush. This task force was made the primary oversight body responsible for reviewing new regulations, assessing existing regulations, and coordinating legislative regulatory policies. It was to provide regulatory relief by applying cost-benefit analysis to proposed regulations, reviewing regulatory impact analyses submitted by agencies proposing major new regulations, and overseeing a case-by-case cost-benefit review of rules currently in effect.

In August 1982, the task force issued a progress report that included estimates of the resource savings attributable to the regulatory relief efforts

---

16. *Economic Report of the President*. (Washington, D.C.: Government Printing Office, 1982, 1983).

of the Reagan administration during 1981 and 1982.[17] It estimated that businesses had saved $6 billion in annual, recurring operating costs, and $9–11 billion in one-time capital costs.

These estimates became the subject of substantial controversy, with administration representatives claiming that the estimates were quite conservative, and critics charging that the claimed savings were exaggerated. The task force progress report argued that the estimates were conservative insofar as it attributed no resource savings to numerous regulatory changes. For example, the Food and Nutrition Service of the Department of Agriculture modified the cost accounting requirements in connection with the national school lunch program. The task force estimated that this change would save 11.7 million person-hours of labor annually, but did not provide a dollar estimate of these savings.

One area where critics charged the task force with exaggerating resource savings involved Department of Transportation's rescission of the passive restraint (air bag) requirements for motor vehicles. The task force estimated this single rescission to yield one-time investment savings of $400 million and savings of $1 billion in annual operating costs.

Efforts at regulatory relief continued, of course, after August 1982. With one possible exception, however—rules regarding particulate emissions for motor vehicles—the task force report implied that further regulatory relief would yield no significant, estimable resource savings. The August 1982 progress report thus provides the only comprehensive savings estimates available.

Estimating the Productivity Impact: A Growth-Accounting Approach

One approach to evaluating the productivity impact of the Reagan administration's deregulatory efforts is to employ the task force savings estimates in a growth-accounting framework. Following Denison, one assumes that regulation or deregulation affects output per unit of input, but not total factor input.[18] Denison used an estimate of the incremental resource costs attributable to regulation (taken as a percentage of total factor cost) as an estimate of the percentage reduction in total factor productivity that occurred as a consequence

---

17. Presidential Task Force on Regulatory Relief, "Reagan Administration Achievements in Regulatory Relief" (Washington, D.C.: 1982).

18. See G. Christainsen, F. Gollop, and R. Haveman, "Environmental and Health/Safety Regulations, Productivity Growth, and Economic Performance: An Assessment," U.S. Congress, Joint Economic Committee, 1980, for a discussion of the small impact that environmental regulations appear to have on employment and the capital stock.

of regulation. Here, the estimated resource savings (taken as a percentage of total factor cost) are used to calculate the percentage increase in total factor productivity attributable to deregulation.

First, the one-time capital savings are converted into an annual flow sufficient to return the capital and to provide a reasonable rate of return. If one assumes a marginal, annual rate of return of 10 percent and an average investment life of fifteen years, the annualized value of the task force's lower-bound estimate of $8.973 billion in one-time capital savings is $1.180 billion. If one assumes a high marginal return of 20 percent and an average investment life of five years, the task force's upper-bound estimate of $11.023 billion in one-time capital savings yields an annualized value of savings of $3.686 billion.

These estimated annualized values of one-time capital savings can then be added to annual operating cost savings. The task force provided a lower-bound estimate for operating cost savings of $5.971 billion, and an upper-bound estimate of $6.206 billion. The sum of the upper- and lower-bound figures yields an estimate of upper- and lower-bound total annual savings. These are shown in table 5.

Finally, these total annualized savings estimates can be taken as a percentage of national income (total factor cost, including profits) to estimate their impact on total factor productivity. Using total factor cost for 1982 taken from the 1983 *Economic Report of the President*,[19] the task force estimates imply that, because of deregulation during 1981 and 1982, the average level of total factor productivity in 1982 was 0.29 to 0.41 percent higher than it otherwise would have been. This calculation is shown in table 6.

Using the average level of total factor productivity in 1980 as a base, an increase of 0.15 to 0.20 percentage point in the average annual growth

TABLE 5

Upper- and Lower-Bound Estimates of the Annual Cost Savings from 1981–1982 Deregulation Efforts
(*In billions of dollars*)

	Lower-Bound Estimate	Upper-Bound Estimate
Annualized value of capital savings	1.180	3.686
Annual operating cost savings	5.971	6.206
Total annual savings	7.151	9.892

---

19. *Economic Report of the President*, 1983.

rate of productivity for 1980–1981 and 1981–1982 is attributable to the administration's deregulation efforts. If no additional deregulatory savings are to occur, however, this increment to the average annual growth rate will dissipate over time.

This estimated effect of reduced regulatory intensity in the 1980–1982 period on measured productivity is likely to be biased upward to some extent. As distinct from the approach of Denison, we have assumed that the estimated cost savings increase national income by an equivalent amount. This assumption is appropriate in the case of cost savings that affect the business sector. Consider air bags, for example. Requiring air bags would increase automobile costs and prices. The purchase of automobiles by a business will increase its production costs and the GNP deflator, but not measured real GNP. In the absence of the air-bag regulation, the business might well have made purchases that contributed to real output. However, to the extent that the regulation directly affects consumer or government purchases, measured productivity is not affected. The purchase of automobiles with air bags by consumers or government increases measured output by the same amount as measured input. Elimination of the regulation might lead to reallocations of consumer spending, with no net effect on measured output or inputs. Hence, the impact of deregulatory savings on measured productivity should reflect only those savings that apply to businesses. For this reason, the results reported here may overstate the impact on measured productivity. They may, however, indicate the impact on some concept of true productivity—if the included consumer and government savings reflect purchases of low-valued products that these decision makers no longer must make.

In addition to providing a means of estimating the overall impact of deregulation, the task force cost savings estimates permit a partitioning of the

TABLE 6

Estimated Impact of Deregulation on Total Factor Productivity in 1982
(*In billions of dollars*)

	Lower-Bound Estimate	Upper-Bound Estimate
(1) National income	2,436.5	2,436.5
(2) Estimated cost savings	7.2	9.9
(3) National income in absence of deregulation [(1)–(2)]	2,429.3	2,426.6
(4) Productivity increase due to deregulation [(2) ÷ (3)] (× 100%)	0.29	0.41

impact among the major regulatory agencies. Table 7 provides alternative estimates of the portion of the total impact accounted for by each agency.

Table 7 shows that Department of Transportation deregulation, dominated by rescission of the passive restraint rule, accounted for nearly one-third of the deregulatory impact. Deregulation involving the Environmental Protection Agency accounted for about one-fifth of the total. If we exclude the estimated cost savings from rescinding the air-bag rule, the estimated impact of deregulatory savings on the growth rate of total factor productivity from 1980 to 1982 drops to 0.13-0.18 percentage point.

Estimating the Productivity Impact: An Econometric Approach

An alternative assessment of administration deregulation efforts can be developed from econometric estimates that include data from 1981 and 1982, in addition to data from prior years. Such estimation can be performed by updating and refining the methodology used in Christainsen and Haveman.[20]

TABLE 7

Proportion of Deregulatory Impact Accounted for by Various Regulatory Agencies

Agency	Percentage Based on Lower-Bound Estimation Method	Percentage Based on Upper-Bound Estimation Method
Architectural and Transportation Compliance Board	3.5	2.5
Department of Agriculture	8.7	6.3
Corps of Engineers	14.0	10.1
Department of Education	2.7	11.6
Department of Energy	2.8	2.5
Department of Health and Human Services	0.7	0.5
Department of Housing and Urban Development	0.1	0.1
Department of Interior	0.04	0.03
Department of Labor	12.4	10.0
Department of Transportation	33.3	31.4
Environmental Protection Agency	21.0	24.4
Office of Management and Budget	0.7	0.5
Total	100.0	100.0

---

20. Christainsen and Haveman, "Public Regulations and the Slowdown in Productivity Growth."

First, we specify an aggregate production function for the private, non-farm sector of the U.S. economy. The production function relates the flow of output in the private, nonfarm sector (y) to the values of three inputs—the stock of nonresidential structures and equipment used for purposes other than pollution abatement (K), the amount of labor of some standardized level of quality (L), and the stock of research and development capital in existence ($R\&D$). Regulation (R) may affect the ability of producers to transform these inputs into outputs; that is, it may shift the production function.

We hypothesize four other factors that may cause the aggregate production function to shift. First, the composition of output (C) may well affect the aggregate value of output, ceteris paribus. Second, the relative price of energy $\left(\dfrac{P_e}{P}\right)$ is a potential source of production function shifts. Third, the deviation of the rate of inflation from its expected rate ($|\dot{P} - \dot{P}^e|$ is viewed as a potentially disruptive force; if producers misinterpret changes in the general price level as being changes in relative prices, they may make non-optimal decisions. Finally, the production function may shift over time (T) as disembodied technical change occurs. Letting the parameters of the production functions be denoted by β's, we then assume the function takes on the following (first-order) form:

$$y = \beta_1 \cdot K^{\beta_2} \cdot L^{\beta_3} \cdot R\&D^{\beta_4} \cdot \exp[\beta_5 \ln R + \beta_6 \ln C \qquad (1)$$
$$+ \beta_7 \ln \frac{P_e}{P} + \beta_8 \ln |\dot{P} - \dot{P}^e| + \beta_9 T].$$

We assume the amount of labor of standardized quality to be equal to:

$L = q \times l$, where l is hours of raw labor input, and q is an index of labor quality. Substituting this into (1) yields:

$$y = \beta_1 \cdot K^{\beta_2} \cdot (q \times l)^{\beta_3} \cdot R\&D^{\beta_4} \cdot \exp[\beta_5 \ln R + \beta_6 \ln C \qquad (2)$$
$$+ \beta_7 \ln \frac{P_e}{P} + \beta_8 \ln |\dot{P} - \dot{P}^e| + \beta_9 T].$$

Taking the natural logarithm of both sides of (2):

$$\ln y = \ln\beta_1 + \beta_2 \ln K + \beta_3 \ln(q \times l) + \beta_4 \ln R\&D + \beta_5 \ln R \qquad (3)$$
$$+ \beta_6 \ln C + \beta_7 \ln \frac{P_e}{P} + \beta_8 \ln |\dot{P} - \dot{P}^e| + \beta_9 T.$$

Because $\ln(q \times l) = \ln q + \ln l$, we can subtract $\ln l$ from both sides to obtain an estimable equation for labor productivity, as conventionally measured:

$$\ln y - \ln l = \ln\beta_1 + \beta_2\ln K + \beta_3\ln q + (\beta_3 - 1)\ln l + \beta_4\ln R\&D$$
$$+ \beta_5\ln R + \beta_6\ln C + \beta_7\ln\frac{P_e}{P} + \beta_8\ln|\dot{P} - \dot{P}^e| + \beta_9 T. \quad (4)$$

Finally, by adding a cyclical variable to capture business-cycle shocks (as justified by Nordhaus[21]), we obtain:

$$\ln\frac{y}{l} = \ln\beta_1 + \beta_2\ln K + \beta_3\ln q + (\beta_3 - 1)\ln l + \beta_4\ln R\&D + \beta_5\ln R$$
$$+ \beta_6\ln C + \beta_7\ln\frac{P_e}{P} + \beta_8\ln|\dot{P} - \dot{P}^e| + \beta_9 T + \beta_{10}\ln\left(\frac{\text{real GNP}}{\text{real GNP*}}\right), \quad (5)$$

where real GNP* refers to high-employment real GNP. The parameter of primary interest is, of course, β_5.

In log-linear form, the above specification captures most of the factors hypothesized to influence productivity in previous studies. Factors not captured by this specification include the effect of changes in the work ethic and changes in the quality of business management.

A restricted form of equation (5) can be obtained by assuming constant returns to scale. In this case, $\beta_2 + \beta_3 + \beta_4 = 1$, and the restriction that $\beta_4 = 1 - \beta_2 - \beta_3$ can be imposed. The restricted form of equation (5), then, is:

$$\ln\frac{y}{l} = \ln\beta_1 + \beta_2\ln K + \beta_3\ln q + (\beta_3 - 1)\ln l$$
$$+ (1-\beta_2-\beta_3)\ln R\&D + \beta_5\ln R + \beta_6\ln C + \beta_7\ln\frac{P_e}{P}$$
$$+ \beta_8\ln|\dot{P} - \dot{P}^e|$$
$$+ \beta_9 T + \beta_{10}\ln\left(\frac{\text{real GNP}}{\text{real GNP*}}\right). \quad (6)$$

We estimated both the free and restricted forms of the productivity equations [equations (5) and (6)] with annual data for the 1947-1982 period.[22] Data for

---

21. W. Nordhaus, "The Recent Productivity Slowdown," *Brookings Papers on Economic Activity*, 3 (1972), pp. 473–546.
22. The data for 1982 are subject to revision.

y, l, and q were obtained from the Department of Labor; q equals the percentage of the civilian labor force composed of males, ages 25 through 54. Data for K were obtained from Data Resources Inc. The stock of R&D is computed as in Kendrick[23] and Nadiri and Schankerman,[24] using data obtained from the National Science Foundation. C is the percentage of total, private, nonfarm output produced in the economy's manufacturing sector, computed from data compiled by the Department of Commerce. For $\frac{P_e}{P}$, P is the Department of Labor's producer price index, and P^e is the Department of Labor's producer price index for "fuels and related products, and power." Then $\dot{P}$ is the annual rate of change in the producer price index, and $\dot{P}^e$ is assumed, as it is for the Citibank Economic Database, to be formed adaptively;
$$\dot{P}^e = .50\,\dot{P}_{-1} + .30\,\dot{P}_{-2} + .15\,\dot{P}_{-3} + 0.5\,\dot{P}_{-4}.$$

The three alternative series for (R) are constructed as shown in table 2. Although each of the R series is a crude measure of regulatory intensity, all are highly correlated and, in our view, provide the best available characterization of regulatory trends.[25]

Exogeneity tests suggest simultaneity between the dependent variable and each of the input variables in both the free-form and restricted equations. Thus we estimated the equations by a two-stage least-squares procedure in which the logarithmic value of each input variable was first regressed on its lagged logarithmic value, a time trend (T), T^2, and the cyclical variable. High-employment GNP was computed as in Gordon.[26] We then estimated the productivity equations using the fitted values of the input variables obtained from the first-stage regressions. As in Christainsen and Haveman,[27] we estimated a two-year lag for R_1 and one-year lags for R_2 and R_3 using a Bayesian technique suggested in Geweke and Meese.[28] At an aggregate level, we could not justify distributed lags according to this technique. We corrected for serial

---

23. J. Kendrick, *The Formation and Stocks of Total Capital* (New York: National Bureau of Economic Research, 1976).

24. M.I. Nadiri and M.A. Schankerman, "Technical Change, Returns to Scale, and the Productivity Slowdown," *American Economic Review* (May 1981), pp. 314–319.

25. As noted by the Center for the Study of American Business, *1982 Directory*, "No perfect measure of the size and cost of these [regulatory] activities has been found. We have discovered, however, that direct measurements of the budgets and staffing of the regulatory agencies provide a useful 'barometer' of the regulatory 'climate.'"

26. R. Gordon, *Macroeconomics*, 2d. ed. (Boston: Little, Brown and Company, 1981).

27. Christainsen and Haveman, "Public Regulations and the Slowdown in Productivity Growth."

28. J. Geweke and R. Meese, "Estimating Regression Models of Finite But Unknown Order," Social Science Research Institute Paper no. 7925, University of Wisconsin-Madison, 1979.

correlation detected in both the free-form and restricted models via the procedure outlined in Amemiya.[29]

On the basis of an F-test, the hypothesis that $\beta_2 + \beta_3 + \beta_4 = 1$ could not be rejected at a 5 percent significance level. Hence, the results from the restricted model are presented in table 8. All of the parameter estimates have the expected sign except for the coefficient on the inflation variable. Various tests indicated that the estimated standard errors were significantly affected by multicollinearity.

The results suggest some role for regulation, but indicate that the biggest noncyclical factor influencing productivity since 1973 has been relative energy

TABLE 8

PARAMETER ESTIMATES FOR RESTRICTED MODEL
(t-statistics in parentheses)

Variable	Using R_1	Using R_2	Using R_3
ln$K$	.261** (1.32)	.257** (1.23)	.257* (1.23)
ln$q$	.691** (1.32)	.695** (1.34)	.696** (1.35)
ln$R\&D$	.048	.048	0.47
ln$R$	−.043* (1.11)	−.024** (1.36)	−.026** (1.34)
ln$C$	.120* (1.05)	.117* (0.99)	.115* (1.00)
$\ln\left(\dfrac{P_e}{P}\right)$	−.063*** (−1.84)	−.053*** (−1.76)	−.053*** (−1.76)
$\ln \|\dot{P} - \dot{P}^e\|$	.005 (0.36)	.004 (0.35)	.007 (0.38)
T	.018**** (4.48)	.018**** (4.49)	.018**** (4.49)
$\ln\left(\dfrac{real\ GNP}{real\ GNP^*}\right)$	.239** (1.33)	.250** (1.42)	.249** (1.40)

* = significant at a 25 percent level.
** = significant at a 10 percent level.
*** = significant at a 5 percent level.
**** = significant at a 1 percent level.

---

29. T. Amemiya, "Generalized Least-Squares with an Estimated Autocovariance Matrix," *Econometrica* (July 1973), pp. 723–732.

prices. Their average impact on the rate of productivity growth since 1973 can be estimated by multiplying the reported regression coefficients by the average annual growth rate of relative energy prices (9.5 percent for the 1973-1982 period). On this basis, relative energy prices served to reduce the growth rate of labor productivity by an average of 0.5 to 0.6 percentage point per year from 1973 to 1982.

Applying the same procedures to regulation, we obtain the results shown in table 9. The estimates in the final column suggest that the growth rate of labor productivity was not seriously affected by regulation from 1947 to 1966 or from 1975 to 1981; the rate of productivity growth was lowered by between

TABLE 9

ESTIMATED EFFECTS OF REGULATION ON PRODUCTIVITY, 1947–1982

Using R_1 Period	(1) Coefficient = $\dfrac{\Delta \ln y/l}{\Delta \ln R_1}$	(2) Average $\Delta \ln R_1$	(1) × (2) Average Effect on $\Delta \ln y/l$
1947–1966	−.04321	.02083	−.00090
1966–1971	−.04321	.03977	−.00172
1971–1975	−.04321	.08544	−.00369
1975–1981	−.04321	.04246	−.00183
1981–1982	−.04321	0	0

Using R_2 Period	Coefficient = $\dfrac{\Delta \ln y/l}{\Delta \ln R_2}$	Average $\Delta \ln R_2$	Average Effect on $\Delta \ln y/l$
1947–1966	−.02408	.03517	−.00085
1966–1971	−.02408	.10533	−.00254
1971–1975	−.02408	.19566	−.00471
1975–1981	−.02408	.04132	−.00099
1981–1982	−.02408	−.06192	+.00149

Using R_3 Period	Coefficient = $\dfrac{\Delta \ln y/l}{\Delta \ln R_3}$	Average $\Delta \ln R_3$	Average Effect on $\Delta \ln y/l$
1947–1966	−.02627	.03102	−.00081
1966–1971	−.02627	.05161	−.00136
1971–1975	−.02627	.018557	−.00487
1975–1981	−.02627	.03552	−.00093
1981–1982	−.02627	−.05129	+.00135

NOTE: R_1, R_2, R_3 are lagged as indicated in table 2.

0.08 and 0.18 percentage point. The more serious effects of regulation on productivity occurred from 1966 to 1971 and from 1971 to 1975. From 1966 to 1971, the effects of regulation lowered the rate of productivity growth by between 0.14 and 0.25 percentage point. From 1971 to 1975, the maximum impact of regulations is recorded; in this period, we estimate regulatory activity to have reduced productivity by between 0.37 and 0.49 percentage point per year.

Table 9 indicates that a stable or decreasing level of regulatory intensity in 1980–1981 raised the growth rate of labor productivity by 0 to 0.15 percentage point for the 1981–1982 period.

We ran several other regressions in addition to those already mentioned. First, we entered the regulatory measures interactively with K, l, $R\&D$, C and/or T in some regressions in order to estimate any second-order effects that regulation might have. We also entered the relative price of energy and K interactively in some specifications. Finally, we used a variable for worker absenteeism obtained from the Department of Labor as a proxy for the work ethic as an added variable in some regressions. With the exception of one run in which the coefficient for the interaction of the relative price of energy and K was significant, none of the regression coefficients for these variables was significant at the 25 percent level. Nor was the sum of the possible second-order regulatory effects ever significant at a 25 percent level, using an F-test. In some cases, the second-order coefficients did not have the expected sign.

Taking the results shown in table 9 at face value, and recalling the fact that the regulatory variables were entered in lagged form, the deregulation in 1981–1982 indicated in R_3 and R_2 implies, ceteris paribus, an increase in the rate of productivity growth of between 0.20 and 0.22 percentage point for 1982–1983.[30]

Table 10 summarizes our estimates of the impact of the Reagan administration's deregulatory efforts on the rate of productivity growth.

Conclusion

Beginning in 1981, the nation's inflation rate declined dramatically. The consumer price index, which had risen 12.4 percent during 1980, rose only 3.9 percent during 1982. At the same time, however, the economy suffered

---

30. The growth rates of R_3 and R_2 from 1981 to 1982 were -7.61 and -8.96 respectively. R_1 cannot yet be updated sufficiently to estimate its impact.

TABLE 10

THE ANNUAL PERCENTAGE-POINT EFFECT OF REAGAN ADMINISTRATION'S
DEREGULATORY EFFORTS ON THE RATE OF PRODUCTIVITY GROWTH

Basis of Computation	1980–1982	1981–1982	1982–1983
Growth-accounting approach	0.15–0.20		
Econometric approach using:			
R_1	0	—	
R_2	0.15	0.22	
R_3	0.14	0.20	

NOTE: The growth-accounting approach was applied to total factor productivity in the economy as a whole. The growth-accounting estimate compares the growth rate of total factor productivity to the growth rate which, it is assumed, would have occurred had regulatory intensity not been affected to the extent indicated by the Task Force on Regulatory Relief. The econometric approach was applied to labor productivity in the nonfarm business sector. The econometric estimates compare the growth rate of labor productivity with that which would have occurred had the level of regulatory intensity in effect during the time period in question been unchanged from the previous time period.

a depression, a development that advocates of supply-side economics hoped could be avoided. This depression occurred despite a moderation in relative energy prices, a factor that undoubtedly contributed to the improved inflation picture. During 1982, the nation's output of goods and services declined 1.8 percent (according to a Department of Commerce estimate that is subject to revision), and the unemployment rate reached 10.8 percent.

The substantial decline in the nation's aggregate supply of goods and services can be explained in two ways. One can argue that supply-side economics policies were not implemented as planned; or one can argue that, even if implemented as planned, supply-side economics promised more than it could reasonably hope to deliver. Our estimates support both lines of argument.

On the one hand, monetary restraint was not carried out gradually, as planned, but occurred with unexpected suddenness. During the last six months of 1980, the money supply (M1) grew at an annual rate of 10.8 percent. From April to October of 1981 it grew at a rate of negative 0.2 percent. At the same time, the country did not experience a major decline in effective personal tax rates. Nominally, federal personal tax rates were reduced, but this was offset by "bracket creep" and increased tax rates for Social Security. In addition, many states and localities raised taxes. Excise taxes were raised at both the federal and local levels.

As for deregulation, the administration reduced budgets and staffing in federal regulatory agencies, but, at least during 1981 and 1982, it devoted little effort to amending major regulatory statutes. Our estimates suggest that the deregulation that did occur brought about a modest improvement in the rate of productivity growth of not more than 0.22 percentage point.

These results must be interpreted with caution. In the case of the growth-accounting approach, the estimated impact was derived from cost savings estimates that many believe to be overstated. Moreover, this approach included large estimated savings from repeal of the air-bag rule and did not distinguish those cost savings that affect measured output from those that do not.

In the case of the econometric approach, the maximum impact on the growth rate of productivity (0.22 percentage point) was obtained from a crude regulatory measure—budgetary expenditures by regulatory agencies—which probably overstates the actual amount of deregulation taking place. If one looks at actual change in statutes, much less deregulation has occurred.

The available evidence suggests that the impact of regulation and deregulation on productivity growth is clearly not zero. Our estimates are consistent with studies that suggest that regulation may have reduced the growth rate of productivity (by whatever measure) by as much as 0.5 percentage point in the early-to-mid-1970s. This impact appears to have tapered off during the late 1970s, however. A reasonable assessment of the impact of Reagan administration deregulation is that it increased the growth rate of measured productivity by about 0.1 percentage point above what it would have been had the 1980 level of regulatory intensity continued.

As noted previously, the beneficial effects of individual post-1980 deregulation efforts are but short-lived. Only continued efforts to reduce constraints on private decisions are likely to have persistent impacts on productivity growth.

Finally, we should emphasize that regulatory policies not only adversely affect productivity growth, costs, and prices, but also convey benefits related to the objectives for which they were established. These benefits—better health and, hence, reduced health care costs, reduced materials damage and increased crop yields, increased recreational activities, and so on—are real and must be offset against adverse productivity effects in reaching any full evaluation. Evidence suggests that the costs of many regulatory measures are more than covered by the real benefits attributable to them, even though many of these benefits are not captured in national income and product account statistics.[31,32]

---

31. L. Lave and E. Seskin, *Air Pollution and Human Health* (Baltimore: Johns Hopkins University Press, 1977).
32. A.M. Freeman, *The Benefits of Environmental Improvement* (Baltimore: Johns Hopkins University Press, 1979).

We conclude then, that government regulation of the private sector does diminish productivity, but not enough to make one optimistic that regulatory relief could bring about major reductions in the inflation rate without the usual slowdown in real output (and employment). A major program of regulatory relief and reform could, perhaps, mitigate the output loss that normally occurs during the disinflation process.

COMMENTS

Martin Neil Baily

Haveman and Christainsen tackle a very difficult issue—the effects of regulation and deregulation on productivity growth. The authors make a systematic effort to compare alternative analytic methods and to come up with hard numbers. This effort was well done and worthwhile, but I wish more resources were available to research this question in greater depth. The paucity of hard data available to the authors indicates that regulatory decisions, like many other policy decisions, are made without the benefit of the necessary data.

The authors start with an overly simplified and misleading discussion of the supply-side approach to fighting inflation. The debate about productivity is not closely related to the debate over inflation. Policies to enhance productivity are desirable whether or not there is inflation and whether or not demand is below supply. The principal criticisms of Reagan's supply-side economics are that it erroneously claimed that very large supply effects would result from cutting taxes and that inflation would be ended without creating slack capacity and unemployment. Since there is nothing in the Haveman-Christainsen results to blunt these criticisms, there is no need for them to defend supply-side economics.

The authors next review various explanations of the slowdown in national productivity growth. I disagree somewhat with their emphasis. My own work and that of Dale Jorgenson do not find shifts in the composition of nonfarm output to be a significant cause of the slowdown. Contrary to their thesis, the share of output produced in the different industries is the variable that counts, not the share of employment. The share of output produced by the manufacturing sector has not declined by very much (this sector produced 30.7 percent of nonfarm business output in 1948 compared to 30.4 percent in 1981). Moreover, the opportunities for mass production and economies of scale in the service sector are much better than the authors indicate. Give this issue some thought next time you visit McDonald's, or an automatic bank teller, or your local electric power plant. The fastest productivity growth in recent years has been in the communications industry—also a part of the service sector.

It is also hard to attribute much of the slowdown to a decline in research and development spending. First, much of the decline in spending cited by the authors occurred because of decreased defense expenditures. Federally funded R&D that goes to develop new weapons has no direct effect on measured productivity growth because the new weapons are valued at factor cost. There may be spillover or secondary effects from defense R&D, but these are bound to be smaller than direct effects. Second, the level of private industrial R&D spending in constant dollars in the 1970s was one and one-half times the level of the 1960s.[1]

The authors then suggest that the increased cost of energy after 1973 was a contributing cause of the slowdown. I have argued the same point myself, but energy is only a small fraction of total production costs. It makes no sense to give up two dollars of output to save one dollar of energy costs.[2]

Christainsen and Haveman consider the impact of regulation and deregulation on productivity. The authors present estimates from various studies and then use their own regression analysis to provide the main results. They explain the logarithm of average labor productivity using capital, labor quality, R&D, the composition of output, the relative price of energy, unexpected inflation, a time trend, and the ratio of GNP to potential GNP. The results are not very good. Using the usual rule-of-thumb that a coefficient should be twice its standard error, only the time trend is statistically significant.[3] The relative price of energy comes close to significance. The alternative measures of regulatory intensity have the correct sign, but have small and insignificant coefficients.

One reason for the weak results is that the authors use two-stage least-squares. I find it hard to visualize the fully-identified structural model that would explain variables such as the relative price of energy or the ratio of actual GNP to potential GNP. Since good instrumental variables are not available, their approach loses a lot of information. They would have done better to swallow some endogeneity.

I doubt that the authors' measures of regulatory intensity can tell us much about the impact of regulation on productivity with an econometric formu-

---

1. These data are from the National Science Foundation, *Science Indicators 1980*, 1981, table 204, page 268.
2. If, however, producers were afraid of supply interruptions, the shadow price of energy might be much higher than the actual price.
3. Since the authors use two-stage least-squares, it would have been better to give the estimates of the asymptotic standard errors than to report the ratios of the coefficients to these standard errors. These ratios do not in general have a t-distribution.

lation. Government expenditures on regulatory agencies or number of pages in the *Federal Register* are rather weak proxies for the real impact of regulation on business. These variables might properly be cited in a footnote or mentioned in an op-ed piece, but they are not a solid foundation for statistical work. They may be the best available variables, but they are inadequate.

The authors' list of deregulations achieved by the Reagan administration includes some items that will have no effect on measured productivity. The costliest item on the list is the repeal of the air bag requirement. If air bags are introduced, the effect on measured productivity will be very small. Under current practice, mandated safety devices are assumed to raise the quality of automobiles sold in the United States. Each automobile sold with air bags installed will represent a larger real output in the official data. As the authors note, to the extent that automobiles are producer goods, air bags would raise the measured capital stock, but would not raise the ability of the capital to provide output-producing capital services. This would be quite a small effect, however.

Let me emphasize that I am not saying that the Haveman-Christainsen estimates of the impacts of regulation and deregulation are overstated. Their numbers are quite small, perhaps even too small. Some of the most severe productivity slowdowns have occurred in industries such as refining, chemicals, coal mining, and public utilities, where the cost of complying with regulations has been significant. But I do not know how large the effect of regulation has been, and I doubt the ability of the econometric analysis to tell me, given the available data. I would like to see more work done on an industry-by-industry basis or perhaps a comparative international study.

COMMENTS

Isabel V. Sawhill

The Haveman-Christainsen paper is heroic in terms of its willingness to attempt to quantify the impact of regulations on productivity. It certainly pushes existing analysis to the limits of what it can tell us. I think this is a useful approach as long as the caveats are noted, as they are, although more discussion of the problems with the task force numbers and with the indices of regulatory intensity that are used in the paper may have been appropriate.

The paper's value, I think, lies in its detailed description of the way research on this topic has been done, enabling the reader to put the findings in perspective, and to take the numbers with a large grain of salt. I would not criticize the authors for failing to have done new research. What they have done is give readers a sense of the state of the art in this area.

The business community has made outrageous claims from time to time about the cost of regulation, while environmentalists have made equally outrageous claims about the benefits of regulation. Ultimately we want to know, not how costly regulation has been, but how cost-effective it has been. Haveman and Christainsen give the usual nod to the benefit side of the equation, but focus almost exclusively on the cost side. Both need to be kept in mind.

In the balance of my comments, I will try to use this paper to draw some conclusions about the effects of the administration's regulatory initiatives and, then, point out those areas that I think we need to understand better before we can make a more definitive assessment.

Beginning first with the administration's accomplishments, we must first ask what the course of regulatory history would have been if Ronald Reagan had not been elected. I doubt we would have seen an explosion of regulatory activity such as we saw in the first half of the 1970s. This paper shows clearly that regulatory growth had already tapered off in the late 1970s and was not significantly greater in the late 1970s than it had been in the 1947–1966 period. This slowdown in the growth of both regulation and government spending in many areas in the latter half of the 1970s rarely gets the emphasis it deserves.

If you accept that the growth of regulation was already slowing, you can infer from this paper that Reagan's regulatory relief program may have increased labor productivity by perhaps two-tenths of a percentage point. This is the number that Christainsen and Haveman show in table 10 for the years 1982–1983.

The impact would be greater than this if you were to assume that Reagan's program succeeded not only in undoing some existing or proposed regulations, but also in forestalling a new spurt of regulatory activism. One might argue that the Reagan administration has kept environmentalists, civil rights activists, and others so busy protecting past gains that they have been, and will continue to be, diverted from pursuing a more positive agenda. Or one could argue the reverse—that the public outcry in response to the policies of James Watt and Anne Gorsuch will create more activist fervor in the long run. Whichever way you argue this, it is an important intangible in trying to evaluate the ultimate legacy of the Reagan regulatory era.

Because Christainsen and Haveman take seriously the supply-side rhetoric about regulatory relief, I feel compelled to elaborate on it a little further. I think any notion that the supply-side benefits of regulatory relief could significantly offset the demand-side costs of disinflation has to be dismissed outright. Even if you assume somewhat optimistically that you can improve labor productivity and unit labor costs enough to bring down the rate of inflation by half a percentage point, that would offset only about 6 percent of the 8.5 percentage point reduction in the Consumer Price Index that has been achieved since 1980. The other 94 percent would have to be attributed to luck or pure pain. I conclude from this that Reagan's deregulatory program could never be justified as a short-term supply-side measure. However, even viewed as a long-term growth measure, there are limits to how much additional deregulation can occur. If all existing regulatory restraints were eliminated, the impact of this deregulation on the rate of growth of productivity would quickly fade. Any long-term benefits are constrained by this fact.

While I am on this subject, I think the paper could distinguish more between short-run and long-run impacts. In some areas the short-run impacts of regulatory relief on productivity are positive, while the long-run impacts may be negative. For example, the authors' review of the literature on the productivity slowdown suggests that energy price shifts have been a factor in the slowdown. This suggests to me that a relaxation of fuel efficiency standards might have some positive short-run impact; but it might also increase the likelihood of a future price shock, with adverse long-term effects on productivity.

Now let me move to a set of questions that I think need answering before we can make a more complete and definitive assessment. First, and most important, I think we have to understand the microeconomic underpinnings of these macroeconomic analyses. Martin Baily's point about the effect of air bags on productivity would be one example here. I don't think we know very much about how regulations affect measured productivity. I suspect there may be some intangible, hard-to-measure ways in which regulations affect business entrepreneurship or employee productivity that the macroeconomic approach can't adequately capture. Perhaps careful case studies of firms and industries would yield such information.

Second, I would like to know more about the effects of *economic* deregulation on productivity, where there are no potential social benefits being forgone in the process of achieving greater efficiency. I am not sure how well the economic deregulation of the 1970s was captured and measured in the Christainsen-Haveman paper. I gather from their brief description that railroad deregulation, for example, was taken into account. But, if so, the rising tide of social regulations must have completely swamped the partial dismantling of economic regulation. This leads me to wonder how each type of regulation is weighted in the authors' rather crude measures. A related issue is where we draw the line between regulation and other forms of government activity. Are voluntary import restraints, for example, a form of regulation? Murray Weidenbaum includes them, although I probably wouldn't.

Third, to what extent have recent declines in federal regulatory activities been offset by increasing regulatory activity at the state and local level? How does this transfer affect businesses which are then faced with complying with up to fifty different sets of regulations? Christainsen and Haveman address themselves only to federal regulations.

Finally, are the effects of increased and decreased government regulation symmetrical? Christainsen and Haveman seem to make the simplifying assumption that they are. But, for example, if companies are required to retrofit buildings to provide access to the handicapped and later that regulation is voided, what effect (if any) does this deregulation have? The issue here is one of sunk costs. Moreover, it may be that, in the absence of legislative change, reductions in spending and in the staffing of regulatory agencies have perverse effects as Murray Weidenbaum earlier suggested.

Overall, I think that this paper is a valuable attempt to quantify the effects of the regulatory relief program on productivity. Too much of the discussion of the Reagan program has suffered from a failure to look at the evidence. I commend the authors for putting the debate on a little firmer basis.

REGULATORY RELIEF AND THE AUTOMOBILE INDUSTRY

Robert A. Leone

Ronald Reagan came to the presidency with a strong commitment to economic recovery and industrial growth. His administration acknowledged its pro-business sentiments without apology. To advance the general interests of industry, the administration adopted a highly publicized program of regulatory relief under the direction of the vice-president. The auto industry was among the first industries receiving high-level attention under this policy.

Faced with severe unemployment and unprecedented competitive pressure from Japan, the problems of this industry became the focus of White House attention literally within days of the new president's inauguration. On April 6, 1981, the Reagan administration announced a major program of regulatory relief for the auto industry which it called "Actions to Help the U.S. Auto Industry."[1] A little more than two years later, it is appropriate to ask whether these regulatory policy initiatives have, in fact, helped the industry they were designed to assist.

To understand the regulatory aspects of the Reagan administration's auto industry policy, we must keep several political factors in mind. For one thing, the administration's highly touted program of regulatory relief had few candidates for relief that were more in the public eye than the severely depressed auto industry. A quick and visible success in this industry was therefore important to the political success of the overall regulatory relief effort.

In addition, the same political forces that elected Ronald Reagan had not been lost on the Carter administration. On July 8, 1980, the Carter administration had announced a program of regulatory relief for the auto

---

1. White House, Office of the Press Secretary, "Actions to Help the U.S. Auto Industry," April 6, 1981.

industry. On January 11, 1981, only ten days before the new administration took charge, Carter Transportation Secretary Neil Goldschmidt, apparently on his own initiative and without the usual interdepartmental coordination afforded formal "administration policies," had released a report that also included proposals for an auto industry relief effort.[2] These various recommendations provide a benchmark against which any Reagan program might be evaluated.

One pair of analysts has described Carter's July 8 policy statement as an "empty box [with] no regulatory relief for the auto industry over and above what the industry was already going to get."[3] In contrast, the Goldschmidt report, while not official administration policy, established a much more challenging benchmark for evaluating the Reagan plan.

In fact, the Goldschmidt report included several specific recommendations that posed political and ideological challenges to the new administration. For example, Goldschmidt called for a program of import restraint to protect domestic producers. This proposal was not only contrary to the Reagan ideology, but some officials saw early capitulation on a trade restraint issue as a politically dangerous precedent for the new administration. (See Weidenbaum's paper in this volume.) Much of the Reagan administration's haste in producing extensive proposals for regulatory relief for the auto industry was clearly motivated by the desire to reduce the political pressure for restraint of trade.

Second, Goldschmidt called for tax changes targeted to the interests of the auto industry and its suppliers. Although the Reagan team advocated lower taxes in general, they opposed targeted changes in the tax code, fearing that the politics of such efforts might jeopardize the overall tax reduction effort.

Third, Goldschmidt called for a change in the adversarial relationship between the auto industry and government. For an administration with an announced policy of "getting government off the back of business," cooperation was not much more attractive than confrontation.

Fourth, Goldschmidt recommended increased funding for worker retraining and community redevelopment programs. These costly programs were explicit targets of proposed Reagan budget cuts.

And finally, Goldschmidt called for regulatory relief. As the only part of the Goldschmidt proposal acceptable to the new Reagan team, it became

---

2. "The U.S. Automobile Industry," A Report to the President from the Secretary of Transportation, January 1981.

3. G. Eads and M. Fix, "Regulatory Oversight in the Reagan White House," Chapter 6, (draft) (Washington, D.C.: The Urban Institute, 1983), pp. 34–35.

necessary politically to outdo the entire spectrum of Carter proposals in substantive impact using only a single instrument of policy—regulatory relief.

Reagan versus Carter Regulatory Proposals

Reagan's April 6 policy statement included thirty-four specific regulatory actions (table 1), as well as some proposed changes in the Clean Air Act and a list of regulations for more intensive review.[4] Many of the specific actions had been proposed or actively studied during the Carter administration. A comparison of the Reagan regulatory program with proposals likely to have been forthcoming under Carter is instructive.

In the case of changes in environmental regulations, the Reagan proposals were far more generous to the industry's interests. During late 1979 and early 1980, auto producers had presented the Carter administration with virtually the same regulatory "wish list" later presented to Reagan.[5] None of the items on the list was included in the Carter administration's policy statement on regulatory relief for the auto industry issued on July 8, 1980, whereas the Reagan program included most of them. Even considering the passage of a year's time and the growing plight of the auto sector, the Reagan program was presumably much more generous to automakers than Carter's would have been.

For example, Reagan proposed to explore deferral of standards for paintshop emissions—a regulation expected to cost the auto industry approximately $300 million in capital investment between 1981 and 1983. Because Carter administration analysts considered paintshop emissions control to be very cost-effective and because the administration had a strong political commitment to environmental improvement, a proposal to defer these standards would have been unlikely under Carter.

The Reagan proposals with regard to safety regulation were also more responsive to the auto industry's interests than were those likely to have emerged from the Carter White House. In particular, the Carter administration probably would not have proposed a relaxed bumper standard because, as will be discussed later, many Carter analysts felt that the economic arguments for stringent standards were persuasive. These arguments were not overwhelming, however, and, given that this was a "big ticket" item, it is not surprising that the Reagan administration proposed the change.

---

4. White House, "Actions to Help," pp. 4–5.
5. Eads and Fix, "Regulatory Oversight", p. 35.

TABLE 1

SUMMARY OF THE APRIL 6, 1981, POLICY ACTIONS
OF THE REAGAN ADMINISTRATION

Environmental Protection Agency (EPA)	National Highway Transportation Safety Administration (NHTSA)
1. Revise hydrocarbon and carbon monoxide standards for heavy-duty trucks	17. Explore deferral of paintshop standards
2. Relax assembly-line test procedures	18. Delay passive restraints for large cars
3. Delay assembly-line testing for heavy-duty engines	19. Review all passive restraints
4. Relax nitrogen oxides emission limits for heavy-duty engines	20. Modify bumper standards
	21. Rescind "field of view" requirements for cars
5. Institute nitrogen oxides averaging for trucks	22. Terminate "field of view" rule making for trucks and buses
6. Institute emission averaging for diesel particulates	23. Withdraw post-1985 Corporate Average Fuel Economy mileage proposals
7. Eliminate 1984 high-altitude requirements	24. Amend tire grading regulations
8. Adopt self-certification for high-altitude vehicles	25. Amend seat-belt comfort regulations
9. Forgo assembly-line testing at high altitudes	26. Terminate rule making for multi-piece tire rims
10. Consolidate nitrogen oxides waiver proceedings	27. Rescind speedometer/odometer standards
11. Consolidate carbon monoxide waiver proceedings	28. Defer theft protection standards
	29. Modify brake standards
12. Adopt equivalent non-methane hydrocarbon standards	30. Terminate rule making on low-tire-pressure warning devices
13. Do not require controls of emissions while fueling	31. Eliminate tire information requirements
14. Streamline certification program	32. Terminate rule making on batteries
15. Relax test vehicle exemptions	33. Streamline fuel economy reporting
16. Reduce number of assembly-line test orders	34. Change vehicle identification requirements

SOURCE: White House, Office of the Press Secretary, "Actions to Help the U.S. Auto Industry," April 6, 1981.

We can only speculate on the fate of passive-restraint standards under the Carter administration, but certainly the rescission, if it had come, would not have been so hasty as that of the Reagan team trying to demonstrate responsiveness to its new political mandate. Carter appointees in the National Highway Transportation Safety Administration (NHTSA) were clearly much more disposed to passive restraints than Reagan appointees, but both administrations had strong advocates and well-developed arguments for and against the existing regulations. Again, given the Reagan administration's self-imposed limitation to use only regulatory relief to aid the auto industry and given its overall political commitment to reducing the regulatory burden on industry, rescission of this controversial rule was far more likely under Reagan.

In sum, the Reagan administration had several objectives in its regulatory relief program for the auto industry: (1) to aid the troubled auto industry itself; (2) to demonstrate a successful regulatory relief effort; and (3) to avoid a politically distasteful and economically inefficient capitulation to advocates of trade restraint. Given this combination of goals and the self-imposed limitation to achieve these goals only through regulatory relief, the Reagan proposals for regulatory relief were quick in coming and much more generous in proffered relief than a less conservative administration would likely have recommended.

Policy Assessment from an Industry Perspective

Although the preceding discussion suggests that some elements of the Reagan program might have been forthcoming had Carter been reelected, the following assessment of the Reagan policy will not attempt to adjust for this likelihood. Rather, the analysis will attribute all the proposed changes and any associated impacts to the Reagan program.

The following assessment is also intentionally limited to an evaluation of the policy's impact on auto manufacturers and not on auto buyers or the public-at-large. This orientation reflects the aim of the relief program, which was to aid the industry, whatever other impacts it might also have had. If the program failed in this dimension, it failed.

And although our primary interest here is in regulatory relief, a look at other administration policies that were targeted to the auto industry may help place the regulatory relief program in a broader policy context. Most important to the current discussion are subsequent Reagan policies of trade restraint and gasoline taxation.

Two ways of assessing the Reagan policy present themselves. The first is to take the administration's policymakers literally, and simply ask whether the goals they established for the industry have been achieved. The second, more judgmental approach is to ask whether the industry is substantively better off—the quantitative goals of the Reagan policy notwithstanding—as a consequence of administration actions. Both approaches are pursued below.

The Literal Test

The U.S. auto industry in 1981 faced a serious situation. In 1980, sales of U.S.-manufactured cars had dropped to a nineteen-year low, and domestic companies had incurred unprecedented losses of $4.3 billion. The administration estimated that 580,000 auto workers, employees of auto suppliers, and individuals in the dealer network were unemployed.[6]

Reagan envisaged a program of economic recovery and regulatory relief that would improve sales, profits, employment, and productivity. The Reagan administration forecast that new car sales in 1983 would increase by three million units (foreign and domestic), operating income of domestic auto producers would increase by $6 billion, and "most" auto industry unemployment would be eliminated. Higher production volumes would lower unit production costs, and personal income tax cuts would moderate pressures for costly wage settlements.[7] Table 2 summarizes the key industry statistics as of April 6, 1981, and the forecasts reported in the Reagan policy.

Table 2 also reports the actual performance of the industry two years later. The Reagan administration's ambitious sales and employment forecasts did not materialize. The economy has not rebounded as forecast in those optimistic first months of the Reagan term. To the extent the economy has improved, auto sales have not even done as well as in previous economic recoveries.[8] Although sales in 1983 are expected to increase 12 percent over 1982 levels, they are not expected to exceed the 1980 sales volume of 9 million units. This is well below the administration's ebullient forecast of 12 million cars.

Unemployment in the manufacturing sector of the industry has increased rather than decreased, although in fairness to the Reagan policy, this outcome was both inevitable and predictable.[9] The productivity improvement necessary to turn the U.S. auto industry around was simply incompatible from the very outset with the goals for reemployment of large numbers of furloughed auto industry workers unless sales volumes soared to record highs—something not even the most optimistic Reagan forecasters were prepared to predict.

In 1981, labor productivity differed vastly between the newer model lines and the more traditional and larger vehicles in the U.S. fleet. Even in

---

6. White House, "Actions to Help," p. 1.
7. Ibid., p. 3.
8. Thomas Oliphant, "Feldstein Says Upturn Dependent on Tax Hike," *Boston Globe*, May 8, 1983, pp. 1, 17.
9. Jose A. Gomez-Ibanez, Robert A. Leone, and Stephen A. O'Connell, "Restraining Auto Imports: Does Anyone Win?" *Journal of Policy Analysis and Management*, vol. 2, no. 2 (1983), pp. 204, 218n.

TABLE 2

Key Auto Industry Statistics: Actual and Projected Figures, 1980–1983

Year	Actual	Administration Forecast
	Sales	
	(millions of passenger autos)	
1980	9.0[a]	—
1981	8.5[b]	—
1982	9.0[b]	11.0[c]
1983	9.0[b]	12.0[c]
	Unemployment	
1980	580,000[d]	—
1983	657,000[e]	290,000 or less[f]
	Industry Income	
	(billions of dollars)	
1980	−4.3[g]	—
1983	+3.0[h]	+1.7[i]
	Capital Cost Reductions Due to Deregulation	
	(billions of dollars)	
1981–1983	1.13[j]	1.4[k]

Sources: The data were derived as follows:

a. White House, "Actions to Help the U.S. Auto Industry," April 6, 1981, p. 3.

b. *Automotive News 1982* and *1983 Market Data Books*. For 1983, the figure is the author's estimate based on a range of published estimates: "A Modest Auto Recovery?" *New York Times*, January 2, 1983, p. III, 1 (estimate of 8.8-9.2 million unit sales); and "Cost Cutting is Buoying Detroit," *Business Week* (May 9, 1983), pp. 31–32 (estimate of 8.9 million unit sales).

c. White House, "Actions to Help the U.S. Auto Industry," p. 3.

d. Ibid., p. 1. This figure includes both furloughed autoworkers and workers in related industries.

e. This is the author's estimate based on the following assumptions: (1) total vehicles sold in 1980 and 1983 are comparable; therefore, unemployment in the dealer network is assumed unchanged at 100,000; (2) 230,000 auto workers were on extended layoff in April 1983, according to *Ward's Automotive Reports*, May 2, 1983; and (3) supplier industry unemployment is estimated to be 346,000, assuming that unemployment in the supplier sector increased in proportion to unemployment in the primary manufacturing sector.

f. White House, "Actions to Help the U.S. Auto Industry," p. 3. The April 6 policy statement indicated that "most" unemployment would be eliminated by 1983. For this table, "most" has been interpreted to mean at least 50 percent.

g. Ibid., p. 1.

h. *Standard and Poor's Industry Surveys: Auto—Auto Parts* (January 6, 1983), p. A131.

i. White House, "Actions to Help the U.S. Auto Industry," p. 3. The April 6 document refers to a $6.0 billion dollar increase in "net operating income." Given that the $4.3 billion loss for 1980 equals the aggregate consolidated losses (all operations) for the major U.S. automakers in 1980, this table assumes the $6.0 billion increase applies to consolidated earnings as well.

j. See table 4.

k. White House, "Actions to Help the U.S. Auto Industry," p. 5. These are savings projected to occur over a five-year period.

the absence of further productivity improvement, the shift in mix from larger vehicles to smaller, newer designs would have meant less employment for the equivalent number of vehicle sales. However, productivity was not stagnant; on the contrary, the U.S. industry was adopting new methods, installing new equipment, and consciously pursuing efforts to lower fixed administrative costs. As a result of these productivity advances, U.S. automakers built about the same number of cars in March 1983 as they had in April 1980, but with about 70,000 fewer workers.[10]

Since industry analysts well appreciated the potential for a dramatic advance in productivity at the time the Reagan auto policy was put in place, the stated employment goals must be attributed more to political exigency than to real expectations about the outcome of the administration's policy. However, administration officials did apparently think that the sales levels were realistic and attainable, although they clearly have been wide of the mark.

Although the administration's employment and sales forecasts have not been met, its operating income levels for the industry have been exceeded. Even with the currently depressed levels of auto sales, domestic auto producers are expected to earn $3 billion in 1983.[11] This figure represents an improvement in operating income of $7.3 billion for the major U.S. producers over 1980 levels (table 2).

Table 3, however, suggests that the Reagan administration cannot claim credit for this turnaround in industry income. Because total automobile sales in 1983 are not likely to exceed sales in 1980, the increase in net operating income is not associated with increased sales volume.

Even if we accept the administration's estimates of the capital savings associated with its deregulation initiatives, table 4 shows that deregulation can, at most, explain only $1.13 billion of the $7.3 billion improvement in operating income. This sum reflects the capital savings attributable to those regulatory actions announced in Reagan's April 6 policy statement that have actually been implemented—and assumes the entire one-time benefit will accrue to 1983 income. It includes $400 million for savings due to the rescission of the passive-regulation and $300 million due to the deferral of certain environmental controls for paintshops.

If we assume that through pricing practices the industry was able to capture 100 percent of the savings that the administration forecast would fall

---

10. Based on calculations from data in the following issues of *Ward's Automotive Reports*: (for April 1980) May 5, 1980, pp. 141, 144; April 21, 1980, p. 124; and April 14, 1980, p. 116; (for March 1983) May 9, 1983, p. 152; April 4, 1983, p. 108; March 21, 1983, p. 92; and March 7, 1983, p. 76.

11. *Standard and Poor's Industry Surveys: Auto–Auto Parts* (January 6, 1983), p. 131.

TABLE 3

Speculation As to Sources of Improvement in Auto Industry Income
1980 versus 1983
(Billions of dollars)

Increase in income	7.30[a]
Contributing factors	
Increased sales volume	0[b]
Capital savings due to deregulation	1.13[c]
Industry capture of consumer savings due to deregulation	1.44[c]
Benefits of auto import restraint	0.44[d]
Productivity, price, consolidated corporate earnings improvements, etc.	4.29[e]

    a. See table 2.
    b. While total sales are comparable in 1980 and 1983, U.S. market share is expected to increase slightly in 1983. (See *Automotive News 1982 Market Data Book* and "A Modest Auto Recovery?" *New York Times*, January 2, 1983, p. III-1.) This volume effect is attributed to import restraint policies and counted elsewhere in the table.
    c. For the regulatory actions reported in table 4, this is the sum of associated annual savings to consumers estimated by the Department of Commerce, "Assessing the President's Program for the Automotive Industry," (Draft), May 1983.
    d. Jose A. Gomez-Ibanez, Robert A. Leone, and Stephen A. O'Connell, "Restraining Auto Imports: Does Anyone Win?" *Journal of Policy Analysis and Management*, vol. 2, no. 2 (1983), p. 203. These are the authors' extreme estimates of the annual benefits to automakers of the Reagan import restraint policy.
    e. This is the change in income not explained by other entries in the table.

to consumers as a consequence of this deregulation, this sum constitutes an additional $1.44 billion of increased operating income attributable to regulatory actions.

Finally, the administration's program of import restraint presumably added to the income of domestic producers. The $440 million estimate of this impact (shown in table 3) is based on the assumption that import restraint arrested the secular decline in market share for domestic firms and allowed automakers to increase prices more than they might have otherwise.

Even with these very generous assumptions, we cannot attribute much more than 40 percent of the earnings turnaround in the auto industry to Reagan administration policy. The turnaround resulted mainly from improved productivity and actions by auto industry management to create lower breakeven levels of production in U.S. manufacturing facilities.[12] These factors, more than any others, explain the respectable levels of profit by U.S. manufacturers at sales volumes, which by any historic measure remain depressed.

---

    12. "Cost Cutting is Buoying Detroit," *Business Week* (May 9, 1983), pp. 31–32.

TABLE 4

Capital Cost Savings Attributable to Reagan Administration's Deregulation Effort

Action	Capital Saving (millions of dollars)
Elimination of gastank vapor controls (EPA)	103
Eased motor vehicle certification procedures (EPA)	5
Eased assembly-line test orders (EPA)	1
Self-certification for high-altitude vehicles (EPA)	1
Elimination of assembly-line testing at high altitudes	0.035
Deferred air standards for paintshops (EPA)	150[a]
Rescission of passive-restraint rule (NHTSA)	400
Withdrawal of field-of-view regulations (NHTSA)	160
Withdrawal of multipiece rim regulation (NHTSA)	300
Relaxation of test for hydraulic brakes	10[b]
TOTAL	1,130

SOURCE: Department of Commerce, "Assessing the President's Program for the Automotive Industry" (Draft), May 1983.

a. The administration estimates that the expenditure of $300 million will be deferred two to three years. At a 20 percent cost of capital, this is approximately a $150 million savings in capitalized interest charges.

b. The administration estimates that this will be an annually recurring savings in testing. At a 20 percent cost of capital, this represents a present value of $50 million.

The administration, however, might take credit for part of this improved productivity. Deregulation has not saved the industry as much as originally intended, but it has eliminated much governmental red tape. The resulting reductions in fixed costs for automakers presumably helped the industry's efforts to reduce fixed costs across the board. Although this analyst is not inclined to assign a great deal of weight to this factor, clearly management's task would have been more difficult if the administration had not taken the actions it did.

Despite the administration's optimistic sales forecasts, the automakers' aggressive move to lower breakeven production levels suggests that management did not expect or plan for a revival in industry volume, but instead anticipated and planned for lean corporate organizations capable of earning money at low levels of production. Indeed, since lean production strategies imply the sacrificing of maximum attainable profits at cyclical peaks, profit-oriented managers, however favorably disposed they might have been to administration policy, clearly did not see the fruits of that policy in higher sales volumes.

Interpreted literally, then, the Reagan policy has not achieved its objectives: automobile sales have not revived, and the prospect for a substantial improvement in industry employment is dim. While operating incomes have increased, this improvement is most readily explained by management efforts to reduce fixed costs and bring the U.S. industry to a leaner, lower breakeven production level.

The Judgmental Test

Ultimately, the ability of any domestic industry to compete successfully for the consumer's dollar depends on three factors that can serve as the basis for evaluating the Reagan auto policy. The first factor is cost. The lower an industry's costs, the more readily it can price its product attractively to the consumer and profitably to itself. In competitive markets, costs are only high or low relative to the competition; in this case, the relevant competitors are foreign manufacturers. Therefore, we must consider what impact the Reagan policy has had on the second factor critical to competitive success: international competitiveness. The third criterion for evaluating the Reagan program is to consider to what extent it has helped or hindered the efforts of individual domestic firms to maintain their "strategic focus"—that is, their specific strategies for successful competition in the marketplace.

Costs. One specific objective of the Reagan administration policy was to reduce the costs of auto manufacturing.[13] To the extent that both existing and prospective regulations have been eased, costs facing manufacturers undoubtedly fell. The administration claims that deregulation has eliminated about 10 percent of the capital costs of federal regulation facing the auto industry.[14] This decline in costs is clearly significant even though it represents only about 75 percent of the cost reduction Reagan forecast would be forthcoming from his program of regulatory relief.

All other things being equal, lower costs mean a greater opportunity to price aggressively to achieve volume increases while still operating profitably. But all things are rarely equal. In complex markets like those for automotive services, shifts in costs among segments of the industry often have great

---

13. White House, "Actions to Help," p. 3.
14. Department of Commerce, "Assessing the President's Program for the Automotive Industry," (draft) May 1983, p. 17.

competitive significance.[15] For example, the Reagan administration raised the gasoline tax five cents per gallon on April 1, 1983. By raising the cost of automobile operation, it shifted costs from one sector of the economy to another. Auto users can reduce these costs by purchasing more fuel-efficient cars. This is an important incentive in a market in which auto producers must compete for the consumer's automotive dollar with service stations, insurance companies, financial institutions, and petroleum companies. Just as artificially low gasoline prices in the mid-1970s frustrated industry attempts to shift the product mix to smaller and more fuel-efficient cars, higher gasoline costs will encourage consumers to substitute more costly, but fuel-efficient, automotive capital for more expensive gasoline.

An illustrative calculation helps to put this economic incentive in perspective. According to automakers, consumers attempt to keep the real operating cost per mile relatively constant.[16] A gasoline tax of five cents per gallon increases operating costs by about $20 per year, assuming the typical new vehicle attains 25 miles per gallon and is driven 10,000 miles annually. At a 20 percent interest rate, a consumer can pay an additional $100 for a more fuel-efficient car to obtain the desired stability in operating costs without increasing the total costs of automotive services. If, on the margin, 50 percent of the additional revenues to automakers are contributions to gross income, this nets the automakers $50. Given a typical gross margin on the average vehicle of perhaps $2,000, this $50 is a substantial increment to the industry's earning potential.

This calculation assumes that total costs of auto use remain the same or drop with the gasoline tax. This is likely because the tax money is earmarked primarily for improvements in highway maintenance. These improvements presumably more than justify the costs of higher taxes.

Of course, some of the savings attributable to the gasoline tax come from reduced maintenance and longer vehicle life as a result of a reduction in the number of potholes, for example, which decreases sales of replacement parts and sales of some new vehicles, with consequent reductions in gross profits. But, just as higher gasoline prices encourage purchasers of new cars to buy more costly, fuel-efficient vehicles, this same competitive stimulus encourages owners of fuel-inefficient older vehicles to retire their cars earlier than otherwise. On balance, the effect of the gasoline tax on automakers' income is likely to be positive.

---

15. Robert A. Leone, "Competition and the Regulatory Boom," in *Government Regulation of Business: Its Growth, Impact, and Future*, Council on Trends and Perspectives, Chamber of Commerce of the United States, pp. 27–39.

16. General Motors Corporation, "General Motors Fuel Economy: 1983 Model Year Status," January 7, 1983, p.8.

Ironically perhaps, this seemingly favorable tax policy was not aimed at aiding the U.S. auto industry. Nor, for that matter, were the implications of the gasoline tax for auto producers the subject of much political debate. The political discussion surrounding this policy focused on the trucking and construction industries, not the automobile or petroleum industries.[17]

Some of the regulatory changes that were part of Reagan's April 6 program had impacts on cost structure similar to the impact of the gasoline tax. Consider the deferral of air emissions standards for paintshops. This regulatory change defers for two to three years—and maybe permanently, if legislation is forthcoming—the expenditure by automakers of $300 million.[18] Whether this reform is good for the environment is another question, but without doubt the deferral lowers the total cost of automotive services and reduces the cost of the vehicle relative to the other costs of auto use. These changes, like the gasoline tax, benefit auto producers.

The impact of other changes, such as bumper standards, is more ambiguous. According to NHTSA, the move from a bumper standard of 5 miles per hour to a standard of 2.5 miles per hour lowered consumers' vehicle costs by about $24 to $55 per vehicle, reduced fuel costs on a lifetime basis by $28 to $70, but increased insurance costs by $45 to $83.[19] This shift in costs works to the competitive advantage of automakers. Moreover, if NHTSA is correct that total consumer costs also fell, the industry will ultimately benefit indirectly from the resulting stimulus to auto use.

Not all observers agree with NHTSA's estimates. Insurance interests have argued that the more stringent bumper standards lowered total consumer costs, hence their rescission raises the total cost of auto ownership.[20] Thus, any benefits to auto producers from improvements in cost *structure* have to be weighed against the losses due to increases in the overall cost *level* for automotive services. Because the overall impact on the cost of auto services is unclear, the net impact on producers remains ambiguous.

The rescission of passive restraint requirements may fall into the same category. Advocates of passive restraints contend that the total cost of automotive services declines with regulation. William Nordhaus, for example,

---

17. See, for example, "Reagan Endorses Gasoline Tax Increase of 5 Cents a Gallon to Fix Roads, Bridges," *Wall Street Journal*, November 24, 1982, p. 3; and Judy Sarasohn, "Congress Approves Transportation Funding," *CO Weekly Report* (December 25, 1982), pp. 3044–45.

18. Department of Commerce, "Assessing the President's Program," p. 25.

19. National Highway Traffic Safety Administration (NHTSA), *Final Regulatory Impact Analysis: Part 581 Bumper Standard*, May 1982, pp. vi-10, vi-17, vi-37, vii-38, and vii-46.

20. Albert R. Karr, "Eased New-Car Bumper Rules Could Save Some Auto Costs But Raise Insurance Fees," *Wall Street Journal*, May 17, 1982, p. 14.

testifying before Congress on behalf of several automobile insurance companies, contended that passive-restraint regulations would increase the vehicle cost to the consumer by $60, but would decrease insurance costs by $225.[21] This yields a total cost reduction of $165 per vehicle on a lifetime basis. In a world in which the overall demand for automobile services has approximately a unitary price elasticity,[22] this $165 is "up for grabs" by those sectors of the industry that can compete for it. Clearly, auto insurers will capture a portion, given the decline in the relative cost of insurance in the automotive service bundle. Some of it will also be captured by petroleum companies through higher fuel use necessary to carry passive restraints around.

Possibly the remainder can be captured by automakers in higher markups or sales of more accessories or vehicles. Assuming an incremental contribution to earnings of 50 percent of sales, the industry can overcome the $60 cost increase by capturing three-quarters of the total cost reduction. If so, the total cost reduction in auto services that Nordhaus predicts could plausibly benefit automakers.

NHTSA, however, does not believe that restraints lower total costs of automotive services. NHTSA claims that passive restraints increase total lifetime costs by $89 per vehicle. This includes a $75 increase in the price of the car and added fuel costs, less $29 to $87 in insurance costs.[23]

Although the Nordhaus and NHTSA studies disagree on the overall cost impact—and hence can lead to different conclusions regarding the net impact on automakers—they do agree on one key point: passive restraints shift more of the cost of automotive services to automobile manufacturers. The increased cost of the vehicle encourages less frequent purchases of new cars or the purchase of otherwise less costly vehicles—in either case to the detriment of manufacturers. Any lowering of total costs may encourage overall consumption of automotive services, but as the calculation above illustrates, most of the savings would need to accrue to automakers to offset this cost structure impact.

Automakers' opposition to passive restraints strongly suggests that they believe that the negative impact on cost structure dominates any beneficial consequences of lower total costs for automotive services.[24] Even if passive

---

21. U.S. Congress, House, Subcommittee on Telecommunications, Consumer Protection, and Finance of the Committee on Energy and Commerce, *Automatic Crash Protection Standards*. Hearings. April 27 and 30, 1981, serial no. 97-10, pp. 132–33.

22. Gomez-Ibanez et al., "Restraining Auto Imports," p. 218n.

23. National Highway Traffic Safety Administration, *Final Regulatory Impact Analysis: Amendment to FMVSS Occupant Crash Protection—Rescission of Automatic Occupant Protection Requirements*, October 1981 (DOT HS-806 055) pp. v-8, vi-48.

24. U.S. Congress, *Automatic Crash Protection Standards*, pp. 256–67.

restraints raise the total costs of auto use, the reduction in auto insurance costs may explain the enthusiasm of insurance companies for these regulations. On balance, this analyst concludes that rescission is favorable to auto manufacturers.

International Competitiveness. The cost changes associated with Reagan's auto policy have had mixed consequences for U.S. auto manufacturers. The impact of regulatory changes on international competitiveness is similarly ambiguous because the policy changes that benefit U.S. firms also benefit foreign manufacturers. The consequences for international competitiveness depend on the relative improvement accruing to each group of competitors.

Because U.S. manufacturers tend to produce more heterogeneous fleets for sales in the U.S. market than their foreign competitors do, any policy changes that complement fleet diversity tend to work to the advantage of U.S. firms. For example, the Reagan administration's move to emission averaging for diesel particulate emissions is one such policy. Averaging will allow some vehicles in a manufacturer's fleet to have excessive emissions provided other vehicles exceed the environmental standard. Averaging is of little value to a manufacturer that produces only one kind of vehicle. For producers with diversified fleets, however, the scheme can result in cost savings because some vehicles would not need the most costly emission control devices.

In contrast, any policy that encourages foreign producers to move away from their traditionally narrow product lines and seek greater fleet diversity, especially by shifting to higher-priced vehicles, works against the long-term competitive interests of U.S. producers. The Reagan administration's import restraints on Japanese vehicles, although intended to aid the U.S. auto industry, clearly creates this perverse incentive. Indeed, the estimated $440 million increase in industry income due to import restraint reported in table 3 is a bit misleading. The authors of this estimate also contended that the induced strategic shift in mix of Japanese vehicles to higher-margin, luxury cars would hurt the U.S. industry in the long run—so much so that the net present value of import restraint might actually be negative, despite a substantial income increase in 1983.[25]

On balance, the Reagan auto industry policy may not have improved the domestic industry's competitive position worldwide. The benefits resulting from its deregulation initiatives may have been more than offset by the negative effect of its trade policies.

---

25. Gomez-Ibanez et al., "Restraining Auto Imports," p. 210.

Strategic Focus

The last criterion for measuring the success of the Reagan administration's automotive industrial policy is its impact on strategic focus. A basic principle of sound management states that no organization can do all things well. Thus, it must focus its efforts on a limited number of objectives and marshal its limited resources to these ends.

Federal policy toward the auto industry has historically been a disaster when viewed from the perspective of strategic focus. Environmental policies in the early 1970s established uniform requirements for all vehicles, thus discouraging U.S. manufacturers from producing the diverse fleet of vehicles for which they were well organized. In contrast, corporate average fuel economy (CAFE) regulations later in the decade were established on a fleet-weighted basis, thus actively encouraging diversity in vehicle sizes while generally supporting a move to smaller cars. Safety requirements emphasized crashworthiness as opposed to on-the-road performance, thus encouraging the manufacture of heavier, less fuel-efficient vehicles. Gasoline price controls for several years discouraged producers from manufacturing the small, fuel-efficient vehicles that represented the industry's future.

Indeed, when coupled with stringent CAFE standards, gasoline price controls penalized domestic firms with the foresight to plan for the inevitable shift to smaller, more fuel-efficient cars.[26] As long as gasoline prices were kept artificially low, consumers wanted to buy large cars. To sell large cars, U.S. firms also had to sell small cars with high mileage to meet the CAFE standard. But small cars had to be sold at low prices to induce consumers to buy them, severely limiting the profitability of small cars.

The historic picture of federal regulation is a sorry one of conflicting strategic signals constantly frustrating managements' efforts to achieve strategic focus. The Reagan policy has helped reduce this strategic confusion. For example, no changes in CAFE standards are planned beyond 1985, thus reducing the conflict between the economic imperatives of the energy market and the political imperatives of fuel-economy regulation.[27] The movement toward fleet-weighted averaging in the auto emissions area complements traditional U.S. skills in producing a diverse fleet. The administration claims to be committed to free-market energy prices even under emergency conditions, thus reducing an additional element of political uncertainty.

---

26. Robert A. Leone, and Stephen P. Bradley, "Federal Energy Policy and Competitive Strategy in the U.S. Automobile Industry," *Annual Review of Energy*, vol. 7, 1982, pp. 61–85.

27. Department of Commerce, "Assessing the President's Program," p. 35.

Although many of these changes are favorable to the auto industry's interests, other administration actions continue to frustrate the attainment of strategic focus. Its rescission of the passive-restraint requirement is perhaps the best example of such a policy.

The arguments for and against passive restraints can be debated endlessly, but two things are certain. Ultimately, the only way the auto industry can resolve the passive-restraint issue itself is to begin installing them. Not surprisingly, the Japanese, who allegedly have a substantial cost advantage in producing passive restraints, are most inclined to pursue this avenue to reduce regulatory uncertainty.[28] Any resolution of the passive-restraint issue other than industry capitulation requires government action.

Second, the merits and demerits of passive restraints notwithstanding, the notion of improved vehicle safety has an underlying political legitimacy. Politicians, not industrialists, need to address these political issues.

The Reagan administration has failed to resolve the passive-restraint issue precisely because it has ignored this political reality. Its heavy-handed policy of rescission in April 1981 was a paper victory for advocates of deregulation. By paying little attention to the analytical, legal, and political support necessary to sustain the policy, the administration created for itself—and the auto industry—the very uncertainty that the "once and for all" decision was designed to eliminate. Because the administration failed to do its analytical and political homework before announcing the rescission, the issue was brought before the Supreme Court, which reversed the rescission on points of law and due process.[29] The issue is once again before Congress,[30] where the proindustry interests are not nearly so strong as in the executive office of the president.

Actions Not Taken

In addition to reviewing the Reagan administration policy on the basis of specific actions taken, we can also evaluate its policy on the basis of actions not taken. Indeed, some analysts argue that the substantive benefit of the Reagan administration's regulatory relief program to the U.S. auto industry is not mea-

---

28. Daniel Rapoport, "Air Bags—Made in Japan?" *National Journal* (September 11, 1982), p. 1566.

29. David M. Kennedy, "The Rescission of the Passive Restraints Standards," Case C16-82-455, Kennedy School of Government, Harvard University.

30. Helen Kahn, "Wide Ranging Safety Bill Calls for Airbags in '86," *Automotive News* (April 25, 1983), pp. 1, 46.

sured in rollbacks of existing regulations but in the slowdown in growth of new regulation. On this score, the Reagan policy has been beneficial to automakers. Although the number of new regulations facing this industry is difficult to judge, the complexity of compliance has apparently declined during the Reagan term.[31]

Inaction is not always a plus, however. It often represents lost opportunities. For example, the Reagan program of economic recovery was intended to sell more cars, but the administration failed to pursue available means to further this objective. For example, environmental regulations apply to new vehicles with increasing stringency over time. This creates a substantial bias against the purchase of new vehicles. One analyst has estimated that the bias against new car sales created by the tougher 1981 emissions standards for passenger cars reduced potential sales by almost 3 percent in 1983.[32] This represents about $400 million in lost income for the industry.

Not only does the industry lose income, but the reduction of new vehicle sales means that more polluting older cars stay on the road longer—with negative near-term consequences for the environment. (All this for a regulation that Professor Lawrence White finds cost-ineffective.)[33] The Reagan administration has done nothing to address this bias against new car purchases.

To cite another example of a missed opportunity, the Reagan administration's program of regulatory relief was intended to lower production costs, but it has not aggressively pursued opportunities to lower costs in this sector. Consider the cost of steel. Automobile manufacturing utilizes 21 percent of the nation's steel output.[34] The United States has long had a cost disadvantage in steel vis-à-vis the Japanese. Policies of trade restraint in steel raise the cost of U.S. producers and lower it to foreign suppliers (by increasing the supply available to their domestic markets), thereby exacerbating rather than ameliorating an important cost disadvantage facing U.S. competitors. Despite public commitments to free-trade principles, the administration has not attacked this and other policies that raise automakers' costs.

The Bottom Line

Over all, this analyst concludes that the Reagan administration's policy toward the auto industry has been far stronger in its stated intentions than in

---

31. Department of Commerce, "Assessing the President's Program," pp. 6ff.
32. Howard K. Gruenspecht, "Differentiated Regulations: The Case of Auto Emissions Standards," *American Economic Review* (May 1982), p. 330.
33. Lawrence J. White, *The Regulation of Air Pollutant Emissions from Motor Vehicles* (Washington, D.C.: American Enterprise Institute of Public Policy Research, 1982).
34. Department of Transportation, "The U.S. Automobile Industry, 1980," January 1981, p. 1.

its actual performance. Many actions have benefited the industry, but they have been limited in scope and mixed in their long-term competitive consequences for U.S. producers. The administration has made little attempt to consider the international competitive implications of its various initiatives and has paid still less systematic attention to the strategic consequences of its policies.

Few administrations have succeeded in stimulating individual industrial sectors—especially declining ones—and this administration is no exception. Ironically perhaps, trade restraint—the one policy aimed unapologetically at aiding the industry—may well have hurt the industry, whereas higher gasoline taxes and improved highway maintenance policy—the Reagan policy arguably most favorable to the industry's interests—was formulated with little thought to its potential benefit to the auto industry's economic prospects.

Inattention to the Political Process

The Reagan administration's biggest failures have not been associated with a lack of commitment to the automobile industry, but rather with the failure of its policymakers to effectively manage the political process for which they are responsible. The full slate of legislative reforms promised in the April 6 policy document simply has not been forthcoming. Nothing has come of administration promises to reform the Clean Air Act, for example.

The passive-restraint debacle is perhaps the best example of a well-intended initiative that backfired by adding to the uncertainties of public policy. These uncertainties have always been the biggest single objection of businesses to government's involvement in industry affairs.

In sum, the probusiness sentiments of the Reagan administration have not greatly benefited the U.S. auto industry. The economics of competition are too complicated to allow good intentions to resolve industrial policy problems. This administration's regulatory relief initiatives have lacked systematic competitive analysis and detailed attention to the realities of political process.

COMMENTS

E. Woodrow Eckard

I agree with the main conclusion of Leone's paper that recent improvements in auto industry performance (i.e., through early 1983) are due primarily to industry's efforts to increase efficiency rather than to the Reagan administration's deregulation efforts. For example, General Motors was profitable in 1982 despite a very depressed output level of about 4.0 million units, significantly below the 1980 level of about 4.8 million units and more than 40 percent below the last cyclical peak of 6.9 million units. Leone's projections of increased industry profitability in 1983 are reasonable.

Although I agree with Leone's basic conclusion, I think he is somewhat overly critical of administration performance. He notes that the Reagan administration has not dramatically reduced auto industry regulation since 1980, and that such reductions seem unlikely in the near future. But the Reagan administration may have succeeded in arresting the trend toward increasing regulation. If so, the appropriate basis of comparison is not actual levels two to three years ago (when Reagan took office), but instead the presumably higher levels that would have existed by now had Reagan lost the 1980 election.

When evaluating the performance of this administration (or any other) vis-à-vis the auto (or any other) industry, we must remember that government options for positive, constructive help are limited. In fact, the principal option available is to maintain a favorable competitive environment. This means eliminating unnecessary regulations and assuring that the remaining regulations are enforced at levels where costs don't outstrip benefits. It also means maintaining a stable macroeconomic environment, thereby reducing the risk and uncertainty of long-term business planning. This is particularly important to the auto industry, given its long product-development lead times and the magnitude of investment.

The principal problem now confronting U.S. auto firms is strong competition from Japanese automakers. This competition would exist regardless of administration successes or failures in deregulation policy or in fighting recession and inflation. The government can do little directly to solve the competitive problems of U.S. auto firms in the areas of product cost and quality. Only the firms themselves can make the necessary design and manufacturing improvements. In sum, we should be careful not to expect too much when assessing the impacts of government policy on the auto industry.

The one area in Leone's discussion of cost impacts of deregulation where I had problems is his argument that the recently imposed gas tax will benefit the auto industry. This is quite unlikely, given the fundamental economic proposition that the demand for a good falls if the price of a complementary good increases. Thus, the demand for cars should fall as gas prices increase, a situation not likely to benefit auto firms.

To illustrate this point, assume a two-segment car market—large cars and small cars. Ignoring for a moment the substitution between large and small cars, the demand curves for both market segments shift inward when the price of gas rises because of the tax. But if we consider substitution between the large- and small-car markets, the gas tax causes small-car demand to rise (i.e., to shift back out), whereas the large-car demand curve shifts further inward. The net overall effect is negative. Moreover, the shift toward smaller cars because of the gas tax is *away* from U.S. strength and toward Japanese strength. Thus the initial impact on the U.S. firms is compounded.

Leone notes that part of the proceeds from the gas tax is slated for highway maintenance. However, unless U.S. roads have deteriorated to the point at which car sales are affected, road improvements will not produce offsetting increases in sales. The bottom line is that policies yielding higher gas prices hurt, rather than help, U.S. auto firms.

I also disagree with Leone's, claims, in his discussion of international competitiveness, that government regulations have the same impact on domestic firms as on foreign firms. I think regulatory relief can, to some extent, help U.S. competitiveness insofar as U.S. firms have historically specialized in producing cars larger than those built abroad. Thus, policies that increase gas prices favor small-car specialists (i.e., foreign firms). The Corporate Average Fuel Economy (CAFE) standards also penalize large-car producers. Automakers can meet auto emission standards at lower cost in small cars since smaller engines have lower emission levels to begin with. This is an area in which a fleet-averaging concept, similar to that used in CAFE regulation, could lower compliance costs without sacrificing regulatory objectives. Finally, as originally planned, the air bag was to have been introduced on large cars first (in 1984) and then on small cars (in 1985). All these regulations adversely impact the competitiveness of U.S. auto firms.

In Leone's discussion of opportunities for additional regulatory relief, a review of CAFE standards would have been worthwhile. The law requires that each firm meets the fuel economy standard on an average basis for all cars sold. The standard is 26 miles per gallon in 1983, 27 miles per gallon in 1984, and 27.5 miles per gallon in 1985 and thereafter. The penalty is five dollars per car for each 0.1 miles per gallon the fleet average falls below the standard. That's five dollars per car for *all* cars sold. According to published sources, Ford this year (1983) expects an average 24.3 miles per gallon, 1.7 miles per gallon below the standard, while GM is forecasting a CAFE of 23.6 miles per gallon, 2.4 miles per gallon below the standard. On the basis of depressed 1982 sales levels, these figures imply penalties of $163 million and $402 million for Ford and GM respectively. These penalties may be covered this year by previously earned "carry-forward" credits. However, automakers may have to pay substantial cash fines in 1984, 1985, and perhaps later years. Of course, the ultimate losers are those consumers who must pay higher prices for large cars.

In an era of deregulated energy, a law regulating auto fuel economy is clearly an anachronism. The deregulation of oil was begun under Carter and completed under Reagan, suggesting a bipartisan recognition that the free market can effectively allocate energy resources. Events over the past decade demonstrate that a free market also works for auto fuel efficiency. Consumers have responded to the dramatic increase in gas prices with an equally dramatic shift to smaller, more fuel-efficient cars; in fact, prior to this year consumer demand for fuel economy has caused fleet fuel economy to exceed the mandated standards.

More important, no economic rationale exists for auto fuel economy regulation. A concern over U.S. dependence on oil from the politically volatile Middle East might form the basis for an externalities argument. In terms of policy action, however, this would suggest no more than a tariff on oil imported from the unstable source. Furthermore, this argument has been undermined by recent substantial reductions in such oil imports, which coincided with domestic energy deregulation. In any event, this concern provides no basis for regulating specific forms of domestic oil consumption.

Nevertheless, the CAFE standards exist and will continue to increase until 1985. Meanwhile, fuel prices have moderated, and so has consumer demand for fuel efficiency. As suggested previously, this situation could be very costly in the near future and could serve to needlessly disadvantage domestic automakers.

I shall conclude with a brief comment on macroeconomic policy. Automobile sales are particularly vulnerable to high interest rates, unstable prices, and recessions. The currently lower inflation and interest rates have been beneficial, with even greater benefits possible as recovery proceeds. However, the recovery must be engineered without reigniting inflation or high interest rates. If the Reagan administration succeeds here, the long-term benefits to the U.S. auto industry could well exceed the benefits of even the most successful deregulation program.

FEDERALISM AND REGULATION

Jerry L. Mashaw and Susan Rose-Ackerman

The Reagan administration urges a reconstitution of the federal system with more regulatory authority given to state governments.[1] Its rhetoric, however, has not been followed by any concerted efforts to repeal laws that preempt or supplement state initiatives. Instead, it has implemented the "new" federalism by cutting funds and freezing budgets in health, housing, and other social welfare areas,[2] and, as Michael Fix's paper in this volume shows, by increasing the pace of formal delegation and relaxing federal oversight of state implementation of environmental and health and safety laws.[3] At the same time, the administration has espoused contrary policies, reasserting

---

The authors thank Jose Berrocal, Stephen Calabresi, Peter Keisler, Jonathan Rich, and Edward E. Steiner, whose independent study projects in the spring of 1983 helped us in the preparation of this paper.

1. "One of the most important goals of the Administration is to make government more efficient and more responsive to its citizens by restoring an appropriate balance among Federal, state and local governments." David Stockman, "Statement Before the Committee on Finance, U.S. Senate, on President Reagan's Federalism Initiative," (mimeographed) (Washington, D.C.: Office of Management and Budget, March 4, 1983), p. 12. See also Ronald Reagan's 1982 State of the Union Address (H.R. Doc. no. 133, 97th Cong., 2d sess., 1982).

2. Thus, the Reagan administration proposed consolidating thirty-four programs into four block grants with FY 1984 funding of approximately $21 billion (a funding cut of 14 percent, according to the National Governors Association). The proposed legislation would hold funding levels constant until FY 1988. See Rochelle Stanfield, "Revised New Federalism Plan Would Do Little to Change Power, Authority," *National Journal* 487 (5 March 1983), pp. 518–19; Stockman, "Statement on . . . Federalism Initiative"; and U.S. Executive Office of the President, "President's Federalism Initiative Legislation Fact Sheet," (mimeographed), February 24, 1983.

3. For example, the Environmental Protection Agency asked the Justice Department to drop forty-nine pending enforcement actions, arguing (among other things) that enforcement should be left to the states. Under Medicare and Medicaid, the federal government has sharply cut funds for nursing home inspections. Both examples are cited in George Eads and Michael Fix, "Reg-

national authority, for example, in such areas as trucking regulation, interstate transport of hazardous products, and nuclear power.[4]

It is not our purpose, however, to detail the Reagan administration's accomplishments and failures or to provide a balance sheet equating rhetoric and action. Instead, we shall attempt the more conceptual task of providing a framework within which to assess this, or any other, administration's policies concerning the mix of state and federal regulatory authority.

We begin by noting that state and federal regulatory laws can relate to each other in four stylized ways. First, federal law may preempt state laws. In such cases the federal government carries out all rule making and enforcement activity. The federal government, for example, claims exclusive sovereignty over the nation's air space and the exclusive right to regulate federally registered airlines.[5] Second, federal law may contain positive or negative incentives (subsidies or penalties) to encourage states to participate with the federal government in a cooperative scheme. These incentives can be thought of as "prices" charged to change state officials' demands for various types of substantive policies or implementation strategies. Many federal regulatory and grant programs take this form.[6]

Third, state and federal laws that regulate the same conduct may be independently enacted and enforced. Thus, for example, new insurance products

---

ulatory Policy,'' in J. Palmer and I. Sawhill, eds., *The Reagan Experiment* (Washington, D.C.: The Urban Institute Press, 1982), pp. 128–53 and pp. 504–505. For more information on EPA activities, see Environmental Protection Agency, Office of Policy and Research Management, "Improving Delegation of EPA Programs to the States," (mimeographed), December 1982; and Thomas Curtis and Peter Creedon, *The State of the States: Management of Environmental Programs in the 1980s* (Washington, D.C.: National Governors Assn., Committee on Energy and Environment, May 1982).

4. The 1982 Federal Surface Transportation Assistance Act, for example, requires states to accept double-trailer trucks on interstate highways and on roads that provide access to them. In the field of nuclear power, the administration has attempted to prevent states from implementing laws restricting the development of nuclear power and the disposal of radioactive wastes. See Rebecca Smith, "Federal Limitations on State Power to Regulate Radioactive Waste," *Montana Law Review* 43 (Summer 1982), pp. 271–278. But the federal position has not always triumphed. See, e.g., *Pacific Gas and Elec. Co.* v. *State Energy Resources Conservation and Development Comm'n*, 103 S.Ct. 1713 (1983), where California's position was upheld.

5. See 49 U.S.C. Section 1305 (Supp. III, 1979) and 49 U.S.C. Section 1508(a) (1976). Courts have also inferred preemption even if it is not explicitly stated in the legislation. "The key to the scope of federal preemption is the intent of Congress in enacting the applicable federal legislation," *San Diego Unified Port Dist., Port Dist.* v. *Gianturco*, 651 F.2d 1306, 1310, note 8 (1981). Following this principle, the Ninth Circuit found that the Quiet Communities Act of 1978, P.L. 95–609, 92 Stat 3079 (1978), preempted state regulation of aircraft noise.

6. According to the useful taxonomy developed by the Advisory Commission on Intergovernmental Relations (ACIR) "Regulatory Federalism: Policy, Process, Impact, and Reform: Findings, Issues, and Recommendations," (mimeographed), December 1982, p. 12, these incentives are of four basic kinds. The ACIR distinguishes between direct orders backed by civil or criminal penalties; crosscutting requirements, which apply to a large number of assistance

may be subject to marketing approval by both state insurance commissions and the federal Securities and Exchange Commission.[7] Both the federal and state governments charter and regulate banks. And states commonly regulate intrastate activity that is closely associated with federally regulated interstate activity (food, drugs, and securities regulation are examples). Fourth, some areas such as the granting of professional licenses may in principle, at least, be regulated entirely by the states, although activity not subject to any federal overlapping regulation is rare.[8] In the following discussion, we will refer to these various categories of federal and state regulation as a preemptive system, an incentive-based system, a parallel system of regulation, and a states' rights system, respectively.[9]

Devolution of federal regulatory authority means different things in different contexts. The simplest type of devolution is a move from preemption to states' rights—that is, the repeal of a federal statute or concession of federal jurisdiction that permits states to enact their own laws. Alternatively, devolution could involve a move from a preemptive to a parallel system of regulation. The federal standards then effectively become minimum standards that states may exceed. Federal statutes that are either preemptive or parallel may be amended to require a greater reliance on incentives. For example, states can be given more freedom of action by reducing the financial penalty for noncompliance, by relaxing the formal requirements for federal approval, or by approving state plans after only limited analysis. Amending the substance of federal policies or the structure of enforcement schemes may also increase state authority or discretion in mixed systems.

---

programs; crossover sanctions, which threaten the reduction or termination of one type of aid if the requirements of another program are not met; and partial preemptions, which establish federal standards but delegate administration to the states if they adopt plans meeting with federal approval. The Appendix, reproduced from ACIR, "Regulatory Federalism," pp. 76–79, lists the major statutes by category.

7. See, for example, *SEC* v. *Variable Annuity Co.*, 359 U.S. 65 (1959).

8. The Tenth Amendment provides that "the powers not delegated to the United States by the Constitution, nor prohibited by it to the states, are reserved to the states respectively, or to the people." The states of Virginia and Indiana challenged as unconstitutional the Federal Surface Mining Control and Reclamation Act of 1977 (30 U.S.C. Section 1201–1328 [Supp IV 1980]) under the Tenth Amendment. These states contended, and the lower courts agreed, that the law unconstitutionally interfered with the powers of state and local governments to control land use. The Supreme Court, however, upheld the act in *Hodel* v. *Virginia Surface Mining and Reclamation Ass'n*, 452 U.S. 264 (1981) and *Hodel* v. *Indiana*, 452 U.S. 314 (1981). For a discussion, see Dennis Abrams, "The Federal Surface Mining Control and Reclamation Act of 1977—First to Survive a Direct Tenth Amendment Attack," *West Virginia Law Review* 84 (1982), pp. 1069–1092.

9. See Bruce LaPierre, "The Political Safeguards of Federalism Redux: Intergovernmental Immunity and the States as Agents of the Nation," *Washington University Law Quarterly* 60 (1982), pp. 782–1056, for a comprehensive review of recent court decisions governing interstate relations.

In the conceptual analysis to follow, we shall not attempt to explore all the possibilities for statutory and institutional design that preemptive, incentive, parallel, and states' rights systems might allow in the context of particular substantive areas. Instead, we will concentrate on the increasingly common incentive-based relationships that are somewhat optimistically labeled *cooperative federalism*. This emphasis reflects the Reagan administration's efforts which, thus far, have primarily involved incentive-based regulatory schemes.

During the Reagan administration, existing statutes that already gave considerable regulatory authority to the states have been pushed further in that direction in at least four distinct ways. First, Congress, with administration support, cut funding for some programs (e.g., subsidized housing), making compliance with federal rules less important.[10] This form of devolution requires no direct federal action other than a budget reduction. Second, by amending a few laws, Congress suspended many federal regulations and ended matching requirements (e.g., by incorporating social service spending under Title XX of the Social Security Act into the 1981 Omnibus Budget Reconciliation Act).[11] Third, the administration has altered federal practices, thereby effectively shifting the balance of authority. For example, the administration has largely broken the link between the distribution of Medicaid funds and state compliance with federal Medicaid requirements.[12] Similarly, under environmental statutes that mandate heavy state involvement, the administration has attempted to give states more freedom to develop their own plans and more responsibility for enforcement.[13] Finally, where overlapping state and federal statutes exist, the Reagan administration has effected devolution by slowing either the rule making or the enforcement activities of federal agencies. For example, it has moved slowly in promulgating regulations under the Occupational Safety and Health Act (OSHA), and has been sluggish in its enforcement of the Resource Conservation and Recovery Act (RCRA), which regulates toxic substances.[14]

The administration's actions raise several related questions: How far can this process of devolution be expected to proceed? Will many incentive-based systems be pushed into the category of unilateral state control? What resistance

---

10. See Raymond Struyk, John Tuccillo, and James Zais, "Housing and Community Development," in Palmer and Sawhill, eds., *Reagan Experiment*, pp. 403–417.

11. See Michael Gutowski and Jeffrey L. Koshel, "Social Services," in Palmer and Sawhill, eds., *Reagan Experiment*, pp. 315–318.

12. See Judith Feder, John Holahan, Randall Bovbjerg, and Jack Hadley, "Health," in Palmer and Sawhill, eds., *Reagan Experiment*, pp. 285–291.

13. EPA, "Improving Delegation." The EPA has also prepared a package of charts giving the percentage of various activities delegated to the states.

14. See "OSHA Taking Slower Route on Perilous-Substance Rules," *New York Times*, April 18, 1983.

is likely to be met in this process of devolution? Which political forces support, and which oppose, delegating further authority to the states? How should we evaluate the arguments for and against devolution of regulatory authority? What is the "right" mix of state and federal regulatory power?

This paper approaches these issues as follows. We first spell out the normative arguments for regulation at the state versus the federal level and isolate those situations in which an incentive-based scheme has normative appeal. We then move to a positive analysis of the demand for regulation. We examine the interests of state and federal public officials in promoting incentive-based federal regulatory statutes. Finally, we analyze the bargaining power and interests of businesses with respect to the location of regulatory authority.

In the end, both our positive and our normative analyses tend to support the continuation of "cooperative federalism." We cite convincing normative justifications for incentive-based schemes, and show how the interests of businesses and political forces support this type of devolution. These general conclusions help to explain the "make haste slowly" strategy that has characterized the Reagan administration's devolution program and help us evaluate particular initiatives. Nevertheless, the form of the federal-state relationship suggested by normative theory is often not the version enacted into law. We need to adopt a critical view of the regulatory process that moves beyond rhetoric to a careful consideration of the policies actually adopted.

Normative Arguments

In developing our analysis, we shall attempt to keep the issue of regulatory relief (or deregulation) strictly separate from the issue of the appropriate location of regulatory authority. Although the Reagan administration's rhetoric has linked devolution of authority to the states with regulatory relief, the important normative question is where to locate regulatory decision making given a desire to achieve a particular regulatory end. The question of location must address several distinct issues: (1) the effects of externalities, (2) the possible existence of "prisoner's dilemmas," (3) economies and diseconomies of scale in administration, (4) substantive benefits of diversity versus uniformity, and (5) citizen participation in regulatory choice. An analysis of these issues defines a normative structure in which allocative efficiency and consent are primary values.

Externalities

Political jurisdictions have little incentive to economize on regulatory costs or to produce regulatory benefits that do not accrue to that jurisdiction. Ideally the jurisdictional boundaries of regulatory authority should, therefore, be coterminous with the extent of its external effects.[15] Upstream and downstream water users, for example, should be regulated by a single authority. Recognizing that this principle may lead to an unmanageably large number of overlapping governmental entities, many economists have recommended the use of federal matching-grant programs to give states an incentive to take responsibility for their externalities (spillovers) through regulatory action.[16] Managing interstate externalities thus provides the first normative argument for incentive-based, cooperative federalism.

Existing matching-grant programs, however, often have proved ineffective for controlling interjurisdictional externalties. They lower the price of certain inputs (e.g., the capital cost of sewage treatment), but do not directly regulate output. In principle, it would be better to tie the federal subsidy to reductions in interstate externalities (e.g., the interstate transport of water pollution). But performance-based subsidies or fines—although they have long been advocated by economists—may involve serious monitoring problems. For example, models of the interstate transport of air and water pollution exist, but need further refinement before they can be used to levy fines or calculate subsidies. Therefore, the federal government may need to supplement matching grants with direct federal regulation of the choice of technology and the operation of the public system. In the environmental area, uniform matching rates for federal grants can be combined with direct regulations that take account of interstate differences in the impact of discharges.

A desire for regulatory diversity does not require a federal-state program, however. A preemptive federal statute regulating automobile pollution or airport noise, for example, could be designed to take account of geographical

---

15. See, for example, Wallace E. Oates, *Fiscal Federalism* (New York: Harcourt Brace Jovanovich, 1972); Mancur Olson, Jr., "The Principle of 'Fiscal Equivalence': The Division of Responsibilities Among Different Levels of Government," *A.E.R. Papers and Proc.* 59 (May 1969), pp. 479–87; Jerome Rothenberg, "Local Decentralization and the Theory of Optimal Government," in Julius Margolis, ed., *Analysis of Public Output* (New York: Columbia University Press, 1970); and Gordon Tullock, "Federalism: Problems of Scale," *Public Choice* 6 (Spring 1969), pp. 19–29.

16. See, for example, Albert Breton, "A Theory of Government Grants," *Canadian Journal of Economics and Political Science* 31 (May 1965), pp. 175–187; Richard Musgrave and Peggy Musgrave, *Public Finance in Theory and Practice* (New York: McGraw-Hill, 1973), pp. 614–620; and Oates, *Fiscal Federalism*.

differences.[17] Nevertheless, diversity within wholly federal regulatory programs has proved politically difficult to achieve in practice. Regulatory diversity may be easier to achieve by carrying out a federal program in conjunction with state governments. However, all forms of diversity are not necessarily efficient, and it seems unlikely that the diversity produced by cooperative federalism will approximate the optimal mixture.

"Prisoner's Dilemmas"

Redistributive policies are especially vulnerable to erosion in political systems with many competing state and local governments. A kind of "prisoner's dilemma" may operate in which each locale tries to gain at the expense of others, whereas all would be better off if they could work together as a group. This problem arises with particular saliency when state and local governments attempt to redistribute income to the needy and seek to attract jobs. Individual states generally view themselves as unable to carry out a large-scale redistribution of income because they fear that their high-income residents and businesses will relocate in lower tax jurisdictions. Thus, economic analyses of federalism commonly recommend that income redistribution, whether achieved directly through taxation or through regulation, be made a federal responsibility.[18]

Moreover (and here we have the prisoner's dilemma), states may all try to attract businesses to their jurisdictions through tax breaks and regulatory laxness. In this competitive environment, each state tries to outdo the others in offering low levels of taxation and regulation. These considerations, both of which assume that firms are sensitive to cost-increasing regulations, argue for federal regulation in areas where redistributional goals are substantial, such as minimum wages and health and safety in the work place. Some types of consumer protection legislation might also require federal support if businesses respond to state protective laws by refusing to do business in the more strictly regulated states.

Although the case for a federal presence in redistributive programs is convincing, it may nevertheless be desirable to allow some redistributive

---

17. See David Harrison, "Controlling Automotive Emissions: How to Save More than $1 Billion Per Year and Help the Poor Too," *Public Policy* 25 (1977), p. 527; idem, "The Regulation of Aircraft Noise," in Thomas Schelling, ed., *Incentives for Environmental Protection* (Cambridge, MIT Press, 1983).

18. See, for example, Musgrave and Musgrave, *Public Finance*, pp. 606–07; Mancur Olson, "Principle of 'Fiscal Equivalence';" and A. Mitchell Polinsky, "Collective Consumption Goods and Local Public Finance Theory: A Suggested Analytic Framework," *Issues in Urban Public Finance*, Papers and Proceedings of the 28th Conference of the International Institute of Public Finance, New York (September 1972), pp. 166–181 (Urban Institute Reprint 168-1207-8).

diversity both in the levels of transfers and styles of administration. Since tastes for redistribution may not be uniform, an incentive-based system, as opposed to federal preemption, may be a useful method for achieving the desired compromise. Federal grants and minimum standards combined with state administration and "add-ons" could be a means of fulfilling national redistributive goals while taking advantage of the greater sensitivity of state and local governments to local conditions.

Economies and Diseconomies of Scale in Administration

Much regulatory activity requires the production and transmission of information. Some information relevant to the entire country can be most efficiently created by the federal government. National institutes can study public health problems, develop models of ambient air and water quality, and test the safety of products for the benefit of all. In areas such as these, which no state would finance on its own, economies of scale demand national action.

Other information, however, may be specific to a particular time, place, and circumstance and may be virtually useless outside a local area. Furthermore, if information must be transmitted up a long bureaucratic chain to federal decision-making officials, the data may be lost or misinterpreted. Where such diseconomies are important, state administration of federal statutes may be preferable to a decentralized federal administrative structure. The argument for devolution on grounds of administrative efficiency is further strengthened if state governments already have agencies charged with similar tasks. In this case, overlap and duplication are reduced through cooperation.

Nevertheless, "cooperative" and incentive-based schemes are suggested only in areas where the law serves some federal purpose. Otherwise *both* spending and regulatory authority might better devolve to the states under a states' rights system. However, when interjurisdictional externalities or prisoner's dilemmas are present, the possibly greater administrative capacity of low-level governments must be balanced against the danger that the federal purpose may be undermined if too much authority is delegated.

Substantive Benefits of Variety and Uniformity

Uniform national regulation frequently produces economies of scale for private firms in interstate commerce. Search costs are reduced; economies of national scale in production and distribution arrangements are maintained; and the uniform application of national standards tends to produce a more stable and predictable jurisprudence. Constitutional restrictions on state interference with interstate commerce and national preemptive legislation both contribute to the realization of these scale economies. These potential savings, however, are not great enough to override other considerations tending toward state diversity. "Commerce Clause" restrictions on state regulation leave considerable opportunity for state variation. Moreover, the basic framework of laws regulating commercial transactions and business structure (corporations, partnerships, and trusts) are all state rather than federal, as is the regulation of such important industries as insurance. How are these apparent anomalies explained?

State predomination in the areas of commercial law and insurance may simply be historical curiosities. Indeed, the advantages of uniformity in the area of commercial law are so great that all the states (save Louisiana) have adopted uniform laws with only minor variations. Insurance regulation is not so unified, in part because insurance was deemed not to be "commerce" until 1944 (*U.S.* v. *Southeastern Underwriters Ass'n*, 322 U.S. 533) and was therefore immune from federal regulation. By then state regulation was so entrenched that Congress passed the McCarran-Ferguson Act, which delegated power to the states to continue their regulation of the insurance industry. That this situation continues into the 1980s seems to reflect merely advantages to the industry from continued state regulation and the absence of a consensus in favor of any federal regulatory scheme.

Although historical accident, political inertia, and the adaptive powers of business firms may explain the persistence of state regulation in some areas, in others exclusive state jurisdiction may have a firmer normative basis. Competition among the states may produce efficient regulation where no prisoner's dilemma operates and no interstate externalities exist. Indeed Ralph Winter has argued that state competition for corporate charters tends to generate precisely this outcome.[19] The Winter result follows, however, only if it is assumed that the terms of the charters are of interest only to shareholders and corporate managers, that the location of a firm's charter is not tied to any other corporate location decision, that state officials have an incentive to make rules satisfactory to the firms, and that managers are good agents for shareholders. If any of these conditions is absent, the argument that interstate competition produces efficient regulation is unpersuasive even in the absence of externalities. For example, Winter himself argues against permitting states to determine rules governing mergers and takeovers because he fears that in that instance managers may not be good agents for shareholder interests. Moreover, additional examples of efficient regulation through interstate competition are difficult to identify.

---

19. Ralph K. Winter, Jr., "State Law, Shareholder Protection, and the Theory of the Corporation." *Journal of Legal Studies* vol. 6 (June 1977), pp. 251–92.

We are left, then, with a much weaker argument: national uniformity produces economies of scale in compliance but eliminates the possibility that new and useful ideas may emerge when states design their own programs.[20] Given this trade-off, it is desirable to have a mixed system of regulation which imposes some level of national uniformity but which allows state experimentation in those areas that are most uncertain and least open to opportunistic manipulation.[21]

Political Responsiveness and Citizen Participation in Regulatory Choice

In a world of purely private goods, people with a variety of tastes can live side by side without difficulty. Each person simply purchases a different bundle of goods and consumes it privately. When some goods are public goods, consumed and financed in common, people may be better off if they can cluster together in communities with others who have similar tastes. This insight was developed by Charles Tiebout in a now-classic article[22] which has spawned a large literature in economics.[23] So long as this clustering does not create interjurisdictional externalities or undermine distributive goals, diversity in tastes argues for a states' rights system with no central government. Tiebout's result, however, depends on a number of special assumptions: Citizens are well informed and free to move between a large number of communities; the level of public goods provision and taxes is the only determinant of location; and public services become congested so that there is an efficient population size for each level of service.

In reality, because of the link between job location and residence and the importance of existing housing, most people have only a few viable options. Therefore, especially at the state level, the use of competitive pres-

---

20. The incentive to search for new ideas comes from the pressures of interstate competition and there is no suggestion here that the states are "laboratories" carrying out scientifically valid experiments. See Susan Rose-Ackerman, "Risktaking and Reelection: Does Federalism Promote Innovation?" *Journal of Legal Studies*, vol. 9 (June 1980), pp. 593–616, for an argument that state politicians have little incentive to support risky experiments.

21. Cf. Frank Easterbrook, "Antitrust and the Economics of Federalism," *Journal of Law and Economics*, vol. 26 (April 1983), pp. 23–50, who recognizes the limitations of interjurisdictional competition in the regulatory area, but is relatively sanguine about the results.

22. Charles Tiebout, "A Pure Theory of Local Expenditures." *Journal of Political Economy*, vol. 64 (October 1956), pp. 416–24.

23. Susan Rose-Ackerman, "Beyond Tiebout: Modeling the Political Economy of Local Government," in George Zodrow, ed., *Local Provision of Public Services After Twenty-Five Years* (New York: Academic Press, 1983), reviews research on multiple governments and cites the relevant sources.

sures as a substitute for politics is unlikely to produce optimal results. The frictions and imperfections of the system are too large.[24] Nevertheless, the possibility that citizens will leave a jurisdiction is a check on the behavior of state and local politicians. The multiplicity of state and local governments permits variety that is responsive to the tastes of residents even if the costs of migration assure that few governments will consist of people with homogeneous tastes.

In contrast to Tiebout, other scholars emphasize the advantages of smallness over the advantages of multiplicity and variety.[25] Smaller governmental units may be "closer to the people" and more responsive to the political activity of individuals. Yet much citizen participation in state and local activities results from requirements in *federal* statutes and regulations.[26] These requirements indicate that national politicians believe that the ideal of citizen participation is undervalued by state and local officials. The opportunity for participation is apparently not a "natural" result of decentralization. If this is true, an increase in the authority of state governments to set regulatory policy may produce laws that are less, rather than more, responsive to citizen preferences.

Finally, consider James Madison's argument in "Federalist Paper No. 10" that a large republic will be less likely to succumb to the will of narrow, self-interested factions. To extend his argument to a modern context, the advantage of federal lawmaking may not be only the organizational problems of factions in large polities, but also the national publicity that accompanies attempts to pass or amend federal regulatory statutes. Only a few states have populations large enough and diverse enough to support a full range of single-issue-oriented interest groups or an effective stable of statehouse reporters. State government thus may be optimally designed, not for democratic responsiveness, but for capture of the regulatory apparatus by special interests.

Conclusions

Reviewing these arguments we see that externalities, prisoner's dilemmas, certain scale economies in regulation and compliance, and robust participatory competition argue in favor of a strong federal presence. The possibility that diversity promotes freedom of choice, responsiveness, and desirable

---

24. See ibid. for a more detailed critique.
25. See ACIR, "Regulatory Federalism"; and Lewis Kaden, "Politics, Money and State Sovereignty: The Judicial Role," *Columbia Law Review*, vol. 79 (1979), pp. 847 ff.
26. This has been one of the concerns of the EPA in judging state plans. See EPA, "Improving Delegation."

forms of interjurisdictional competition (innovation) argue for state authority. Our general conclusion, nevertheless, is that the Reagan administration's rhetorical commitment to devolution and states' rights has oversold states' rights as the desirable goal for regulatory legislation. Sometimes diversity is a good thing; sometimes states can do a better job administratively; and some federal requirements imposed on state governments serve no useful purpose. Nevertheless, public officials should carefully think through their reasons for favoring devolution. Using the states to administer a federal program has implications very different from those of giving the states authority to carry out a program that has no national purpose or from encouraging decentralization as a way of testing innovative ideas. Moreover, this analysis of conflicting normative claims confronts a practical politics of diverse preferences and scarce resources. We must, therefore, also consider the interests of bureaucrats, politicians, and interest groups in the intergovernmental distribution of regulatory authority. We can then isolate a second set of conflicts: between normative principles and positive political theory.

Positive Analysis

The Incentives of Bureaucrats and Politicians

Delegating authority to the states is a policy choice intended to achieve certain ends—innovation, variety, democratic responsiveness, effective implementation, or scale economies. But how will officials react to these delegations? Surely we do not imagine that all the relevant actors would relentlessly pursue these goals. Indeed, they may seek delegations for purposes very different from those that a normative analysis suggests are desirable.

We begin with the premise that politicians want to be reelected and that bureaucrats want to retain their jobs. Moreover, each group prefers the good things in life (i.e., increased power, resources, leisure, and prestige) to the bad things in life (i.e., decreased power, resources, leisure, and prestige).[27] These common human motivations will sometimes coincide with the pursuit of appropriate normative goals and sometimes they will not. Next we imagine that officials act within the existing federal system in which government functions and tax bases are not clearly demarcated and where the federal

---

27. See the closely related theories of R. Douglas Arnold, *Congress and the Bureaucracy* (New Haven, Yale University Press, 1979); Anthony Downs, *Inside Bureaucracy* (Boston, Little Brown, 1967); and William Niskanen, *Bureaucracy and Representative Government* (Chicago: Aldine-Atherton, 1971).

government's hierarchical superiority has not gone unchallenged.[28] In such a federal system there are many opportunities for strategic behavior. We therefore expect that, at the margin, both state and federal officials will attempt to keep the benefits of cooperative programs for themselves and their governments and to transfer the costs and difficult decisions elsewhere.

Casual empiricism suggests, moreover, that these hypotheses are valid. Consider the four most important actors: federal and state legislators and federal and state bureaucrats. At their most self-interested, federal legislators would want to pass laws that provide "goods" to targeted groups of beneficiaries (e.g., the handicapped) and diffuse "bads" (e.g., taxes) broadly across the population.[29] They might do this, for example, by writing a strongly worded law that orders states to regulate the behavior of localities, private individuals, or firms as a condition for getting certain federal grants. The grants may be tied to the act's purposes, or compliance with the law may be made a condition for receipt of some other type of grant.

If, as is frequently the case, the federal grants in our hypothetical program do not cover the entire cost of the new regulation, Congress has succeeded not only in benefiting a targeted group but also in shifting some responsibility for the diffuse bad (general taxation) to another level of government.[30] Similarly, targeted bads (e.g., enforcement) may also be shifted to the states by giving them the responsibility for implementation. Such laws, however, still allow for casework by federal legislators in aid of their constituents as long as federal bureaucrats oversee state enforcement efforts. Federal officials might thus simultaneously blame states for laxness and intervene in pursuit of reduced enforcement in particular cases. Ideally, each law would permit federal politicians to claim credit both for aiding a particular group and for intervening on behalf of particular individuals while avoiding responsibility for the program's costs.[31] By contrast, formula grants provided to states and localities with little federal oversight provide sharply reduced opportunities

---

28. Morton Grodzins, *The American System: A New View of Government in the United States* (Chicago: Rand McNally, 1966); idem, "The Federal System," in *President's Commission on National Goals for Americans* (Englewood Cliffs, N.J.: Prentice-Hall, 1960); and Daniel J. Elazar, *The American Partnership: Intergovernmental Cooperation in the Nineteenth Century United States* (Chicago: University of Chicago Press, 1962) are the leading exponents of this view of American federalism.

29. See, for example, James Q. Wilson, *The Politics of Regulation* (New York: Basic Books, 1980).

30. ACIR, "Regulatory Federalism."

31. For examples see ibid.; Susan Rose-Ackerman, "Mental Retardation and Society: The Ethics and Politics of Normalization," *Ethics*, vol. 93 (October 1982), pp. 94–96; and Randy Roach, "The Least Restrictive Environment Section of the Education for All Handicapped Children Act of 1975: A Legislative History and Analysis," *Gonzaga Law Review*, vol. 13 (1978), pp. 717–19.

for political returns to federal politicians. Such programs are likely to be approved, however reluctantly, only if most districts benefit.[32]

State and local legislators and chief executives will have preferences that differ from those of federal politicians. They will seek increases in federal grants and reductions in federal regulatory requirements.[33] Because state and local politicians want more money and less oversight, they will not necessarily welcome devolution if it means giving states more authority to regulate while reducing the federal grants in support of such efforts. Thus, state officials typically complain about federal laws that impose regulatory requirements on the states without providing the funds to comply with the new rules.[34] The Education for All Handicapped Children Act, the Rehabilitation Act, and the Highway Beautification Act are examples of federal laws that have been unpopular at the state level for this reason (the acts are cited in the Appendix). Some state opposition to EPA devolution attempts also stems from a concern about funding cutbacks.[35]

Of course, the concerns of state and local politicians are not fully described by the demand, "Give us more money and leave us alone." Nor do national politicians approach intergovernmental relations solely from

---

32. See the discussions of the passage of the revenue-sharing law and its reenactment in Richard P. Nathan, Allen D. Manvel, and Susannah E. Calkins, *Monitoring Revenue Sharing* (Washington, D.C.: The Brookings Institution, 1975); Richard Nathan and Charles Adams, *Revenue Sharing: The Second Round* (Washington, D.C.: The Brookings Institution, 1977); and William Pierce, *Bureaucratic Failure and Public Expenditure* (New York: Academic Press, 1981). On the importance of credit claiming and casework, see M. Fiorina and R. Noll, "Voters, Legislators and Bureaucracy: Institutional Design in the Public Sector," *American Economic Review-Papers and Proceedings*, vol. 68 (May 1978), pp. 256–60; and David Mayhew, *Congress: The Electoral Connection* (New Haven: Yale University Press, 1974).

33. See, for example, ACIR, "Regulatory Reform." David Schnapf, "State Hazardous Waste Programs Under the Federal Resource Conservation and Recovery Act," *Environmental Law* 12 (Spring 1982), pp. 716–17, reports that a committee of the National Governors' Association (NGA) recommended that the EPA be a silent partner in the administration of RCRA. After the EPA authorizes a state program, the NGA recommended that it minimize permit review, enforcement, and inspection. See also Fischer's criticism of state implementation of federal worker protection statutes. He argues that states are motivated only to accept responsibility for enforcement, not to carry it out. Richard Fischer, "Cooperative Federalism and Worker Protection: The Failure of the Regulatory Model," *Texas Law Review*, vol. 60 (1982), p. 960.

34. The Federal Surface Mining Control and Reclamation Act of 1977 (SMCRA) (30 U.S.C. Sections 1201–1328 [Supp IV 1980]) illustrates the difficulties that have arisen under federal statutes which envisage an important role for the states while leaving them little freedom to develop their own programs. See William Eichbaum and Hope Babcock, "A Question of Delegation: The Surface Mining Control and Reclamation Act of 1977 and State-Federal Relations," *Dickinson Law Review*, vol. 86 (1982), pp. 615–46. For the Reagan administration's attempt to give the states somewhat more freedom of action, see U.S. Department of the Interior, Office of Surface Mining Reclamation and Environment, *Proposed Revisions to the Permanent Program Regulations Implementing Section 501(b) of the Surface Mining Control and Reclamation Act of 1977, Final Environmental Statement OSM-EIS-1: Draft Final Regulations* (Washington, D.C.: Government Printing Office, January 1983).

35. Curtis and Creedon, *State of the States*.

the perspective of shifting responsibilities for costs and claiming credit for benefits. State politicians, for example, want to be responsive to local constituencies, and they may see that only federal requirements can relieve them of the prisoner's dilemma that limits their responsiveness. Thus a subcommittee of the National Governors' Association welcomed devolution of regulatory authority from the EPA, but argued that "successful delegation of programs can only be accomplished with strong technical and financial assistance from EPA, a national presence of EPA in standards setting and resolving interstate pollution problems, and strong federal research."[36] The subcommittee thus recognized the scale economies in research and technical assistance and feared that, left to themselves, state politicians might try to use their authority both to impose costs on the citizens of other states and to benefit at their expense.

State officials' positions on federal regulations will also depend on whether interstate competition is symmetric or asymmetric. Consider the symmetric case first. In the struggle to attract businesses, a state can benefit if it establishes a low-tax and low-regulation environment when other states do not; but if all the other states follow suit, only the businesses come out ahead.[37] Thus state officials may support federal laws (or interstate compacts) limiting their ability to compete with each other. Because states will also have an incentive to undercut each other at the implementation stage, state officials may also support federal enforcement efforts.[38] Where asymmetry exists, one group of states (e.g., upstream polluters or energy-producing states) may try to impose costs on other states (e.g., downstream water users or energy-using states) in situations where the disadvantaged states have no corresponding costs they can impose on their upstream neighbors. The states' interests in

---

36. National Governors' Association, Environment Subcommittee, "Report of Work Group on Delegation and Oversight" (mimeographed), December 1982.

37. T. Schellhardt Jacobs, "War Among the States for Jobs and Business Becomes Even Fiercer," *Wall Street Journal*, February 14, 1983; and "Great Lakes Governors Split Over Truce on Industry Raids," *Wall Street Journal*, July 18, 1983. See also Rose-Ackerman, "Does Federalism Matter? Political Choice in a Federal Republic," *Journal of Political Economy*, vol. 89 (February 1981), pp. 152–65, for an analysis of the implications of this competition for support for federal laws.

38. Consider, for example, the federal law that requires states either to form regional interstate compacts to handle the disposal of low-level nuclear waste or to dispose of it within their own states (Low Level Radioactive Wastes Policy Act of 1980, 42 U.S.C. Section 2021 d(a) [Supp IV 1980]). No state in the Northeast has yet expressed a willingness to acccpt a waste disposal site; Massachusetts has passed a referendum making approval of the state as a waste disposal site subject to a statewide vote (Eugene Carlson, "States Scramble to Find Places for Disposal of Nuclear Waste," *Wall Street Journal*, March 1983). In the West, Washington and Montana have passed laws to limit all types of radioactive waste disposal. The Washington law was successfully challenged in federal court (Smith, "Federal Limitations").

federal versus local control are clearly opposed in the asymmetric situation. Economic efficiency requires federal legislation to correct the externality but, without some form of logrolling (e.g., federal grants), only the disadvantaged states will favor a federal law.[39]

Federal and state bureaucrats have equally complex motivations. On the one hand, devolution may permit a federal agency to turn over difficult problems to the states while keeping the relatively easy or popular issues for itself. This may cause problems if federal agencies themselves determine which tasks are delegated. On the other hand, if bureaucrats are professionals who believe they have a stake in operating a high-quality program, they may oppose devolution because they fear lower-quality, unequally enforced, and poorly administered programs.[40]

State bureaucrats may wish to maintain federal financial and political support for their functions, while retaining sufficient authority to respond to local political pressures. Indeed, some sort of federal-state mix may be ideal for state administrators. The complicated politics of federal-state relations may make threatening changes (such as abolition of the agency's function) difficult, may maximize opportunities for credit claiming and blame shifting, may give state bureaucrats federal allies with similar professional backgrounds,[41] and may give state bureaucrats independently funded budgets—thus providing them more freedom to make independent patronage arrangements. Conversely, dedicated state professionals may chafe at the loss of independent policy or enforcement authority and may therefore favor either a pure state-controlled or a parallel system rather than a mixed, incentive-based one.

In summary, positive analysis of the likely behavior of bureaucrats and politicians based upon perceived self-interest leads to roughly the same conclusion as a normative analysis of the appropriate location of regulatory authority. Mixed or incentive-based systems will often appear attractive. However, creating the specific structure demanded by government officials will

---

39. Outside the regulatory area, this issue has arisen most clearly in the severance taxes levied by coal-producing states on minerals produced within their borders. In *Commonwealth Edison Co.* v. *Montana*, 101 S. Ct. 2946 (1981), these taxes were held to be constitutional. See Mike McGrath and Walter Hellerstein, "Reflections on Commonwealth Edison Co. v. Montana," *Montana Law Review*, vol. 43 (Summer 1982), pp. 165–79; and Wray Victor Voegelin, "Commerce Clause v. Coal Severance Taxation" *West Virginia Law Review*, vol. 84 (1982), pp. 1123–1134.

40. These concerns were apparently important at the EPA in the past (Harry Lieber, *Federalism and Clean Water* [Lexington, Mass.: D.C. Heath, 1975]) and remain important to officials (EPA, "Improving Delegation").

41. See generally Martha Derthick, *The Influence of Federal Grants: Public Assistance in Massachusetts*. (Cambridge, Mass.: Harvard University Press, 1970).

not necessarily improve the public welfare. Governors may want their states to gain at the expense of others. Congress may want to take credit for a law's benefits while imposing the costs elsewhere. Bureaucrats at all levels may seek to enhance their agencies' independence while avoiding painful choices. Federal and state officials may obtain rewards from misallocation, as well as from appropriate allocation, of regulatory authority.

Political Incentives of Firms and Interest Groups

Government officials are, of course, not the only relevant political forces. Private interests outside of government may seek the passage of legislation favorable to them in spite of costs imposed elsewhere. They may also try to influence the implementation of state and federal laws.

To understand the behavior of private firms and individuals, we must first recognize that regulation is a generic term applying to a wide range of public policies. Scholars disagree over whether existing regulatory laws typically serve the public interest, or benefit the regulated industries.[42] In fact, some laws aid industry, while others are costly hindrances.

Instead of seeking a single positive theory of regulation, we concentrate here on the interests and bargaining power of private firms and citizens in response to three categories of regulation. We then examine the bargaining power of firms at the state level under each type of regulation. Next, we consider the relationship between the benefits and costs of regulation and the level of government that promulgates the law. Our discussion focuses on the choice between a preemptive law and a pure states' rights scheme. Much of the argument, however, applies to the more complex and common incentive-based schemes under which federal laws can be written to give more or less freedom of action to state governments.

Finally, we consider the possibility of intraindustry conflicts. Within a single industry some firms may favor federal preemptive legislation while others prefer to be regulated at the state level; some firms may support substantial devolution of authority to the states, while others prefer federal

---

42. See Richard Posner, "Theories of Economic Regulation," *Bell Journal of Economics*, vol. 5 (1974), pp. 335–58, for a review of the existing theories. For a recent attempt to revive a public interest theory of regulation see Michael Levine, "Revisionism Revised? Airline Deregulation and the Public Interest," *Law and Contemporary Problems*, vol. 44 (January 1981), pp. 179–95.

mandates.[43] We conclude our positive analysis by applying our ideas to the regulation of insurance, an industry that is regulated almost entirely at the state level.

Our analysis demonstrates that businesses will not always be in favor of devolution of the kind implied by the Reagan administration's rhetoric. State regulation is likely to appeal to most firms only in situations in which externalities and prisoner's dilemmas ensure that state authority will reduce the stringency and costs of regulation below the existing level. Even then, the nonuniform allocation of regulatory costs within the industry and the different effects of regulatory diversity on particular firms may produce a powerful coalition to maintain or institute federal regulation. A firm's position on devolution will depend on (1) the industry's bargaining power at each level of government, (2) the benefits of regulatory uniformity as opposed to interstate diversity within the industry, and (3) an individual firm's political influence and regulatory costs relative to that of its competitors.

The Bargaining Power of Firms at the State Level

The bargaining power of firms depends on the distribution of the benefits and costs of regulation across a state's citizenry. Thus, we must first locate a firm's allies and opponents, and next consider the magnitude of the benefits and harms they suffer. Finally, these gains and losses must be translated into politically relevant effects. An organized political reaction to regulation is more likely to have the greater the impact on particular individuals and groups.[44]

Allies and Opponents. A firm's allies (or opponents) may consist of consumers, employees, owners of other inputs, and other affected citizens. Regulations impose costs that fall into three broad categories: (1) costs imposed on consumers through higher prices; (2) reductions in employment opportunities or wages; and (3) reductions in profits and returns to other factors, including creditors. In the subsequent discussion, we assume that the basic goal of firms is to maximize profits and that rents are earned by some

---

43. See Robert Leone, "Competition and the Regulatory Boom" in Paul MacAvoy et al., *Government Regulation of Business: Its Growth, Impact and Future* (Washington, D.C.: Council on Trends and Perspectives, Chamber of Commerce of the United States, 1979), pp. 111–18, for a discussion of the way various federal regulations benefit some firms in an industry relative to others.

44. A firm's or industry's influence may also depend on its willingness to contribute to state political campaigns. Some evidence exists that federal deregulation combined with controls on corporate gifts to congressional candidates have increased the campaign contributions made by industry to state-level races. See Timothy Schellhardt Jacobs, "Corporate PACs Turning Attention to the States as Deregulation Gains," *Wall Street Journal*, October 28, 1982.

firms in all markets (thus, while regulation may cause an industry to contract, it will not disappear altogether).

Let us now consider three types of regulations: process, employee protection, and product. Process regulation, such as environmental controls, presumably benefits the general public but may impose costs on workers and input owners. If firms respond by reducing operations within a state, the state's citizenry may also bear some costs if tax revenues fall as a result. The effect of process regulation on consumers depends on the relationship between local producers and out-of-state firms that sell in the local market. If prices are set nationally, the affected firms cannot pass the costs of the regulations on to consumers and consumers will, therefore, be indifferent. In contrast, if the market is a local one, increased regulation may result in price increases, and local consumers might well support business efforts to limit regulatory actions. (For example, home purchasers may oppose efforts by environmental groups to impose strict controls on builders.)[45]

Employee protection legislation is costly for input owners if it implies a general contraction of the industry. In some cases, however, such laws may cause firms to substitute capital or other inputs for labor. Then even if industry output falls, the demand for certain inputs could increase. Like process regulation, employee protection legislation may or may not affect consumers, depending on whether prices are set locally or nationally. Even if such legislation reduced the long-term growth prospects of the industry in a state, existing employees will benefit. Thus employees will oppose such laws only if their employing firm threatens to shut down, sharply curtail activities, or move away.

Both process and employee protection regulation are imposed on a firm by the jurisdiction in which a product is manufactured. Product regulation, in contrast, is imposed on all goods of a certain type sold in a state. Consumers may have mixed views about such regulations. Some favor them because of the quality improvements expected. Others oppose them because of the expected increase in price. The impact on local workers and resource holders is also ambiguous and depends both on the overall stringency of the regulations and on whether the regulations permit local firms to gain relative to national firms. Thus employees and local input owners may shift from opposing regulation to supporting regulation as it becomes more protective of local producers. Table 1 summarizes the response of the affected parties to various types of regulation, indicating the expected direction, but not the magnitude,

---

45. Bernard Frieden, *The Environmental Protection Hustle* (Cambridge, Mass.: MIT Press, 1979).

TABLE 1

Support for The Position of Local Firms

	Type of Regulation		
	Process	Employee Protection	Product
Consumers			
With prices set nationally	0	0	?
With prices set locally	+	+	?
Employees of Firms	+	−	+
Local Owners of Nonlabor Inputs, Creditors, and Stockholders	+	+	+
Other Citizens			
As beneficiaries	−	0	0
As taxpayers	+	+	+

+ = support
− = oppose
0 = neutral
? = ambiguous

of each group's support for the position of local firms. Note that we assume here that product regulation helps local inputs.

The Level of Benefit or Harm. Having isolated groups (consumers, employees, etc.) whose interests are either congruent with or opposed to those of regulated firms, we now turn to examine the amount of benefit or harm imposed on these groups. A price increase (or a wage decrease) of 50 percent will have quite a different political impact from an increase (or decrease) of 1 percent. Similarly, an increase in the price of automobiles or housing is more likely to arouse consumers to political action than an increase in the price of paper clips.

First we will consider process regulation. Such regulation reduces the demand for inputs within the state. To measure the magnitude of this effect, we need to know two things: (1) the elasticity of the regulated firm's input demand in the state with respect to the level of regulation and (2) the underlying elasticity of input supply. The first measure of elasticity is determined not only by the severity of the regulation, but also by the cost of moving out of state. The second depends on the competitiveness of the input markets. Even a large fall in input demand in the state will be largely irrelevant to employees and input owners if comparable jobs are plentiful and lucrative alternative uses for resources are available. A large fall in input demand from the firm might then produce only a small fall in returns to input factors.

Furthermore, if the firm moves its operations out of state, some input owners and employees may not suffer very much if they can simply follow the relocating firm. In contrast, some inputs may be immobile and specialized to the requirements of the firm. Owners of these inputs (e.g., mineral-rich land) will strongly support the firm's positions.

The same basic points apply to employee protection legislation. Employees are obviously least likely to support such laws if large reductions in wages and jobs are expected.

Product regulation can be analyzed in a similar way, but by concentrating on the behavior of output, rather than input, markets. We need to know the elasticity of supply with respect to the regulation, the underlying price elasticity of demand, and the product's budget share for consumers. The drop in the supply curve in response to regulation depends upon the importance of a state's market to the affected firms. A firm may be able to refuse to sell in a small state with little adverse effect, but to give up the New York or California market may mean not only lost sales but higher unit costs of production. Even if the shift in supply is large, however, consumers may be relatively indifferent if good substitutes exist within the state or if purchases can be made out of state; that is, if demand for the regulated firms' products offered for sale within the state is very price elastic. Conversely, product regulations, even if they improve quality, may be opposed by consumers if they cause prices to rise significantly, especially where purchase of the regulated product accounts for a significant share of consumer budgets.[46]

Per Capita Effects. To complete a political-economic analysis of a regulatory issue, we must express gains and losses to a state's citizens in per capita terms, and we must be able to measure the number of people affected in each group. We suppose that a firm's political power to oppose regulation (or to shape its effects) directly corresponds to the proportion of the population adversely affected, to the proportion of state income accounted for by those who are harmed, and to the overall loss to the state's economy. To some extent, of course, differences in organizing ability independent of these levels of support may reinforce or work against these indices of political clout. Numbers and wealth could be overcome, for example, in employee protection legislation, by powerful union organization.

Examples. We turn now to consider several examples. Resource-based industries generally have many local inputs and owners, high moving costs,

---

46. Of course, most businesses with local markets also produce their output locally. In addition to the savings in transportation costs which importantly determine this phenomenon, our analysis also suggests a political-economic rationale if firms with local inputs can gain the support of employees and local owners in opposing restrictive regulation.

and prices set nationally (or even internationally). An industry's ability to resist process regulation will depend on (1) how important it is to the local economy (e.g., the coal industry will be most influential in Kentucky and West Virginia), (2) how unprofitable it is (i.e., the more credibly it can threaten to shut down or reduce operations), and (3) how difficult it is for its employees (miners, in our example) to move or develop new skills. Thus, West Virginia largely ignored the environmental damage of coal mining because of the importance of the industry to the state and the fear that regulation in West Virginia would favor producers in other states.[47]

Environmental control affects all industries which use the air and water. Industry coalitions, therefore, have had substantial impact on state environmental regulation. Before the passage of the federal water and air pollution control acts in 1970 and 1972, many states included representatives of the polluting industries on boards charged with overseeing environmental control.[48] Even without such representation, the interests of industry have been given considerable weight by state officials.[49] Still, some states have been willing to pay substantial costs for improved environmental quality. In the state of Washington, where lumbering and pulp and paper mills are major sources of both employment and water pollution, the paper mills vigorously opposed water quality control. By 1975, however, stringent pollution controls were in effect—and two of the eight mills in the Puget Sound area had closed.[50]

In the mid-1960s the coal and automobile industries were not powerful enough in New York City and California, respectively, to prevent pollution control laws that damaged their markets. Neither industry was a major employer in the regulating jurisdictions, and environmental interest groups overcame consumer resistance to higher prices for electric power and automobiles. Both industries responded by supporting federal legislation since each was more powerful nationally than at the state level and environmental groups were not yet a powerful national force. In the end, however, these industries lost control at the national level as well when a strong air pollution law was passed in 1970.[51]

---

47. D. Michael Harvey, "Paradise Regained? Surface Mining Control and Reclamation Act of 1977," *Houston Law Review*, vol. 15 (1978), pp. 1147–1174.
48. The case of Mississippi is discussed in Lieber, *Federalism and Clean Water*, pp. 138–47.
49. Ibid., p. 152.
50. Ibid., pp. 175–177.
51. For a detailed analysis of this case which emphasizes the importance of the federal system to the outcome, see Bruce Ackerman, Donald Elliot, and John Millian, "Toward a Theory of Statutory Evolution: The Case of Environmental Law," Columbia University, draft, March 1983.

Intraindustry Conflicts Over the Locus of Government Regulation

Firms in the same industry do not necessarily have shared political goals. The firms that join together in a trade association are in other contexts rivals and competitors; and these interfirm rivalries sometimes affect the stability of their political coalitions. George Stigler, however, has argued that when firms in the same industry have somewhat divergent interests, this gives each one an incentive to be part of an industrywide lobbying effort.[52] But when individual firms can choose between state and federal political action, their divergent interests may weaken the industry's overall political influence. Local diversity that discriminates against national firms can be obtained, if at all, only from state legislatures; national uniformity may be available only through political action at the national level. Some local firms may therefore choose to ignore the national political arena to concentrate on state politics. If this preference is widespread, an industry may be unable to establish a strong national influence. Conversely an industry may be ineffective at the state level if major firms emphasize federal lobbying efforts.

Product Regulation. Sometimes firms may seek state or national product regulation as a way of improving their competitive position vis-à-vis other firms in the same industry. Let us first consider regulation at the state level designed to aid local firms in competition with national firms.[53] If a local firm has a product mix somewhat different from that of its national competitors, it may seek regulation that will increase its market share at the same time that it raises prices or lowers the product variety available. Such a firm will be more likely to achieve the desired regulation if it is locally owned, if its use of inputs is important to the local economy, and if it can move out inexpensively. Even a firm with relatively low bargaining power at the state level might push for protective state regulation if regulations having the desired anticompetitive effect are not available at the national level. Such firms will

---

52. George Stigler, "Free Riders and Collective Action," *Bell Journal of Economics*, vol. 5 (Autumn 1974), pp. 359–365.

53. There are, of course, constitutional limits to state action in this area. Although a law forbidding nonresidents from selling insurance was upheld over sixty years ago, *La Tourette v. McMaster*, 278 U.S. 465 (1919), changes in the interpretation of the Commerce Clause have made some of the more extreme forms of state protection illegal (Henry Monaghan, "The Supreme Court 1974 Term. Forward: Constitutional Common Law," *Harvard Law Review*, vol. 89 [November 1975], pp. 12–19). Nevertheless, the possibilities for developing state regulatory impediments to out-of-state competition remain substantial. See *Pacific States Box Corp. v. White*, 296 U.S. 176 (1935) and *Florida Avocado Growers v. Paul*, 373 U.S. 132 (1963). See generally Laurence H. Tribe, *American Constitutional Law* (Mineola, NY: Foundation Press, 1978), Chapter 6, pp. 318–412.

also oppose any federal attempts to reduce their monopoly power at the state level.[54]

This analysis implies that regulations of certain sorts may be more stringent when federal laws are repealed and states are left to their own devices. Not only may powerful local industries obtain protective laws, but other groups may also obtain state-specific benefits.[55]

Second, let us consider firms that sell in national markets (e.g., railroads, trucking, and telecommunications) and especially those that compete with local firms in some markets (e.g., supermarket chains and producers of beer, mineral water,[56] dairy products, or prefabricated houses). Even if a firm's bargaining power is high in most states, it may still seek national regulation because the benefits of uniformity may outweigh the costs resulting from a higher average level of regulation.[57] National regulation may increase scale economies and thereby provide larger national concerns an advantage over their smaller local or regional competitors. In short, large national firms may actively seek federal preemptive legislation to avoid the costs of diversity.

The interstate trucking industry, for example, has litigated and lobbied for federal preemption of state laws governing such things as weight limits, tandem trailers, and mud guards. Airlines have supported federal preemption of state standards governing airport noise,[58] shippers of hazardous wastes want the EPA and the Department of Transportation to impose uniform, preemptive federal rules governing the manifests required of all shippers,[59] and the chemical industry joined with OSHA to impose uniform national labeling standards.[60]

---

54. Funeral home owners' lobbying against Federal Trade Commission regulations may be a recent instance of such political action. The regulations finally promulgated by the FTC were upheld by Congress, but they were considerably less stringent than the original FTC proposals. See Funeral Practices Rule, vol. 40, *Federal Register* 39901, August 25, 1975, and Michael Pertschuk, *Revolt Against Regulation: The Rise and Pause of the Consumer Movement* (Berkeley: University of California Press, 1982).

55. See Eli Noam, "The Interaction of Federal Deregulation and State Regulation," *Hofstra Law Review*, vol. 9 (Fall 1980), pp. 195–210; and Susan Rose-Ackerman, "Does Federalism Matter?" Nuclear power and nuclear waste disposal are areas where state regulations are often more stringent that those of the Nuclear Regulatory Commission. State efforts in these fields have recently been upheld by the Supreme Court in *Pacific Gas and Electric Co.* v. *State Energy Resources Conservation and Development Comm'n*, 103 S. Ct. 1713 (1983).

56. See "Mineral Water Could Drown Regulation," *Business Week*, p. 11, June 1979.

57. See Rose-Ackerman, "Does Federalism Matter?" p. 161, note 16.

58. Eads and Fix, "Regulatory Policy," p. 152. See *San Diego Unified Port District* v. *Gianturco*, 651 F. 2d 1306 (9th Circuit, 1981), where the Air Transport Association of America intervened as a plaintiff in a case challenging a flight curfew imposed by the California Department of Transportation. The plaintiffs argued and the court agreed that the Federal Quiet Communities Act of 1978 preempted state regulation of aircraft noise.

59. Schnapf, "State Hazardous Waste Programs," pp. 726–727.

60. Eads and Fix, "Regulatory Policy," p. 152.

Process Regulation. Firms having manufacturing facilities in a single state will be opposed to state-level process regulation if it puts them at a competitive disadvantage relative to national firms that can concentrate their production in low-regulation states. Even if such local firms are major employers and wield relatively high bargaining power in their home states, they may well favor federal regulation. This regulatory climate is the reverse of what we see in the case of product regulation, where national firms typically seek uniform federal regulations. In the case of process regulation, some local firms may seek federal laws while national firms benefit from interstate competition for business. Or mobile national firms and local firms in low-regulation states both may favor interstate regulatory diversity, while less mobile national firms and local firms that are highly regulated at the state level will favor federal preemption.[61]

For example, in the case of the chemical industry even large national firms appear to have a relatively weak bargaining position at the state level: moving costs are high once capital is in place, and the industry is very capital intensive. Thus, large chemical companies have actively supported uniformity. Under the Resource Conservation and Recovery Act, the Chemical Manufacturers Association (CMA) favored uniform federal standards both to avoid the costs of complying with a multiplicity of requirements and to maintain "competitive balance" among firms in the industry. The CMA worried that "variations in state priorities could result in cost disadvantages for existing facilities due to geographic location."[62]

In national politics, however, the industry must agree not only on the desirability of national legislation but also on its content. In practice, such unity may be difficult to establish. Thus a federal law might, for example, set only minimum standards that states may exceed. Or it might give states considerable freedom in designing standards, thus preserving interstate diversity and benefiting some sectors of the industry more than others (e.g., the Surface Mining Control and Reclamation Act).[63] A federal law might also

---

61. In many industries national firms compete with locally based businesses. Thus groceries, restaurant meals, gasoline, appliances, and other household products are sold both by national franchise or chain operations, and by local operators with one or two stores. Beer, dairy products, and soft drinks produced locally compete with nationally advertised brands. Department and discount stores may be either locally owned or part of a chain operation. The print and broadcast media share this pattern: many are part of national chains, while others remain independent. In the area of personal or professional services, few national firms exist, with the exception of several large law and accounting firms. The interests of mobile practitioners may conflict with the interests of those with similar training who are not mobile and wish to limit entry.
62. From Comments of the Chemical Manufacturers Association (CMA) on EPA's proposed Consolidated Permit Regulations #189, 9/12/79, p. 181, cited in Schnapf, p. 712, note 136.
63. Harvey, "Paradise Regained?" pp. 1147–1174.

set federal standards, but provide for state monitoring and enforcement—a practice that could lead to another sort of interstate diversity. In this case, firms located mainly in lax states may favor devolution of regulatory authority, while others, even if they have considerable bargaining power at the state level, may oppose devolution because they will lose relative to their competitors. Each firm must decide for itself whether it stands to gain anything from federal legislation that is administered by state governments.[64]

Conclusions

The political economy of federal and state regulation cannot be understood without taking into account the market structure of the affected industries and of supply and demand conditions in both input and output markets. Central to the analysis is the conflict of interest between firms that prefer federal controls and other firms in the same industry that prefer state regulation because of the strong coalitions they can form with local citizens. Not all firms seek to minimize regulation. Some may prefer stringent rules if such regulations improve their position relative to their competitors. In particular, devolution of regulatory authority from the federal government to the states may not, as the Reagan administration expects, reduce regulatory levels. Instead, local firms may seek restrictive state rules, similar to existing licensing requirements for professionals, which reduce the competition these firms face. Conversely, in industries in which firms face active citizen opposition at the state level (such as nuclear power generation) cost-increasing regulations may accompany the devolution of authority.

---

64. Suppose that in a single state the industry has two types of firms all producing under competitive conditions. S_1 is the supply curve of out-of-state firms that sell in the state and S_2 is the supply curve of local firms. $S = S_1 + S_2$, and D is demand. At price P_a, $q_1{}^a$ is produced by national firms and $q_2{}^a$ is produced by local firms. A regulation is promulgated which imposes higher relative costs on national firms leading to supply curves S_1' and S_2'. The new equilibrium price is P_b with $q_1{}^b$ and $q_2{}^b$ produced by each sector. In this example, q^b is less than q^a, but $q_2{}^b$ is greater than $q_2{}^a$.

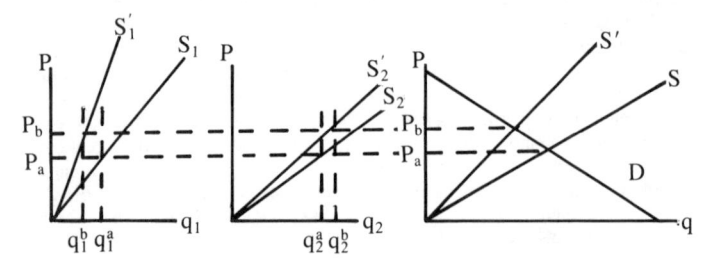

Devolution and Regulatory Relief: The Case of Insurance Regulation

Insurance regulation is of particular interest because it is an example of almost complete devolution of authority to the states. If the Reagan administration were to match its states' rights rhetoric with political action, insurance regulation would presumably be a model for a massive legislative program delegating regulatory authority to the states. Yet insurance regulation also demonstrates the potential divergence between regulatory devolution and regulatory relief. Regulatory relief for the insurance industry does appear to be warranted, but such relief is likely to be achieved only through assertion of national regulatory power.

Insurance has always been regulated at the state level and has never faced substantial, industry-specific federal control. States established insurance commissions in the nineteenth century under an interpretation of the Commerce Clause of the Constitution which excluded insurance from the scope of federal regulatory power.[65] When the Supreme Court finally reversed that interpretation in the mid-twentieth century, Congress enacted the McCarran-Ferguson Act, which reasserted the states' exclusive regulatory authority over insurers. This situation continues to the present despite repeated evidence of discrimination in favor of local companies[66] and the interest in uniform regulation of some national, high-volume companies (e.g., Allstate, State Farm). Yet even these firms have not mounted serious campaigns in favor of federal regulation.

Much of the regulatory apparatus at the state level is difficult to justify on distributional or efficiency grounds. Perhaps the best that can be said for state insurance regulation on the efficiency side is (1) that rate regulation has not tended to prevent price competition from breaking out and (2) that state approval or specification of the terms of insurance contracts *might* promote informed consumer choice where prices vary.[67] On the distributional side, state FAIR (anti-redlining) requirements may have (by cross-subsidy) increased the availability and decreased the cost of property casualty insurance for the poor and disadvantaged minorities. State-required assigned-risk pools

---

65. *Paul* v. *Virginia*, 75 U.S. 168 (1868).

66. Indeed, most of the Commerce Clause litigation involving insurance regulation has, like *Paul* v. *Virginia*, involved an attempt by foreign insurers to avoid state discrimination. See, generally, E. Patterson, *The Insurance Commissioner in the United States* (1927); H. Grant, *Insurance Reform: Consumer Action in the Progressive Era* (1979).

67. See, for example, Paul Joskow, "Cartels, Competition and Regulation in the Property Liability Insurance Industry," *Bell Journal of Economics*, vol. 4 (Autumn 1973), pp. 375–427.

also subsidize high-risk drivers, but the positive public welfare implications of this practice are less obvious.

Several factors seem conducive to the maintenance of the status quo. First, national firms do have some bargaining power at the state level because they can threaten to stop writing policies in a state if its regulations are too onerous. Although this practice could result in a costly loss of business, this is a credible threat in all but the largest states. In contrast, local firms with no national reputation cannot realistically move out of state, but they are likely to have the political power that comes from being a locally owned and operated firm. In fact, perhaps because of local firms' need to exert political influence, insurance agents not uncommonly become politicians[68] or make a point of being well connected with politicians.[69]

Local firms would, of course, prefer that states establish regulations favoring them at the expense of the large national companies. Although early regulation of insurance in some states (such as Wisconsin) took rather extreme forms,[70] current judicial interpretations of the Commerce Clause forbid explicit favoritism. Moreover, explicit favoritism at the state level may not be in the interest of local firms that wish to expand across state lines. Most states now have retaliation provisions whereby if one state discriminates against another state's insurance companies, the second state retaliates in kind. Therefore, most state insurance regulations apply uniformly to all companies. Nevertheless, state insurance commissions can, and do, use their broad implementing discretion to provide substantial protection to local firms. (During some past political regimes, for example, the Ohio Insurance Commission routinely "lost" applications from out-of-state firms seeking to do business in that state.)[71]

National firms also obtain some advantages from state regulation of insurance. Although interstate diversity increases their compliance costs, the

---

68. In 1979, 5 percent of all state legislators were employed by the insurance industry. In North Carolina, the state with the largest percentage, 11 percent were insurance agents (Insurance Information Institute, *Occupational Profile of State Legislatures, 1979* [New York, 1979], pp. 41, 51).

69. See, for example, Robert Caro's biography of Robert Moses, which reports how Carmine DeSapio, head of Tammany Hall in the 1950s, obtained insurance commissions in return for the exercise of political influence (Robert A. Caro, *The Power Broker* [New York: Alfred Knopf, 1974], p. 719).

70. In Wisconsin, in the early twentieth century, the state legislature enacted laws discouraging out-of-state insurance companies from doing business in the state. Although no tariffs could be levied, "foreign" companies were required to deposit the value of their Wisconsin policies with the state treasuries, and the state attorney general harassed their customers. In 1913, the state voided all insurance contracts with unregistered (i.e., out-of-state) companies, making them unenforceable in state courts (Spencer Kimball, *Insurance and Public Policy* [Madison: University of Wisconsin Press, 1960], pp. 270-88).

71. The insurance commissioner's discretion to discriminate is supported by the limited reviewability of an administrator's failure to act in most states. For a hundred years of uniform jurisprudence in Ohio, see, *State ex rel. Ins. Co. v. Moore*, 42 Ohio St. 103 (1884) and *State ex. rel. Life of Maryland v. Katz, Supt. of Ins.*, 4 Ohio St. 3d 140 (1983) (per curiam).

regulatory climate at the state level is stable and familiar. Promoting new federal legislation would run risks of unfavorable outcomes and would demand new adaptations.[72] Moreover, loss of state regulation might well mean loss of immunity from federal antitrust actions.[73] A uniform federal system of regulation might also aid such noninsurance competitors as banks, broker-dealers, and mutual funds, who may find mastering the nuances of fifty jurisdictions' insurance regulations too costly given their desire to offer only a few quasi-insurance products.[74]

Finally, although insurance firms are divided over the benefits and costs of state diversity, state insurance commissions are not. The National Association of Insurance Commissioners (NAIC), formed in 1871, is one of the oldest nationally organized interest groups representing public regulators. The NAIC was responsible for the organizational efforts that produced the McCarran-Ferguson Act and for the proposal and adoption of comprehensive regulatory statutes governing insurance in each state.[75] The state insurance commissions also remain an important source of patronage for state chief executives. Given these political and bureaucratic interests in the maintenance of state regulation, Congress has never seriously reconsidered its delegation of virtually complete insurance regulatory authority to the states in McCarran-Ferguson.[76] Yet this same configuration of interests suggests that regulatory relief in the insurance field may require federal preemption.

Policy, Incentives, and Normative Principles

Although federalism is in many ways an awkward and cumbersome form of government, it has decided advantages in a large, pluralistic society. In the regulatory area the challenge for federal policy makers is to design cooperative programs that give state governments an incentive to correct interstate externalities while at the same time permitting them to organize the compliance effort themselves. Such a delicate mixture may not be easy to achieve, even in principle. In practice, the task is further complicated by the

---

72. This may by a realistic concern. See Ackerman et al., "Toward a Theory of Statutory Evolution," for an example from the environmental field.
73. See, generally, Easterbrook, "Antitrust and Economics of Federalism."
74. See, generally Robert Clark, "The Soundness of Financial Intermediaries," *Yale Law Journal* 86 (1976), pp. 1 ff; and Paul Verkuil, "Perspectives on the Reform of Financial Institutions," *Yale Law Journal*, vol. 83 (1974), pp. 1349 ff.
75. See, for example, *SEC v. Variable Annuity Co.*, 359 U.S. 65 (1959), which declared a "wrap around" variable annuity to be a "security" subject to SEC jurisdiction.
76. See R. Keeton, *Basic Text on Insurance Law* 538 (1971).

self-interest of public officials and private individuals and firms. Our positive political-economic analysis makes clear that even if public officials at all levels express support for "cooperative" or incentive-based federalism, they may have in mind programs rather different from those that fit the normative goals outlined previously. Let us look at some possible divergences between our normative ideals and our positive predictions.

First, one of our fundamental normative principles is the internalization of externalities, either through the drawing of political boundaries or through federal policies that induce state and local governments to take account of the costs and benefits imposed on others. Yet we have pointed out that federal politicians and bureaucrats may themselves try to export costs to the states while claiming credit for benefits, and firms and interest groups may support state regulation in order to impose costs on competitors. The distribution of benefits is unlikely, then, to correspond to the distribution of burdens.

Second, devolution of some types of regulatory authority may be desirable when it facilitates the search for new and better ways of administering programs. Yet the incentive to innovate can be blunted by each state's interest in gaining relative to others and by the interest of firms in regulations that increase location-specific rents. The innovation argument has the most force where a selection mechanism operates which preserves good ideas and rejects bad ones. This may occur in a competitive interstate environment, but only if (1) regulations have few or no external effects on groups not involved in the decision-making process, (2) those adopting regulations have incentives to draft regulatory provisions which promote efficiency, and (3) those choosing to submit themselves to particular regulatory regimes are motivated to choose efficient constraints.

Third, if states are considered good administrators, incentive-based schemes should have performance standards that permit states to reach regulatory goals any way they wish. Such a policy, of course, requires not only that federal goals can be articulated but also that they can be easily monitored. Otherwise, federal oversight will be ineffective and the interests of state officials and powerful interest groups may dominate the process.

Performance standards backed by effective sanctions or incentives may nevertheless be difficult to adopt, for they are not always in the interests of either government officials or of the industries being regulated. Some state officials have welcomed performance standards as a way of obtaining more freedom of action. However, when performance standards are implemented by means of aggressive federal oversight instead of a negotiated, more "cooperative" relationship, state support is likely to decline. Federal bureaucrats may oppose performance standards because they remove the federal agency's control of day-to-day implementation, turning federal officials into inspectors rather than policy makers. Regulated firms may welcome performance standards if they promise cost reductions,[77] but oppose them if they replace existing, more restrictive rules that were poorly enforced. Thus, although economists generally support performance standards because they are economically efficient and because they permit decentralized administration with no loss of federal purpose, political support for performance standards may not be forthcoming. In short, devolution is frequently undesirable on normative grounds, but even when it may be beneficial, regulators acting out of self-interest may oppose or subvert it.

Finally, an ideological commitment to states' rights in the design of regulatory regimes is clearly misguided. Devolution may have unfortunate consequences, not only for efficiency but also for the perceived legitimacy of democratic governance. "Closeness to the people" must be carefully weighed against the increased possibility of "capture" and the potential for small units to become powerful minorities. Moreover, sensible regulatory relief might as easily demand a stronger federal presence as delegation of power to the states.

---

77. For example, the Environmental Protection Agency's "bubble" policy promises such savings. See L. Rhinlander, "The Proper Place for the Bubble Concept under the Clean Air Act, *Environmental Law Reporter*, vol. 13 (December 1983) pp. 10406–10417.

APPENDIX

Major Federal Statutes with a Regulatory Impact on State and Local Governments

Title	Objective	Public Law	Type[1]
Age Discrimination Act of 1975	Prevent discrimination on the basis of age in federally assisted programs	94-135	CC
Age Discrimination in Employment Act (1974)[2]	Prevent discrimination on the basis of age in state and local government employment	93-259; 90-202	DO
Architectural Barriers Act of 1968	Make federally occupied and funded buildings, facilities, and public conveyances accessible to the physically handicapped	90-480	CC
Civil Rights Act of 1964 (Title VI)	Prevent discrimination on the basis of race, color, or national origin in federally assisted programs	88-352	CC
Civil Rights Act of 1968 (Title VIII)	Prevent discrimination on the basis of race, color, religion, sex, or national origin in the sale or rental of federally assisted housing	90-284	CC
Clean Air Act Amendments of 1970	Establish national air quality and emissions standards	91-604	CC,CO,PP

APPENDIX (continued)

MAJOR FEDERAL STATUTES WITH A REGULATORY IMPACT ON STATE AND LOCAL GOVERNMENTS

Title	Objective	Public Law	Type[1]
Coastal Zone Management Act of 1972	Assure that federally assisted activities are consistent with federally approved state coastal zone management programs	94-370	CC
Davis-Bacon Act (1931)[3]	Assure that locally prevailing wages are paid to construction workers employed under federal contracts and financial assistance programs	74-403	CC
Education Amendments of 1972 (Title IX)	Prevent discrimination on the basis of sex in federally assisted education programs	92-318	CC
Education for All Handicapped Children Act (1975)	Provide a free, appropriate public education to all handicapped children	94-142	CO[4]
Emergency Highway Energy Conservation Act (1974)[5]	Establish a national maximum speed limit of 55 miles per hour	93-239	CO
Endangered Species Act of 1973	Protect and conserve endangered and threatened animal species	93-205	CC,PP
Equal Employment Opportunity Act of 1972	Prevent discrimination on the basis of race, color, religion, sex, or national origin in state and local government employment	92-261	DO
Fair Labor Standards Act Amendments of 1974	Extend federal minimum wage and overtime pay protections to state and local government employees[6]	93-259	DO
Family Educational Rights and Privacy Act of 1974	Provide student and parental access to educational records while restricting access by others	93-380	CC
Federal Insecticide, Fungicide, and Rodenticide Act (1972)	Control the use of pesticides that may be harmful to the environment	92-516	PP

APPENDIX (*continued*)

MAJOR FEDERAL STATUTES WITH A REGULATORY IMPACT ON STATE AND LOCAL GOVERNMENTS

Title	Objective	Public Law	Type[1]
Federal Water Pollution Control Act Amendments of 1972	Establish federal effluent limitations to control the discharge of pollutants	92-500	CC,PP
Flood Disaster Protection Act of 1973	Expand coverage of the national flood insurance program	93-234	CC,CO
Hatch Act (1940)	Prohibit public employees from engaging in certain political activities	76-753	CC
Highway Beautification Act of 1965	Control and remove outdoor advertising signs along major highways	89-285	CO
Marine Protection Research and Sanctuaries Act Amendments of 1977	Prohibit ocean dumping of municipal sludge	95-153	DO
National Energy Conservation Policy Act (1978)	Establish residential energy conservation plans	95–619	PP
National Environmental Policy Act of 1969	Assure consideration of the environmental impact of major federal actions	91-190	CC
National Health Planning and Resources Development Act of 1974	Establish state and local health planning agencies and procedures	93-64	CO
National Historic Preservation Act of 1966	Protect properties of historical, architectural, archeological, and cultural significance	89-665	CC
Natural Gas Policy Act of 1978	Implement federal pricing policies for the intrastate sales of natural gas in producing states	95-621	PP
Occupational Safety and Health Act (1970)	Eliminate unsafe and unhealthy working conditions	91–596	PP
Public Utilities Regulatory Policies Act of 1978	Set federal standards in the pricing of electricity and natural gas	95–617	DO

APPENDIX (*continued*)

MAJOR FEDERAL STATUTES WITH A REGULATORY IMPACT ON STATE AND LOCAL GOVERNMENTS

Title	Objective	Public Law	Type[1]
Rehabilitation Act of 1973 (Section 504)	Prevent discrimination against otherwise qualified individuals on the basis of physical or mental handicaps in federally assisted programs	93-112	CC
Resource Conservation and Recovery Act of 1976	Establish standards for the control of hazardous wastes	95–580	PP
Safe Drinking Water Act of 1974	Assure drinking water purity	93–523	CC,PP,DO
Surface Mining Control and Reclamation Act of 1977	Establish federal standards for the control of surface mining	95–87	PP
Uniform Relocation Assistance and Real Properties Acquisition Policies Act of 1970	Set federal policies and reimbursement procedures for property acquisition under federally assisted programs	91-646	CC
Water Quality Act (1965)	Establish federal water quality standards for interstate waters	88-668	PP
Wholesome Meat Act (1967)	Establish systems for the inspection of meat sold in intrastate commerce	90-201	PP

SOURCE: Advisory Commission on Intergovernmental Relations, "Regulatory Federalism: Policy, Process, Impact and Reform" (mimeographed), December 1982, Appendix Table.

1. Crosscutting requirement (CC), crossover sanction (CO), direct order (DO), partial preemption (PP). Defined in footnote 6 in text.

2. Coverage of the act, originally adopted in 1967, was extended to state and local governments.

3. Although the Davis-Bacon Act applied initially only to direct federal construction, it has since been extended to some seventy-seven federal assistance programs.

4. Although participation is voluntary, the failure of a participating state to comply with federal requirements can result in the withholding of funds from several federal handicapped education programs. The requirements of P.L. 94–142 are nearly identical to those established by the Department of Education under Section 504 of the Rehabilitation Act, a crosscutting requirement.

5. A permanent national 55 mph speed limit was established by the Federal-Aid Highway Amendments of 1974 (P.L. 93–643), signed into law January 4, 1975.

6. Application was restricted by the Supreme Court in *National League of Cities* v. *Usery*, 426 U.S.

COMMENTS

David Harrison, Jr.

The topic of federalism and regulation is timely since it intersects the dual themes of devolution of authority to the states and industry relief from burdensome regulations. Proponents of the new federalism point to the massive growth in regulation—particularly social regulation—in recent years, as well as to the dramatic shift to federal authority. Many analysts would argue that these trends have created an enormously expensive system that is largely unresponsive to the needs and desires of individual citizens. The new federalism initiative articulated by the Reagan administration implies a shift both in the size of the regulatory effort and in the locus of responsibility. Its regulatory relief measures are designed to (1) reduce the number and extent of regulations and (2) to increase the decision-making role of state governments, which are closer to the people than the federal government is and therefore more likely to reflect the will of the people.

The new federalism appears desirable because it embodies the democratic ideal of a government closer to its people. But the need for an analysis of the advantages and disadvantages of state versus federal control becomes apparent when one considers specific regulations. Should the federal Environmental Protection Agency set air and water standards for large industrial dischargers, or should the standards be set by the state in which the discharger is located? What if the discharge pollutes beyond the state boundary? Should states be allowed to ban certain trucks on their highways, or should the federal government preempt such rules? Should banking regulations be set by individual states, or should there be some national uniformity? None of these questions can be resolved with a simple appeal to the new federalism. The choice between state or federal authority is, after all, but a means to the end of effective, efficient, and fair regulation.

Major Findings

The paper by Mashaw and Rose-Ackerman provides an important perspective on this new federalism initiative. Rather than assess the Reagan initiative, the authors attempt to develop a framework for analyzing any policies that concern the mix of state and federal regulatory authority. Their methodology consists of both normative and descriptive analyses. They first consider the normative factors that affect the choice of an appropriate level of government, assuming that each level is free from improper political influences. They then consider the real world of politicians and businessmen and the likelihood that regulatory decisions will be made to further private rather than public goals. Finally, they provide a case study of insurance regulation to illustrate some of their normative and descriptive analyses.

Virtually all of the authors' analyses indicate that regulations are better set at the federal rather than the state level. Because most normative criteria call for federal controls, little deductive evidence exists in favor of state control beyond the intuitive notion that states are "closer to the people." The authors acknowledge that uniform federal regulations fail to account for diversity, which may be particularly important in the case of environmental regulation because the benefits and costs of controls may vary widely from place to place. But any argument for state control becomes less persuasive when one considers the likely performance of state agencies, particularly when faced with industry pressures to relax or modify regulations. Thus, in many cases, regulatory reform will require a strengthening of the federal presence to reduce inefficiencies caused by interest group pressures to dilute desirable regulatory initiatives.

The same recommendation for a stronger federal role results from the authors' analysis of regulations that may not serve the public. The recent trend toward deregulation of transportation, financial markets, and telecommunications reflects a consensus among analysts that regulation has insulated companies from the discipline of the competitive marketplace. Thus, for example, in the case study of insurance regulation, Mashaw and Rose-Ackerman point to the advantages of eliminating regulation and thereby reducing the economic rents that are earned by insurance carriers that have obtained protective regulations. In this case, the issue is whether the states or the federal government is more likely to effect deregulation. The authors' discussion of the influence of industry officials on state officials suggests that insurance deregulation will probably require a federal initiative, even if federal regulation of the insurance industry is not itself desirable.

The authors' general conclusions are sound, and their analysis is helpful in assessing arguments for and against the new federalism. I want to point out an additional criterion not specifically addressed by the authors that tends to reinforce their recommendation for federal control in many of the new areas of social regulation, and then suggest a reform of the current federal approach that promises to obtain the advantages of diversity while maintaining the advantages so clearly articulated by the authors.

Mashaw and Rose-Ackerman indicate that state regulatory requirements may be inefficient when the following conditions hold: (1) there are substantial externalities (or spillovers) from one jurisdiction's regulation, (2) a prisoner's dilemma leads to state acquiescence to threats by businessmen to leave if standards are not relaxed, (3) there are large economies of scale in administration so that individual state programs are costly to design and enforce, and (4) there are dangers that state and local officials will be "captured" by special interest groups. Although these are the most important factors when the choice of authority is raised *de novo*, the additional criterion of continuity may be important for existing programs. Particularly in technical areas such as environmental or health and safety regulation, switching regulatory control from one level of government to another may be confusing and costly. The social legislation enacted in the past fifteen years has created strong federal agencies with substantial technical and regulatory expertise. In contrast, many state agencies are understaffed and underfunded. Shifting major responsibility to the states would thus involve a substantial start-up expense, whatever its long-term merits.

The "New" New Federalism

The general skepticism surrounding greater state involvement in regulation creates a dilemma for people interested in regulatory reform. Must we continue with inflexible regulations set without regard for the circumstances of individual jurisdictions? I believe that such a dilemma is not inevitable. Instead, I would propose a major reform of existing regulations involving, not devolution to the states, but increased flexibility of federal regulations. I suggest that the federal government set *differential* regulatory requirements based on state or local circumstances. I refer to this alternative as the "new" new federalism to denote its concern for greater regulatory flexibility (hence the "new federalism" label) while recognizing the advantages of federal controls in many areas. Mashaw and Rose-Ackerman mention this alternative but devote relatively little attention to it.

The growth of federal regulation in the last fifteen years has created an enormous body of standards and guidelines regulating industrial behavior. As federal regulators designed these systems, they faced a trade-off between tailoring regulations to individual situations and creating uniform regulations that could be more easily developed and implemented. Most legislators and regulators realized that the costs and benefits of regulation would often vary with individual circumstances. For example, some pollution is discharged into streams with so much assimilative capacity that the benefits of control are slight. Similarly, some air pollution is of little consequence to health or welfare because it results in concentrations below threshold levels. On the cost side, some firms are able to reduce pollution with modest expenditures, while others must spend large sums. On the other hand, tailoring regulations to individual circumstances would be costly and time-consuming.

This dilemma was particularly prominent in the case of the Environmental Protection Agency (EPA), which had to administer complicated air and water statutes under tight deadlines. For example, the Clean Water Act required the EPA to set standards for new sources within one year of passage of the act. Taking into account both new and existing sources, the EPA was faced with setting approximately 30,000 individual discharge standards under the water program alone.[1] The agency had a strong incentive to develop standards that could be enforced quickly in order to maintain the momentum for environmental protection begun by the statutes' enactment and to show industry that the ground rules had changed.

Not surprisingly, therefore, Congress and EPA chose to rely primarily on uniform standards applicable to all polluters in broad industry classes. For example, a single set of water effluent guidelines applies to all steel companies discharging into U.S. rivers and streams. A single set of air emission standards applies to new power plants. Companies discharging a particular toxic air pollutant meet the same emission standards. And the same automobile emission standards will eventually apply to all new cars regardless of where they are driven. There are exceptions—for example, the Clean Air Act provides for states to allocate responsibility among polluters for meeting ambient air quality standards. But most of the environmental standards developed in the 1970s are nationally uniform standards with little or no flexibility to account for differences either in costs or benefits.

Critics have tended to focus on the costs of this regulatory explosion—$700 billion being spent to meet the air and water standards alone from 1979 to 1988. Economists and others have emphasized the excessive cost of ignoring cost differences among various sources of pollution; they point out that overall costs could be greatly reduced with no sacrifice in environmental quality if regulations were more flexible—imposing more stringent controls on low-cost sources and more lenient limits on high-cost sources of pollution. Efficiency-minded critics commonly prescribe emission charges or marketable permits that would "automatically" allocate control efforts in accordance

---

1. David Harrison, Jr. and Robert Leone, *Federal Water Pollution Control Policy* (Washington, D.C.: American Enterprise Institute, forthcoming).

with costs. These arguments have had some effect on policy. Although effluent charge schemes have not yet been developed, the EPA has in recent years introduced some cost-based flexibility into its regulations—for example, its "bubble" policy, emissions offsets in nonattainment areas, and "banking."[2] These modifications may yield significant gains in efficiency.

A parallel effort is needed on the benefit side. Over the past decade I and my colleagues have considered the advantages of developing federal standards that take into account differences in the benefits of control. The empirical evidence includes studies of air pollution, water pollution, aircraft noise, and—most recently—toxic substances and hazardous wastes. This evidence has led me to the following conclusions:

1. Setting different standards for emissions in different geographic areas (and, in some cases, different times) would yield large efficiency advantages.

2. Most of the efficiency advantages could be achieved with a small number of geographic categories, perhaps two or three for most pollutants.

3. Such a reform would avoid the disadvantages of state control while retaining the advantages of federal control that are outlined in the Mashaw and Rose-Ackerman paper.

4. The obstacles to developing such regulations—primarily the accusation that they would unfairly stifle industrial growth in high-control areas—appear less persuasive than might appear at first glance.

These notions can be illustrated by the case of automotive emission standards.[3] Currently all automobiles are required to meet one set of emission standards regardless of where they are driven. Although the cost of meeting emission controls varies somewhat with the type of car (pollution control is typically somewhat more expensive for large cars than for small cars), there

---

2. Robert Crandall, *Controlling Industrial Pollution: The Economics and Politics of Clean Air* (Washington, D.C.: The Brookings Institution, 1983).

3. This case is based on David Harrison, Jr., *Who Pays for Clean Air* (Cambridge, Mass.: Ballinger Publishing Company, 1974); and idem, "Controlling Automotive Emissions: How to Save More than $1 Billion Per Year and Help the Poor Too," *Public Policy* 25 (Fall 1977). For a more detailed discussion raised by such a proposal, see David Harrison, Jr. and Albert L. Nichols, "Benefit-Based Flexibility in Environmental Regulation," Discussion Paper E-83-06 (Cambridge, Mass.: John F. Kennedy School of Government, April 1983); David Harrison, Jr. and Paul R. Portney, "Who Loses from Reform of Environmental Regulation?" in Wesley A. Magat, ed., *Reform of Environmental Regulation* (Cambridge, Mass.: Ballinger Publishing Company, 1982), pp. 147–79; and David Harrison, Jr., "Regulation of Aircraft Noise," in Thomas C. Schelling, ed., *Incentives for Environmental Protection* (Cambridge, Mass.: MIT Press, 1983).

is much greater variation in the benefits of emission control. The benefits of controlling emissions are large in dense cities like New York and Boston, while the benefits are small in rural areas and smaller cities—both because the air is already relatively clean and because lower population densities mean that fewer people are affected by a given car's emissions. I estimate that switching to a "two-car" strategy—in which more lenient standards would apply to cars purchased for use outside the heavily polluted metropolitan areas—would reduce long-run costs by 35 percent, with only a 9 percent reduction in benefits. The cost savings would amount to more than $1 billion per year.

The two-car strategy bypasses several objections that a state-controlled scheme might encounter. The federal government would have to determine which areas would require the more stringent standards, taking into account the influence of prevailing winds to avoid spillover of one area's pollution on another. Automakers would not be able to bargain with individual jurisdictions to obtain more favorable standards. Since every car would be subject to a single set of standards, the administrative costs of developing and enforcing the standards would not rise. Some city dwellers might cheat by buying a car in an area with more lenient standards, but registration procedures could be devised to discourage cheating. Indeed, we already have a two-car strategy for interim standards in which California cars must meet more stringent standards, and no major administrative difficulties have arisen.

The major objections to varying standards for cars or for industry in general would probably relate to the issue of fairness. Is it fair to provide less environmental protection to residents of sparsely populated areas? Is it fair to require firms located in densely populated areas to pollute less than other firms? Is it fair to put densely populated regions at a competitive disadvantage in seeking new industry? The answers to these questions will necessarily depend on the definition of fairness.

Clearly a shift to differential standards would generate some losses. If fairness implies protecting individuals and firms from the vagaries of change, the shift could be viewed as unfair. But many people would conclude that setting standards to reflect the environmental damage done is fairer than treating all emissions alike. Firms already pay vastly different prices for land and labor, depending upon their location. The prices imposed by regulation could reflect the opportunity costs of the environmental resources consumed, just as land prices reflect relative scarcity.

In addition, some of the objections diminish when subjected to closer scrutiny. For example, fears that differential standards would lead to major regional dislocations are almost certainly overdrawn. Decisions about where to build a new plant hinge on many factors: wage scales and other aspects of local labor markets, transportation costs to final markets, access to raw materials, and state and local taxes; differences in environmental regulations are unlikely to be the main determinant in most cases. Moreover, if firms were to decide not to build polluting plants in dense areas, residents would gain from lower health risks and other environmental improvements.

Conclusions

Government regulation of industry is in a period of transition, buffeted by a variety of forces and objectives. Arguments for regulatory relief, increased regulatory responsiveness, greater enforceability, greater effectiveness, and greater efficiency create a large agenda. The Reagan administration's new federalism represents one effort to achieve some of these objectives.

Mashaw and Rose-Ackerman have contributed to the discussion of regulatory reform by considering whether devolution to the states would effectively achieve these reform objectives. They acknowledge that some trade-offs are involved, but they conclude that the new federalism is unlikely to accomplish most of the reform objectives. Both from the standpoint of normative analysis, in which one assumes that a priori objectives are achieved, and from a consideration of the practical obstacles to effective decision making at the state and local levels, one is hard-pressed to put much faith in devolution of regulatory authority as a solution. This conclusion does not denigrate the important contribution that state officials can make in a host of regulatory areas, but rather acknowledges the inherent limitations of states in dealing with regulations that often have effects beyond individual state jurisdictions.

My comments have dealt primarily with a suggestion for modifying federal regulation to obtain some of the advantages of diversity that underlie pressures for greater state controls. States and localities do differ in the costs and benefits that accrue to their citizens from regulation. Federal regulations that accommodate this diversity can generate improvements in the efficiency— as well as the effectiveness and enforceability—of regulation. Such reforms should be part of the agenda as regulation continues to evolve in the 1980s.

TRANSFERRING REGULATORY AUTHORITY TO THE STATES

Michael Fix

The 1982 Economic Report to the President by the Council of Economic Advisers states, "One important principle of this Administration is an increased reliance on State and local governments to carry out necessary governmental activities."[1]

The report later develops that theme as it applies to regulation:

> *Regulation should take place at the appropriate level of government.* The primary economic reason for most regulation is the existence of external effects. The costs or tolerance of these external effects may vary among locations. Economic efficiency, therefore, calls for the degree and type of regulation to vary also. National standards tend to be too severe in some regions, while being too lax in others. Federal regulation should be limited to situations where the actions in one State have substantial external effects in other States, constitutional rights are involved, or interstate commerce would be significantly disrupted by differences in local regulations.[2]

The report's clear implication was that the intergovernmental assignment of regulatory responsibilities had not served the goals of economic efficiency. Thus it could be claimed that devolution—that is, transfer—of regulatory responsibilities to lower levels of government would serve both the political goals and the economic goals of the administration. Politically, devolution sustained the administration's efforts in reducing the reach of the federal government and enhancing state autonomy—essentially the goal of the short-lived New Federalism initiative. Economically, transfer of regulatory authority to state and local governments would promote the tailoring of regu-

---

1. *Economic Report of the President and the Annual Report of the Council of Economic Advisers* (Washington, D.C.: Government Printing Office, February 1982), p. 47.
2. Ibid., p. 147.

lations to local conditions—theoretically providing greater benefits at lower costs. Furthermore, the way in which authority was to be delegated would streamline regulatory processes involving multiple layers of government, saving time and money.

This paper provides a discussion of the statutory and procedural background for the transfer of regulatory authority, the advantages and disadvantages of this transfer of authority as a regulatory strategy, and the four transfer techniques employed by the administration. These techniques are (1) accelerating the formal delegation of program authority to the states; (2) promulgating generic regulations; (3) reducing federal oversight of state regulatory activities; and (4) relaxing federal compliance standards.

Background

A growing number of health and safety laws—many in the environmental area—have been structured in a way that has provided the administration an unusual opportunity to realize its regulatory federalism goals. Congress clearly intended these laws to be implemented by means of a formally negotiated, cooperative arrangement that would permit states to play a central role in program administration. Although the statutes differ in the specific responsibilities divided between states and the federal government, certain fundamental structural similarities can be discerned.

The basic design—sometimes referred to as "partial federal preemption" in the literature[3]—calls for the federal government to conduct necessary scientific research and to set minimum national standards. States are authorized to assume responsibility for all or much of program administration within their boundaries so long as they meet two conditions: the states' own implementing regulations must be at least as stringent as the federal government's,

---

3. A recent publication of the Advisory Commission on Intergovernmental Relations described partial preemption programs as "resting upon the authority of the federal government to preempt certain state and local activities under the Supremacy clause and the Commerce power. . . . This is preemption with a twist, however. Unlike traditional preemption statutes, preemption in these cases is only partial. While federal laws establish basic policies, administrative responsibility may be delegated to the states or localities, provided that they meet certain nationally determined standards." See David Beam, "Washington's Regulation of States and Localities: Origins and Issues" (Intergovernmental Perspective, Advisory Commission on Intergovernmental Relations, Washington, D.C., Summer, 1981), p. 11. Examples of partial preemption statutes include the Clean Air Act Amendments of 1970, the Federal Water Pollution Control Act Amendments of 1972, the Occupational Safety and Health Act, the Resource Conservation and Recovery Act of 1976, and the Surface Mining Control and Reclamation Act of 1977.

and the states must appear to have the resources and legal authority to carry out an acceptable program. Federal law and regulations, then, set a floor for state standards and performance but typically no ceiling regarding their stringency or the vigilance with which they are enforced.[4] Federal officials must review and approve all delegations of regulatory authority, and the federal regulatory agency retains authority to override individual state decisions. If, following delegation of authority, a state should utterly fail to adopt or enforce equivalent standards, the appropriate federal agency is authorized to apply federal rules. To help states carry out their responsibilities, the federal government typically provides substantial grants. For example, in fiscal year 1982 federal assistance to state environmental management programs totaled $227.8 million and represented approximately half of all state expenditures in such programs.[5]

The value of this model of shared federal-state regulatory responsibilities within the federal system is clear. Delegation of federal authority preserves to some degree the regulatory sovereignty of the states, permitting them to serve as laboratories for innovation. In addition, the arrangement is designed to promote efficiency in a number of ways. On one level, it does so by assigning to the federal government those tasks for which significant economies of scale may be achieved, such as training, research, and development. On a second, and more important level, this arrangement promotes efficiency by promoting national uniformity or preemption as needed. National uniformity may be desirable when state regulatory autonomy would burden interstate commerce, would expose citizens to widely varying health standards, would stimulate competition among states based on "minimum technology-based requirements," or would lead to parochial vetoes of projects involving important national interests, such as hazardous waste disposal. From a practical standpoint, it is extraordinarily cost-effective for the federal government to enlist state enforcement and administrative personnel because their wages are often significantly lower than those of their federal counterparts.[6]

Furthermore, advocates of increased delegation of authority to the states contend that states have gone through a period of significant reform. As one

---

4. This partial-preemption approach should be contrasted with instances where full federal preemption is invoked by the courts. Full preemption occurs when there is an outright conflict between the federal scheme and the state requirement. State authority is also barred when congressional action would be an implicit barrier, that is, when state regulation would unduly interfere with the accomplishment of congressional objectives.

5. The National Governors' Association Committee on Energy and Environment, *The State of States: Management of Environmental Programs in the 1980s* (Washington, D.C. 1982).

6. The comments in this paragraph are drawn from remarks by Turner T. Smith, Jr., "Opening Address: Reflections on Federalism" (Airlie House, Conference on the Environment), reported in Articles and Notes, *Environmental Law Reporter*, vol. 12, p. 15067, December 1982.

prominent environmental lawyer has written, "Constitutions have been modernized, court systems streamlined, legislatures reorganized and professionally staffed, and governors' authority as chief executives strengthened. States have set up and staffed natural resource protection agencies with experienced and competent staffs." Indeed, staff size has increased tenfold over the past ten years, and education and salary levels have also risen.[7]

Although the merits of this incentive-based cooperative federalism scheme are clear—at least in theory—state officials have claimed that, in practice, little regulatory discretion has been given to the states and that their programs serve as little more than surrogate federal regional offices. The coercive nature of partial preemption is revealed by the highly detailed, prescriptive regulations that set minimum program standards for states. Congressionally authorized procedures give federal officials review or veto power, or both, over virtually all delegated state regulatory activities and decisions. Moreover, cumbersome procedures involving multiple layers of state and federal bureaucracies have slowed reviews and proved an irritant to both the states and regulated parties alike.

Advantages and Disadvantages of a Strategy of Delegation

Besides its philosophical appeal, delegation of regulatory authority to the states has proved a useful strategy to the Reagan administration, in part because of its political and procedural feasibility. The eventual transfer of federal authority to the states is contemplated by many of the health and safety statutes enacted during the 1970s. Thus the transfer of authority can be accomplished by means of administrative mechanisms, and the political vagaries of the legislative process can be avoided. Some policy changes can be made without even having to go through the administrative rule-making process. (For example, the Environmental Protection Agency's state implementation plan [SIP] review guidelines and its new policy on emissions trading were not issued as administrative regulations.) Moreover, given the labyrinthine nature of intergovernmental relations, regulatory responsibilities can often be reshuffled without attracting much attention or controversy.

Not only is delegation workable, it has a developed political constituency. A number of the administration's most important proposed changes—such as EPA's emissions-trading policy guidelines or the revision of regulations imple-

---

7. T. Henderson, "Delegation of Environmental Programs to the States: Ohio's Experience" (Washington, D.C.: Environmental Law Institute, 1982).

menting the Surface Mining Control and Reclamation Act of 1977—built upon on an existing technical and political base. Delegation of authority can be viewed as evolutionary, and thus quite different from more radical policy reversals proposed by administration regulatory reformers.[8] Further, while delegations of authority are by no means immune from legal challenge,[9] many have proved more durable than other regulatory relief actions.

One important aspect of transferring regulatory authority is the practical permanence of delegation. This permanence owes less to the legal status of delegated programs than to the substantial political difficulties associated with revoking program authority. Actions that transfer federal regulatory authority to lower levels of government are, then, likely to be among the longest lived of all the Reagan administration's regulatory changes for two reasons: because they represent a continuation (albeit an accelerated one) of prior federal policies and because their undoing is politically impractical.

Viewed from the perspective of regulatory relief, delegation of regulatory responsibilities has posed some problems. In the first place there is no assurance that giving states increased regulatory responsibilities will lead to fewer inefficient rules. Powerful state-level firms might in some instances lobby for restrictive regulations in order to limit competition from out-of-state firms.[10] Interest groups might exert increased pressure at the state level for sustained or increased regulatory protections. For example, state regulation of nuclear power and nuclear waste disposal is often more stringent than federal regulation.[11]

Delegation has also raised fears that a profusion of state standards, whatever their relative stringency, would prove to be more troublesome and inefficient

---

8. Representative of the continued federal concern in the area of delegation of authority is the existence and work of the Advisory Commission on Intergovernmental Relations, an independent agency committed to examining issues bearing on the proper role of differing levels of government in the federal system. See, e.g., "Regulatory Federalism, Policy, Process, Impact and Reform" (Washington, D.C.: ACIR, December 1982).

9. See *NRDC* v. *Gorsuch*, 685 F.2d 718 (D.C. Cir.), which declared the netting of emissions in nonattainment areas under the Clean Air Act to be illegal. Plainly, the framers of EPA's emissions-trading guidelines did not anticipate that the guidelines' application would be constrained in this manner. See also *Scenic Hudson* v. *Marsh*, USDC D.C. Civ. Act. No. 82-3632, December 22, 1982.

10. See Jerry L. Mashaw and Susan Rose-Ackerman, "Federalism and Regulation," in this volume.

11. The Supreme Court recently upheld state efforts in these fields in *Pacific Gas and Electric Company* v. *State Energy Resources Conservation and Development Commission*, 103 S.Ct. 1713 (1983). At one level, though, the goals of regulatory relief and the Reagan administration's efforts to delegate authority are perfectly complementary. When state and local governments have been deputized to carry out the federal government's regulatory responsibilities and the federal rules governing the performance of those duties are made more flexible, the states, in their role as policemen, have been provided real relief.

for many firms than uniformly imposed and enforced federal standards. This might be especially true for firms that sell and perform in national markets.

Finally, there is the issue of resources. Anne Gorsuch, the former administrator of the EPA (the agency with the greatest number of transferrable programs and responsibilities), announced soon after she was appointed that the agency would within the next four years "zero fund" state administrative efforts. Not surprisingly, this raised a furor among those state officials and environmental activists who saw delegation as a simple code for deregulation. The "zero funding" approach, like Ms. Burford's government career, was short-lived. Delegation, then, could not be looked to for significant federal budget relief.

An Overview of Transfer Strategies

The Reagan administration has relied primarily on four strategies to enhance state regulatory authority in health and safety.[12] This section briefly describes these strategies and provides several examples of their use.

The first, and most obvious strategy has been to accelerate the formal delegation of program authority. In many cases delegations proceed in phases, with states moving incrementally to full delegation status. (For example, program delegation under the Occupational Safety and Health Act [OSHA] follows this model.) To date, administration efforts to promote formal delegation have involved relaxing the conditions and standards that state programs must meet to qualify for program responsibility.

A second strategy for enhancing state discretion has been to promulgate generic regulations. Generic regulations authorize states to conduct predetermined permitting and enforcement actions without being subject to the level of federal scrutiny that such actions would otherwise trigger. Examples include EPA's emissions-trading policy and the Army Corps of Engineers' general permit guidelines issued under Section 404 of the Clean Water Act.

A third strategy for enhancing state regulatory authority has been to reduce federal oversight of state regulatory activities. A notable example is OSHA's removal of federal field inspectors in states with certified occupational safety and health programs. Another example is EPA's new approval procedures for "noncontroversial" alterations of state implementation plans under the Clean Air Act.

---

12. The authors do not mean to imply that the administration's approach to the transfer of authority has been consciously designed. Rather, this typology is simply an attempt to categorize a set of ad hoc actions moving in a predetermined direction.

A fourth strategy for transferring responsibility has been to relax federally promulgated program standards. In order to qualify for delegation, a state must have program standards roughly equivalent to those adopted by the federal government. Therefore, relaxing requirements of all sorts can in effect ease eligibility requirements and should increase the states' administrative flexibility. Since federal rules only set a floor on regulatory stringency, states retain the option of maintaining older, more stringent standards. Because changes in specific program standards are motivated by a wide range of concerns, of which enhanced state discretion is only one, this "strategy" may be more conceptually problematic than the others.

The scope of discretion transferred by individual rule changes will, of course, vary depending on the nature of the waived mandate. For example, elimination of simple reporting requirements can have implications far beyond the preparation of a specified report to the kinds of data kept and the kinds of activities monitored.

The impact of relaxing federal standards varies with the timing of federal action. Standards that are altered after state programs are in place and have weathered state legislative or administrative review are likely to have a much slower, trickle-down effect than changes incorporated as state plans are developed.

Accelerating Formal Delegation of Program Authority to the States

In January 1983, a trade journal reported that since Ronald Reagan assumed office—

- The number of states authorized to carry out the Clean Air Act's prevention of significant deterioration program had increased from sixteen to twenty-six;

- Three additional states had assumed full responsibility for permitting under the Clean Water Act's national pollutant discharge elimination system, and six more states had taken on increased permitting roles;

- The Safe Drinking Water Act's underground injection control program had been delegated to the first four states and full delegations to another twenty states were expected in the upcoming months.[13]

---

13. "On Delegation to the States," *The Environmental Forum*, January 1983, p. 9.

In addition, then–EPA Administrator Anne Gorsuch boasted that delegation of the Clean Air Act's new source performance standards program had increased 38 percent nationwide since the Reagan administration took office, that delegation of the national emissions standards for hazardous air pollutants had increased 32 percent nationwide, and that delegated construction grant activities had increased by 48 percent from January 1981 through October 1982.

Aggregated in this manner, these numbers raise a host of questions. First, no baseline data are provided. Second, the numbers fail to differentiate between interim authorizations and final delegations. Third, the numbers fail to account for program maturity.

EPA: The Resource Conservation and Recovery Act

To provide a better understanding of the EPA's efforts to delegate regulatory authority over the course of the past two and one-half years, we have explored the number of jurisdictions granted interim authorization under Phases I and II of the Resource Conservation and Recovery Act (RCRA).

As of May 26, 1983, twenty-seven of the thirty-seven delegations of Phase I program authority had been completed during President Reagan's term in office. EPA staff point out, however, that the agency's first administrator under President Reagan, Anne Gorsuch, did not assume office until May 1981; at that time, almost 60 percent of all Phase I program delegations had been completed. Twelve of those approvals had taken place within a leaderless EPA after Reagan's inauguration. Increased delegations were, then, primarily a function of program maturity and career-staff activity, and less a function of the political preferences or bureaucratic prowess of administration officials. Regulations implementing RCRA were first promulgated in 1980, and delegation of RCRA program authorization was not possible until late fall 1980, when the Carter administration itself embarked on an effort to rapidly transfer responsibility to the states, granting Phase I authorization to nine states within three months. Phase II authorizations have only recently begun. All ten authorizations were approved by Reagan administration officials during or after March 1982.

OSM: The Surface Mining Control and Reclamation Act

Another agency in which the pace of program delegations has quickened is the Office of Surface Mining (OSM). According to documents provided by OSM, twenty-five state programs have been granted either final or conditional approval under the Surface Mining Control and Reclamation Act of

1977. Thirteen of the twenty-five state programs receiving such approval did so during the first two and one-half years of the Reagan administration. However, once again, aggregate program approvals tell only part of the delegation story; the imposition and removal of conditions to program delegation must be considered.

Under the Carter administration, programs receiving both "final" and "conditional" approvals were heavily freighted with conditions that states would have to satisfy to obtain or retain full program authority. Not only has the Reagan administration attached far fewer conditions to its delegations, it has since waived or otherwise removed virtually all the conditions imposed by the Carter administration.

Two developments helped contribute to this accelerated devolution of program authority to the states. First, the administration successfully recast what is termed the "state window rule." In so doing, OSM officials changed the standard for evaluating state programs from one requiring that they be "no less stringent than federal rules" to one requiring that they be "no less effective than federal rules." The U.S. District Court for the District of Columbia upheld the new standard in *Sierra Club* v. *Watt* (D.D.C. No. 81-3157, 18 ERC 1565) on September 17, 1982. This broad performance standard gave OSM review officers greater flexibility when comparing federal and state programs, and has marginally increased total approvals.

Second, the accelerated rate of delegation is partially due to program maturity, as was the case with the Resource Conservation and Recovery Act. Most of the recent delegations have been in the eastern coal-mining states, which had lagged behind their western counterparts.

OSHA: The Occupational Safety and Health Act

OSHA has one of the most complex and rigidly prescribed of all partial preemption programs. Four steps to full, formal delegation are called for by the Occupational Safety and Health Act. First, a state must develop a comprehensive plan that demonstrates that state enforcement of occupational safety and health standards will be "at least as effective" as federal enforcement. Then, during the plan's developmental phase, OSHA may negotiate an "operational status agreement" if the agency believes the state is capable of enforcing minimum designated standards. Under an operational status agreement, federal enforcement actions that duplicate state efforts are suspended.

When OSHA has concluded that the required legal, administrative, and regulatory elements of a state plan are acceptable, the agency may formally certify that the state has the capacity to operate effectively. Such certification is an essential preliminary to final approval. After certification, OSHA continues to monitor a state plan closely for at least a year in order to determine whether the program is being implemented effectively. If the agency so decides and if the program has been in operation for at least three years, OSHA may grant final approval. At that time, federal enforcement authority ceases for those occupational safety and health standards that are included in the state's program—with the caveat that authority to monitor the program always remains an important responsibility of federal OSHA.

To date, no state program has been granted final approval—largely because of judicially imposed requirements labeled "benchmarks" that states must meet to be eligible for delegation of final program responsibility. This does not mean, however, that the Reagan administration has not been effectively accelerating the transfer of regulatory authority to the states. Since the Reagan administration took office, three of fifty-five eligible states and jurisdictions have progressed to the point at which they are on the verge of being granted final program responsibility;[14] eight have been certified, and ten have signed operational status agreements with the agency.

In addition, administration efforts to revise court-designated standards for the delegation of program authority under OSHA may prove to have particularly significant long-term impacts on the transfer of authority among governments. In 1978, the U.S. Court of Appeals for the District of Columbia held in *AFL-CIO* v. *Marshall* (570 F.2d 1030 [D.C. Cir. 1978]) that OSHA was obligated to establish benchmarks for state-plan staffing levels that would reflect "a fully effective enforcement effort." As developed subsequently by OSHA, the new benchmarks would have required, among other things, a sharp increase in state staffing levels, adding an estimated 305 safety personnel and 1,351 health personnel to state program staffs.[15]

Aided by congressional action,[16] the administration has proposed to revise administratively these staffing standards. The revision calls for approval standards to be set at levels in effect prior to the Court of Appeals decision

---

14. The three jurisdictions, the Virgin Islands, Hawaii, and Alaska, have relatively few hazardous manufacturing industries.

15. See Report to the Court, *AFL-CIO* v. *Marshall*, 570 F.2d 1030 (D.C. Cir. 1978), filed April 1980.

16. P.L. 97-257, 1982, states:

   Provided that none of the funds made available under this head for fiscal year 1982 may be obligated or expended to enforce or prescribe, as a condition for initial, continuing, or final approval of State plans under Section 18 of the Occupational Safety and Health Act of 1970, State administrative or enforcement staffing levels which are determined by the Secretary to be equivalent to Federal staffing levels.

in 1978. It also specifies that state staffing levels need be no higher than current federal staffing levels.[17]

Summary

Looking across program areas, it is quite clear that the Reagan administration has accelerated the pace of program delegations of authority. Although in some instances both program maturity and prior efforts by former administrations have been responsible for a significant proportion of new delegations, in others the Reagan administration has played an important role in restructuring the rules under which eligibility determinations are made. OSM's revision of the state window rule and OSHA's efforts to redefine judicially designated benchmarks for determining state program adequacy are good examples of affirmative, structural changes.

One related finding is that despite proclaimed budgetary fears, a large number of states apparently remain interested in assuming further regulatory responsibilities. Thus, at least to date, the lure of regulatory sovereignty has proved stronger than fears of substantial federal budget reduction—at least for a significant number of states.[18]

Promulgating Generic Regulations

A second, even less conspicuous, approach to enhancing state regulatory discretion has been the promulgation of generic regulations. Generic rules typically return to state control a designated group of transactions formerly subject to case-by-case federal review and approval. In order for states to assume this new authority they are usually required to adopt regulations that conform to broad decision principles set out as federal policy. States are then free to set and implement policy subject only to federal oversight and audit responsibilities. This approach offers states, the federal government, and

---

17. See "Revision of Rules Regarding Final Approval of State Plans," 47 F.R. 50307, November 5, 1982.

18. Mississippi may represent a case in point. In 1982, the state accepted delegation of the prevention of significant deterioration, new source performance standards, and airborne hazardous pollutants programs, despite pervasive fears at the state level that federal grant funds were likely to be severely cut. Moreover, fully 60 percent of that state's air program funds are provided by the federal government. Skeptical that future funds were actually going to be cut and eager to gain more autonomy in the administration of its air program, the state continued to pursue further delegations. As one official noted, "We've never liked to see EPA acting directly against Mississippi industry."

regulated industries a means of conserving resources and mitigating uncertainty because proposed actions become subject to one, rather than two, levels of government review.

EPA: Emissions Trading

The administration's most publicized adoption of a generic approach to standard setting has been its emissions-trading statement promulgated in April 1982.[19] Rather than requiring that firms meet uniform emissions limits, emissions trading allows sources to adopt alternative compliance strategies that would achieve the same or greater reductions in polluting emissions than control strategies that would otherwise be required.

EPA's published statement consolidated a number of closely related, market-based, pollution-abatement reforms, including bubbles, offsets, netting, and emissions-reduction banking.[20] The reforms were intended to make extra pollution control profitable "by letting firms trade inexpensive reductions created at one emission point and time for expensive regulatory requirements on other points at different times, under controlled conditions to assure air quality and enforceability."[21]

Prior to the adoption of EPA's trading rules in April 1982, applications for permits that involved emissions trading could only be approved if state implementation plans were revised. The revision triggered a lengthy and often cumbersome process of public notice, comment, and review at both the state and the federal levels. Under the new generic rules, many trades will be exempt from the SIP revision process and direct case-by-case federal review, although they will remain subject to federal audit and possible override. Trades

---

19. 47 F.R. 15076, April 7, 1982.

20. *Bubbles* allow existing sources to find alternative emissions reductions from other sources to meet a given legal requirement. The term *bubble* arises from the figurative notion that many emission points are aggregated under one umbrella, or bubble. Bubbles may exist within a plant or between plants.

Offsets relate to the requirement of the Clean Air Act Amendments of 1977 that new sources of emissions in nonattainment areas more than offset the emissions they will add.

Netting permits a plant in a nonattainment area to expand and to avoid new source review by reducing emissions at other parts of the plant to below certain threshold levels.

Banking describes those procedures that allow sources to store emission-reduction credits in a legally protected manner for future use or sale.

See P. Domenici, "Emissions Trading: The Subtle Heresy," *Environmental Forum*, December 1982; and "Model Emissions Trading Rule: State Generic Bubble and Banking Provisions" (Washington, D.C.: Environmental Law Institute, August 1982).

21. Michael E. Levin, "Getting There: Implementing the 'Bubble' Policy," in Eugene Bardach and Robert A. Kagan eds., *Social Regulation: Strategies for Reform* (San Francisco: Institute for Contemporary Studies, 1982), p. 59.

that do not fall within the general rules may still be approved but they must be submitted to the same complex administrative process that all such trades once had to clear. (As the following section indicates, however, that process has been simplified and expedited for proposed "noncontroversial" amendments to state implementation plans.)

As noted, emissions trading has been one of the few innovative regulatory techniques embraced by the Reagan administration, and in some ways it appears to have been one of the administration's more successful relief initiatives. As of the end of 1982, 179 bubbles had been approved or proposed or were under development. (This total includes bubbles proposed under state generic trading rules and those advanced as SIP amendments in states that had not adopted generic regulations.) At that time EPA had approved generic bubble rules allowing New Jersey, Massachusetts, Connecticut, North Carolina, Oregon, and Pennsylvania to approve large numbers of bubble applications without prior federal review. EPA had also proposed to approve three other generic bubble rules, and twelve other states and localities were actively developing rules.[22] However, that success has been offset by a successful challenge to the extension of EPA's netting policy to sources located within nonattainment areas. The decision by the U.S. Court of Appeals in *NRDC v. Gorsuch* was described at some length in an earlier volume.[23]

The administration's emissions-trading initiatives differ from many other elements of the regulatory relief effort as EPA's efforts represent a continuation of prior federal regulatory policies rather than a departure from them. As Michael Levin notes in his useful history of the bubble, proposals for its development date back to 1972.[24] Over time, a strong constituency formed supporting the innovation—first among EPA's professional staff, then among key government officials outside the agency, and finally, with the development of the generic rule principle, among state and local officials. Years of careful, diligent groundwork by agency career staff, along with the development of

---

22. Memorandum: Emissions Trading—End of the Year Status Report, April 5, 1983, EPA. However, one recent study of Ohio's air program suggests that EPA's emissions-trading rules are likely to have a somewhat limited impact in that state. Ohio officials claimed that most of the trades likely to be proposed would involve particulate emissions and would call for complex, expensive technical analysis before they could be approved. Faced with uncertain future funding, state officials had determined that it would not be wise to commit the resources necessary to start and administer such a program. See Henderson, "Delegation of Environmental Programs to the States."

23. *NRDC* v. *Gorsuch*, 685 F.2d 718 (D.C. Cir. 1982). *cert.* granted by S.Ct. May 31, 1983 (No. 82-1591), George C. Eads and Michael Fix, *Relief or Reform? Reagan's Regulatory Dilemma* (Washington, D.C.: The Urban Institute Press, 1984).

24. Levin, "Getting There."

a workable implementing mechanism, clearly contributed to the success of this element of the president's regulatory federalism campaign.

The Army Corps of Engineers

Another example of the Reagan administration's reliance on generic regulations is the Army Corps of Engineers' issuance of general permits under the Clean Water Act's Section 404. This section prohibits the discharge of any pollutant, including dredged materials or fill, into the waters of the United States. Those "waters" have been defined to include 80 percent of the nation's wetlands. Section 404(e) authorizes the issuance of general permits on a state, regional, or national basis for categories of activity that are "similar in nature" and "will cause only minimal adverse environmental impacts." Thus, activities covered by general permits would typically be monitored only by state or local governments and would be essentially exempt from federal review.[25]

The Corps' most significant initiative in this area was announced on July 22, 1982, when it issued interim final regulations setting out twenty-seven nationwide permits.[26] From 1977 to 1982 only seven such nationwide permits had been issued. The Corps' action had been spurred by recommendations from the President's Task Force on Regulatory Relief directing the agency to provide increased incentives and simplified procedures for state assumption of the 404 program.[27]

Six of the twenty-seven nationwide permits proved to be particularly controversial and were subsequently challenged in court. The two that received the most attention were proposals to exempt from federal review discharges

---

25. The Corps' general permit rules differ somewhat from the generic rules developed about emissions trading. One of the most obvious distinctions is that states must, in effect, volunteer for enhanced responsibilities under emissions-trading policy guidelines. Not only must they volunteer, they must adopt rules consistent with federally determined decision principles that are to guide program implementation. In the absence of those voluntary actions, state decisions remain subject to federal review. Under the Corps' nationwide general permit rules, the federal government in effect declared that it will no longer review a described set of actions, leaving the states to decide whether and how they will regulate those activities. Under the Corps' state general permit authority, federal deference is conditioned on the existence of an adequate state program. The standards a state program would have to meet were called into question by a memorandum from the Corps' deputy director to all division and district engineers, directing them to implement "State Program General Permits" by May 28, 1982, whether or not the state program "measured up to Corps standards in all respects." (Memorandum cited in "Brief for the Plaintiff," *Scenic Hudson Inc.* v. *Marsh*, p. 59.)

26. 47 F.R. 31794, July 22, 1982.

27. See "First Round 404 'Regulatory Reforms' Reduce Federal Protection of Land, Nontributary Wetlands—Other Changes to be Proposed This Fall," *National Journal*, March 6, 1982, p. 410.

into rivers, streams, and wetlands located above headwaters and discharges into isolated water bodies. The implications of these innocent-sounding exemptions were vast. To illustrate, EPA's Region III estimated that under the proposed nationwide permits, the percentage of wetlands in Pennsylvania's Pocono Mountains covered by general permits and outside federal review would increase from 3 percent to 60 percent.[28] Senator John Chafee claimed that the new permits would remove or reduce regulation of dredge and fill activities in 1 to 2 million acres of lakes and adjacent wetlands in Minnesota, Michigan, and Wisconsin alone. To all appearances, the permits eliminated federal enforcement over thousands of acres of wetlands, were clearly deregulatory in purpose, and represented a sharp break from prior federal policy. No wonder they generated substantial controversy.

In an interesting reversal of willing state acceptance of federal generic regulations and reduced federal oversight, Wisconsin, followed by twelve other states, informed the Army Corps of Engineers that it would exercise its prerogative to deny certification for a number of the most controversial general permits. That is, state officials essentially rejected the Corps' attempt to shift its enforcement responsibilities to Wisconsin. As a result the Corps was forced to retain jurisdiction and to review on a case-by-case basis all permits in the two contested critical areas—headwaters and isolated water bodies.

Despite the fact that Wisconsin and the Corps eventually negotiated a mutually satisfactory settlement, the political manipulation of the 404 general permit mechanisms by the Corps appeared to have undermined its devolution objectives. In the wake of the thirteen-state rebellion and the strong legal challenge filed by environmental groups, the Corps retreated from its two most controversial reforms. A notice published in the *Federal Register* (48 F.R. 21468) on May 12, 1983, stated that the agency was willing to reconsider the wisdom of its proposal in each area.

Summary

The use of generic rules to grant states the authority to oversee emissions trading presents an interesting contrast to the approach taken by the Army Corps of Engineers in trying to shed its enforcement responsibilities. Generic rules for emissions trading were developed after extensive consensus building within the federal government, the states, and, to some extent, the community of public interest groups. The rules represented a continuation of federal

---

28. Memorandum from John R. Pomponio to Paul Cahill, September 15, 1982, cited in "Brief for the Plaintiff," *Scenic Hudson Inc.* v. *Marsh*.

policy—indeed they made the proposed reforms workable for many state governments. In contrast, the rules and permits proposed by the Corps represented a clear departure in federal policy. Their promulgation did not have the support of key federal agencies. Both EPA and U.S. Fish and Wildlife Service officials had gone on record objecting to the proposed permits. State support was also clearly lacking, as the state denials of certification indicate, and the public-interest community was plainly angry—ultimately sixteen co-plaintiffs sued the Corps. Viewed from a number of perspectives, the proposed rules resembled an unwanted abandonment of federal responsibility more than a careful legal and political effort to transfer authority to the states and to eliminate troublesome regulatory delays and costs.

The use of generic rules documented in this brief section raises two arguments for continued federal oversight. First, when regulations (such as those relating to emissions trading) require that states perform sophisticated technological permitting and enforcement activities, federal checks should be sustained—at least until state capacity has been demonstrated. Second, exempting predesignated classes of activities from scrutiny by using mechanisms such as generic rules always creates a temptation to misclassify proposed actions. Some federal oversight will remain necessary to ensure that proposals likely to have significant environmental impacts are not being misinterpreted in order to receive relatively unexamined, expedited treatment.

Reducing Federal Oversight of State Regulatory Activities

In contrast to the formal delegation of regulatory authority and the development of generic rules, diminished federal oversight of state actions does not affect the structure of federal-state relations. And, although reduced oversight may enhance state authority, that result is likely to be a secondary or derived effect of federal policy.

Clearly, reduced federal review of state or local actions can take many forms. It can mean an accelerated, relatively uncritical review of submissions prior to program delegation. It can also mean less second-guessing of state-drawn permits, decisions to prosecute or not to prosecute, settlements, fines, staffing patterns, and resource commitments. Indeed, reduced federal review embraces all those occasions when the federal government can choose to abide by or override state environmental decisions.

The Occupational Safety and Health Administration

One of the first actions of the Reagan administration sent a strong signal that the new team intended to reduce federal oversight of state program performance. That action was OSHA's announcement that it was going to withdraw a proposed revocation of Indiana's occupational safety and health plan.[29] The revocation had been proposed by the Carter administration the week before Ronald Reagan's inauguration[30] and marked the culmination of efforts begun by the Indiana and national AFL-CIO in 1977. The union contended that the state had (1) failed to hire a sufficient number of qualified industrial hygienists, (2) failed to identify and cite a substantial number of hazards in the workplace, and (3) proposed penalties for violations that were substantially lower than those imposed by federal OSHA for the same violations.[31]

The revocation was withdrawn for two reasons. First, OSHA officials claimed that the state's health program had improved substantially. A review of OSHA's evaluation report on the Indiana program for the year ending June 1982 showed that the number of hygienists had risen from three to thirteen (including three federal inspectors working under contract). Still, less than 4 percent of the state's total inspections were in the health area, compared with more than 17 percent for federal OSHA. Furthermore, the number of health inspections concluded in fiscal year 1981 was 50 percent lower than the total number conducted in 1977.[32] Second, the administration claimed that the evidence upon which the planned revocation was based had grown stale. Subsequent legal action taken by the union proved futile and the rescission remained in place.

Following its action in Indiana, OSHA proceeded to remove all federal compliance officers from states that had signed operational agreements with the agency. This reduction in federal monitors was accompanied by a halving of federal staff assigned to monitoring state plans. OSHA officials claim that the development of a field information system (the integrated management information system) for state performance data would provide a more effective means of monitoring state programs. As yet it remains unclear whether the

---

29. 46 F.R. 19009, March 27, 1981.
30. 46 F.R. 3919, January 16, 1981.
31. Ibid.
32. U.S. Department of Labor, Occupational Safety and Health Administration, Region V, "Evaluation Report of the Occupational Safety and Health Program of the State of Indiana for the Year Ending June, 1982" (Chicago).

quality of data fed into the system will be continuously evaluated, and thus whether the system will be an effective substitute for field monitoring.

The Office of Surface Mining

The Office of Surface Mining also appears to have adopted a "hands off" approach toward state enforcement. However, as a result of a settlement agreement in *National Wildlife Federation* v. *Watt* (Civil Action No. 82-0320), the agency was forced to reexamine its deference to states when state officials fail to enforce the law. A new OSM policy announced in March 1983 declared that federal inspectors are to issue violation notices to mine operators when states have been notified of a violation's existence and have failed to take appropriate action or show cause within ten days.[33] Internal data developed by OSM underscores the policy's relevance. One recent OSM report found that Kentucky state inspectors were at least three times more likely to write a violation when accompanied by federal inspectors than when acting alone.[34]

EPA: State Implementation Plans

One key to the Reagan administration's approach to federal oversight has been EPA's successful efforts to reduce the backlog of state implementation plans awaiting agency review.[35] From January 1981 through October 1982, pending SIP revisions dropped 97 percent, from 643 to 20.

The SIP revision process requires that all changes in SIPs, no matter how minor or routine, receive both state and federal approval. At each level the revision must satisfy notice and comment rule-making procedures. Moreover, federal approvals typically go through a two-stage process: Proposed revisions are promulgated first as proposed rules and later as final rules.

---

33. 48 F.R. 9199, March 3, 1983.
34. U.S. Department of the Interior, Office of Surface Mining, Lexington Field Office Quarterly Report, July 1, 1982–September 30, 1982.
35. Under Title I of the Clean Air Act, the federal government is charged with issuing "national ambient air quality standards" (NAAQSs) for any widespread air pollutant that "may reasonably be anticipated to endanger public health or welfare." These standards may be primary (to protect public health) or secondary (to safeguard public welfare). Under the act, states are required to submit implementation plans indicating how federal standards will be met. Those plans are "intended to be comprehensive bundles of strategies and commands, containing all the requirements necessary to attain the NAAQSs in that state." State implementation plans (SIPs) are specific to one of the six pollutants for which the EPA has developed national standards. See William Pederson, Jr., "Why the Clean Air Act Works Badly," *Penn Law Review*, vol. 129 (1981), p. 1059.

Encountering massive backlogs upon assuming office, the current administration made three procedural changes in the management of the SIP program.[36] First, minor proposed changes are now permitted to go directly to final federal review. If any comments are received during the mandated review period, then the revisions are rescinded and submitted to the full, two-stage review process. Second, to the extent possible, state and federal review of proposed SIP revisions are to be conducted concurrently rather than consecutively. This practice permits federal officials to "front load" their suggestions and recommendations and is intended to avoid having to return rejected, fully developed plans to the states for further revision, with all the procedural consequences that revision entails. Third, if no comments are received after a proposed SIP revision has been published in the *Federal Register*, then full responsibility for approving the revision is assigned to the appropriate regional office and no review is undertaken at EPA headquarters.

While better management practices are clearly partially responsible for EPA's accelerated reviews, agency staffers also concede that state plans are now given greater deference than they were in the past.[37]

One example of the relatively uncritical deference accorded some proposed SIP revisions emerged in Texas. There, the Monsanto Company proposed a "bubble" for its Texas City and Chocolate Bayou chemical plants that would require a revision of Texas's SIP. (The proposed bubble could not be approved under any state-adopted, generic, emissions-trading rule.) In short, Monsanto's proposal would have allowed the company to reduce emissions controls on eighteen specified chemical storage tanks, thanks to certain offsetting emission-reduction credits to which the company claimed it was entitled. The Texas Air Control Board approved the proposal and EPA indicated that it intended to do the same.[38]

A challenge to the proposed bubble, however, raised serious questions regarding both the plan's merits and the advisability of relaxed EPA oversight. Attorneys for the National Resources Defense Council (NRDC) have contended that in calculating the amount of offsetting credits to which it was entitled, Monsanto (1) overstated by 100 percent the emissions credit due by relying on figures that reflected *potential* rather than *actual* annual emissions of the source responsible for generating emissions credits[39] and (2) improperly

---

36. 47 F.R. 27073, June 23, 1982.
37. In fact, a staffer termed efforts to eliminate the SIP backlog as "shoveling out all the garbage in order to get the system current"—scarcely indicating a systematic analysis of each SIP's merits.
38. 47 F.R. 27071, June 23, 1982.
39. Letter from David Doniger (NRDC) to John Hypola, Region VI, EPA, January 10, 1983, "Re: Alternative Emission Reduction Plan for Monsanto Chemical Intermediates Co."

took credit for emissions from a plant that had been closed in 1980 and was in the process of being torn down.[40]

If NRDC's claims are proved correct, then it could be concluded that, at least in relatively complex areas such as emissions trading, systematic federal scrutiny of locally developed calculations should probably be retained at least until states demonstrate greater technical competence. Indeed, proponents of the bubble concept worry that the potential benefits of emissions trading will be subverted if a series of unexamined, "tainted" trades are brought to public officials' attention before the value of this innovative regulatory strategy has been demonstrated.

Despite the administration's clear interest in relaxing federal oversight, political pressures have occasionally undermined federal deference to state authority. For example, just before the change in leadership at EPA in spring 1983, an agency directive was issued ordering EPA's regional staff to take enforcement actions against sources not in compliance with emissions regulations—even if those sources were operating under local district variances.[41] The policy was put in effect in all states, even those like California, which for years had been administering more stringent regulatory programs than those of the federal government. In California, variances were usually granted only for compelling reasons. Critics of the enforcement efforts contended that they were driven by a simple interest in increasing politically sensitive enforcement numbers—not by an interest in deterring violators in a meaningful way. Furthermore, this willingness to override state and local decisions appeared to breach administration promises for a new, cooperative federalism. However, as one EPA official stated, "When you're bleeding to death politically, state partnerships go by the board."

Summary

Oversight can provide opportunities for important procedural reforms—as the administration's restructuring of the SIP review process indicates. In addition, federal supervision of state regulatory activities is an area that falls securely within the legal bounds of a responsible agency's administrative discretion. However, as demonstrated by the successful challenge to the Office of Surface Mining's deference to state nonenforcment policies, that discretion

---

40. "Preliminary Comments on Proposed Revisions to the Texas State Implementation Plan," 47 F.R. 27071, June 23, 1982, D. Doniger, S. Smith, NRDC, July 13, 1982, p. 9.

41. See California Air Resources Board, *Memorandum to All Air Pollution Control Officers; EPA Enforcement Program in Nonattainment Areas Concerning Stationary Source Not in Compliance as of December 31, 1982* (Sacramento, March 31, 1983).

is not limitless. Further, as EPA's rapid turnabout on air-pollution enforcement suggests, relaxed oversight, perhaps to an even greater extent than other administrative strategies, is vulnerable to shifting political winds.

Relaxing Federal Compliance Standards

The fourth category of administrative action that effectively enhances state regulatory authority is the relaxation, elimination, or modification of federally promulgated program standards. Such efforts enhance state authority in a number of ways. When regulatory standards are reduced or made less stringent, states gain the option of keeping old rules or adopting new, more lenient regulations.

An interesting and straightforward means of delegating enforcement authority through standard setting is the adoption of performance rather than design standards.[42] Perhaps the most publicized and systematic administration effort to switch from design to performance standards has been the Office of Surface Mining's revision of its 1979 regulations implementing the Surface Mining Control and Reclamation Act. Suggestions that the regulations governing the mining industry should endorse performance rather than design standards originated with reports by the Carter administration's Regulatory Council and the National Academy of Science's National Research Council.[43]

Although the proposals did not receive much attention during the final months of the Carter administration, they found a receptive audience within the Office of Surface Mining and at the Task Force for Regulatory Relief after Ronald Reagan's election. The Reagan administration's rationale for relying on performance standards (and their relationship to its regulatory federalism goals) is suggested by the following paragraph from the environmental impact statement analyzing the effect of proposed OSM rule changes:

> The current design regulations tend . . . to create a relatively inflexible national set of regulations. Because the acceptability of State regulations is based on the permanent program regulations, this approach allows the Federal Government to maintain stringent control over State programs. Although this results in facilities and structures that meet national standards,

---

42. Performance standards regulate according to general performance criteria, rather than by detailed specification of the means of compliance. They are often thought to permit more freedom of action for regulated concerns to reduce compliance costs, and to provide more freedom to discover new and more efficient compliance technologies. See U.S. Regulatory Council, *Regulating with Common Sense: A Progress Report on Innovative Regulatory Techniques* (Washington, D.C., October 1980).

43. "Regulatory Striptease—Watt Takes Aim at Surface Mining Regulations," *National Journal*, May 30, 1981, p. 971.

it also results locally in some facilities and structures being underdesigned while others are overdesigned. . . .

The draft final regulations, on the other hand, emphasize performance standards and general goals. The regulations are more adaptable to variations in climate, geology, topography, and other physical conditions. This technique of regulation maximizes State control of the specifics of each State's regulatory program (often referred to as State primacy) at the expense of national uniformity of State regulations.[44]

One potential disadvantage of shifting from design to performance standards is candidly addressed in OSM's environmental impact statement: "This [performance] approach requires greater technical sophistication on the part of State and Federal employees to interpret and apply such regulations on a mine-by-mine basis, and by the public in perceiving if compliance occurs."[45] Critics of the proposed regulations concur, but conclude that enhanced flexibility will inevitably lead to less effective standards for safety and environmental protection. Noting that reliance on performance standards makes compliance determination more difficult, these critics contend that the change will require greater technical expertise and a greater commitment of resources than most state programs can afford. Moreover, they argue that compliance under performance standards is typically measured retrospectively—after improvements have been constructed, when their modification is more expensive and more complicated politically.[46]

The adoption of performance standards may provide regulated entities with an opportunity to adopt more cost-effective design and engineering strategies, and will certainly vest state agencies with increased discretion. However, that discretion is likely to make good-faith state efforts substantially more complicated, for two reasons: First, states may be required to perform detailed engineering analyses in order to determine whether proposed designs will satisfy performance criteria. Second, negotiations between operators and state bureaucrats are likely to grow more frequent and protracted, and continued monitoring of sites to determine compliance with performance standards will become increasingly important. Both raise real cost concerns. High attrition levels at OSM field offices[47] and widespread funding and staffing difficulties within state agencies[48] raise questions about the general institu-

---

44. U.S. Department of the Interior, Office of Surface Mining, "Proposed Revisions to the Permanent Program Regulations Implementing Section 501(b) of the Surface Mining Control and Reclamation Act of 1977," Final Environmental Statement, vol. I, p. S-3, January 1983.
45. Ibid.
46. See Comments Submitted on Behalf of National Wildlife Federation, August 25, 1982, ibid., vol. II, p. 292.
47. See Chapter 7.
48. See, for example, letters from James Harris, director, Office of Surface Mining, to George Nigh, governor of Oklahoma, and John Carlin, governor of Kansas, March 11, 1982, regarding the inadequacies of those states' programs.

tional capacity at all government levels to adopt the kind of sophisticated techniques required to implement performance standards.

Summary

The focus of this paper has been Reagan administration actions which have, with a few exceptions, enhanced state authority and promoted harmonious federal-state relations. That is not to say, however, that intergovernmental relations under the Reagan administration have not been strained on occasion. Despite the rhetoric of the New Federalism campaign, when administration priorities have clashed with state preferences, state interests have often been overridden.

Even for an administration with a strong states rights bias, sorting out appropriate regulatory roles poses complex legal and economic questions. In some instances, federal preemption of a regulatory field will be necessary to conform to constitutionally based prohibitions on state actions burdening interstate commerce. In other instances the scale-economies offered by federal preemption provide industries and their spokesmen with convincing evidence for the adoption of uniform federal standards.

The economies associated with uniform federal regulation became quite clear to the nation's chemical industry in the wake of the Reagan administration's rescission of pending Carter administration regulations setting standards for the labeling of toxic chemicals in the workplace. The administration based the rescission (ironically) on the grounds that the area was more suitable to state than federal regulation. At the time the rules were revoked—February 1981—five states had their own chemical labeling statutes—often referred to as worker or community right-to-know statutes. However, soon after the administration's action, the nation's unions, led by the AFL-CIO, began an intense lobbying campaign at the state level for legislation covering the politically volatile issue. By winter of 1983 fourteen states had enacted statutes whose stringency and scope of coverage varied widely.

In March 1982 the Occupational Safety and Health Administration reentered the fray with new proposed regulations which applied only to manufacturing industries but which appeared to preempt state regulations whose coverage was significantly broader. Neither the states which had enacted their own statutes, nor labor were at all pleased with the rules (which were made final in November 1983) and litigation over the administration's assertion of preemption as well as other aspects of the rules appeared certain.[49]

---

49. See 47 F.R. 12092, March 19, 1982 and 48 F.R. 53280, Nov. 25, 1982.

Another example of Reagan administration willingness to override state preferences resulted from efforts to defuse trucking industry opposition to the administration's bill imposing a 5¢ per gallon tax on gasoline. In order to offset industry opposition, the administration proposed to increase the national standards for width, length, and weight of trucks allowed on interstate highways and to permit trucks to haul two semitrailers.[50] States which refused to comply would be denied federal highway assistance. The new policies went into effect in April 1983 and met with outright state defiance. The governor of Connecticut signed an emergency order directing state police to set up check points along state highways to enforce the state's existing ban on the larger trucks. Almost immediately thereafter New Jersey, Vermont, Massachusetts, Maryland, Georgia, and Virginia pledged that they too would defy the federal edict.

To assume then that the administration's actions equaled its rhetorical commitment to state sovereignty would be incorrect. As the chemical labeling and truck-size rules demonstrate, some political trade-offs and economic objectives would clearly outweigh state interests.

Administration efforts to shift regulatory authority to the states did, however, result in a number of significant regulatory reforms. Among the most notable described in this chapter are EPA's revised SIP review regulations, EPA's generic emissions-trading policy, OSM's recast state window rule, and OSHA's attempts to redefine the benchmarks state programs must meet to qualify for full delegation. Each reform would to some extent trade the safeguard of comparatively intense multiagency review for more efficient, streamlined procedures that vest states with greater decision-making authority.

It should be noted, though, that the Reagan administration inherited a number of the more significant and successful efforts to transfer regulatory authority to the states. In several instances accelerated delegations of regulatory authority were the result of legislatively designed program structure, program maturity, and the efforts of career agency staff. Thus, administration initiatives represented a continuation of, rather than a departure from, prior federal policy and were evolutionary, not revolutionary.

The Reagan administration has in general appeared committed to its efforts to remove the federal government from the critical, interventionist role it had assumed in the past. However, even in the area of sorting out federal and state regulatory rules, the administration has had mixed success in obtaining significant structural reform. Plainly, its legislative agenda has gone unfulfilled; the president's inability to get a revised Clean Air Act restructuring

---

50. 48 F.R. 14844, April 5, 1983.

the complex mix of federal, state, and local roles under the SIP and permit programs being an obvious example. To the extent that substantial changes have been implemented, they have been achieved by means of administrative action—the rapid approval of state SIPs, the promulgation of nationwide wetlands permits, the issuance of general emissions-trading regulations, and the delegation of federal programs to the states. And when these efforts appear to have been inconsistent with the intent of Congress, they have been vulnerable to court challenge. The D.C. Court of Appeals significantly limited the application of EPA's emissions-trading guidelines, and the National Wildlife Federation and the Natural Resources Defense Council have strongly challenged the Army Corps of Engineers' nationwide permits.

Still, in many instances the transfer of program authority to the states by delegation and other mechanisms may prove difficult to undo, and may be among the more lasting regulatory actions of the administration. Without legislative changes, however, substantial room for federal oversight and intervention remains—and delegated authority could, at least in theory, be rescinded by future administrations. Moreover, transferring enforcement authority for existing programs to the states without changing the underlying rules will not dramatically alter the regulated community's legal obligations. Although the probability that noncompliance will be detected may drop somewhat, causing some "bad actors" to recalculate the costs of noncompliance, potential liabilities will basically remain unchanged—not a reliable prescription for changing long-term corporate strategies.

Another key issue, besides the long-term impact of the Reagan administration's regulatory federalism campaign, is the funding of state programs. William Eichbaum, a Maryland environmental official, has written,

> The federal dollar has become an absolutely essential ingredient in the development of state environmental protection efforts. The magnitude of that contribution is especially significant when one considers that over the last decade state funds going into these programs have remained generally the same or even grown smaller on a proportional basis. . . . In effect, the growth in size and associated responsibility of these programs during the past "decade of the environment" has been almost entirely supported by the infusion of new federal dollars. . . . The sad fact is that environmental protection has not been able to compete for state funds and state regulators have been able to assume expanded responsibility only through the availability of federal funds.[51]

Severe cuts in federal funding—particularly those previously proposed by the Reagan administration for state environmental programs—when coupled with reductions in EPA's own budget and competing fiscal pressures at

---

51. William Eichbaum, "State/Federal Relations in Environmental Protection: How Will They Evolve in the 1980's?" *Environmental Law*, Summer 1982, p. 1.

the state level, may not only have chilled future delegations, but may have led to a substantial reduction in aggregate enforcement capacity. In this fiscal climate the administration's zero-funding option could have wreaked havoc on the states' and nation's capability for environmental law enforcement.

However, given the strong political support enjoyed by proponents of environmental protection, the prospects for the zero-funding option appear dim. Even the proposed 20 percent reduction in state grant funds for fiscal year 1983 proved unacceptable to Congress, which reinstated most of the proposed cuts. Moreover, the House of Representatives has recently voted to reinstate federal funding for state environmental programs at pre-Reagan levels.[52] Although it seems unlikely in the current economic environment that there will be generally increased spending for enforcement of health and safety regulations, future losses are likely to be marginal.

Given this political-economic scenario, what is likely to happen with the continued devolution of federal authority to the states? Edward Strohbehn, Jr., has written,

> In sum, for each environmental regulatory program, each state makes a specific, independent decision whether to undertake responsibility for the program, and the decision is essentially independent of its decision with respect to other programs.[53]

A myriad of factors will determine a state's inclination to accept or pursue delegation, just as a myriad of factors will determine the relative success of delegated programs. Factors such as a state's political history, its fiscal health, the economic value of the regulated resource to the state, the nature of the industry that the state regulates and the type of industry that the state would like to attract, the flexibility of the state's judicial and administrative systems, and the responsiveness of the state's federal regional office will all combine to determine the results of enhanced authority at the individual state level.

At this early stage in the Reagan administration's devolution of regulatory authority, it appears that the success of its efforts may have been subverted to some degree by its budgetary rhetoric. A jurisdiction that might have accepted some delegations of authority may, like Ohio, prove reluctant if program administration would impose incremental costs that exceed the state's economic capacity or fall outside its political interests. In addition, if the administration appears to act unilaterally to rid the federal government of

---

52. "House Votes to Restore EPA Funds to 1981 Level," *Washington Post*, June 3, 1983, p. A-1.
53. Edward Strohbehn, Jr., "The Bases for Federal/State Relationships in Environmental Law," 12 ELR 15094, December 1982.

formerly shared regulatory responsibilities without facing up to the real political and economic problems that could result, strong state resistance is likely to ensue—as it did with the Corps' proposed Section 404 changes.

Finally, viewed from the perspective of corporate planners, the transfer of regulatory authority to subnational levels of government may revive the enduring problems associated with trading less stringent regulations for less regulatory uniformity. Firms in a position to benefit from uniform national rules by standardizing service or product lines may lose that advantage if a general trend to Balkanized regulation emerges.

The conventional wisdom holds that states are rushing in to fill the role formerly played by the federal government, but convincing evidence regarding a broad, general trend in this direction has yet to emerge. There are, of course, discrete areas in which states have been particularly active, the most obvious being the handling and disposal of hazardous and toxic substances.[54] For example, the National Agricultural Chemical Association announced in 1982 that state legislatures would consider 1,000 pesticide-related bills in 1983— 400 more than in 1981.[55] But even given the delegation of regulatory authority undertaken by the federal government over the past two years, states in the aggregate have not assumed the activist role that the federal government is thought to have abandoned. Indeed, rather than supplanting federal regulatory authority, many states have mimicked federal regulatory relief efforts.[56] In areas other than hazardous waste and toxic substances, it appears that, in general, corporate fears regarding the emergence of "fifty little EPAs" may have been exaggerated.

---

54. An example is Minnesota's recently enacted state Superfund law, which, among other things, grants private citizens who have suffered health or property damage from wastes the right to sue parties responsible for their losses. The bill also provides for companies to be held strictly liable for damage and injuries resulting from hazardous waste dumping after January 1, 1973. Companies found to have engaged in "abnormally dangerous" dumping can be held liable as far back as 1960. See "At Last a Minnesota Superfund," *Minneapolis Star and Tribune*, May 10, 1983, p. 6-A.

55. "Chemical Industry Fears Pendulum's Swing Back to the 50 States," *National Journal*, November 13, 1982, p. 1927.

56. Telephone interview with Rick Jones, analyst, National Conference of State Legislators, May 15, 1983.

COMMENTS

James K. Hambright

I want to compliment Michael Fix on his well-researched and thoughtful treatise on devolution of federal regulatory authority to the states. I am going to discuss this subject from the perspective of a state air program administrator who finds himself confronted by the Environmental Protection Agency. The EPA historically has handled its relationships with its state and local "partners" very ineptly.

Fix has identified in his paper various cogent reasons for the Reagan administration's program delegation policy. What is needed now is to incorporate some good faith and trust into these efforts. My observation is that Congress does not trust EPA, EPA does not trust the states, the states don't trust EPA, and the environmentalists and industrialists don't trust anyone.

Air quality program administrators know that whatever pragmatic regulation or solution they may propose for an air problem is likely to be viewed unfavorably by the industry involved, by citizen groups, by EPA, and even by the state administration under which they serve. Why should air program administrators favor delegation of a federal program that will put them in even more impossible situations? Couple this delegation with the proposed reduction in program funds (hence, resources) and you have a situation that provides an incentive for early retirement.

Jerry Mashaw and Susan Rose-Ackerman, in another paper in this volume, correctly state that federal and state bureaucrats have equally complex motivations. Bureaucrats with a professional interest in running a high-quality program may oppose devolution because they fear it will result in a lower-quality program that is enforced and administered unequally. For example, does anyone believe that every state is capable of administering the technically complex and, in some respects impossible, federal program to prevent significant deterioration of air quality? I don't believe that even the twenty-six states that now have delegation are capable of administering this program correctly. Currently there may be ten or fifteen states that could do the program correctly. But that doesn't mean there are only ten or fifteen reasonably good state air programs. Rather, I would say that particulate and sulfur dioxide (PSD) requirements need to be simplified. Quite frankly, the low level of economic activity in this country has delayed progress in this area. If many companies were wanting to move into regions falling under PSD requirements, we would be hearing a lot more criticism of those requirements. The low level of industrial activity has muted the issue.

I also agree that dedicated state professionals may chafe at the loss of independent policymaking or enforcement authority and would therefore favor either a purely state-run or a parallel system rather than a mixed incentive-based one. Most professionals would prefer to do their jobs without external intervention. Since current federal law makes this impossible, we strive to make the best of the existing situation.

A review of EPA delegatory efforts is in order here. A paraphrase of Fix's comments on the subject might be that "theoretically delegation of authority preserves to some degree the regulatory sovereignty of the state. Many state officials claim that impractical regulatory discretion was left to the states. A strategy for granting safe enhanced discretion has been the issuance of generic regulations, etc. And finally, looking across program areas one thing becomes quite clear. The Reagan administration has definitely accelerated the pace of program delegation. The administration appears to have been relatively successful in handing over program authority by means of formal delegation of regulatory responsibilities."

If as much emphasis were given to any program area as EPA has given to program delegation, we would normally expect some positive results. If the emphasis on assuming delegation included a less discriminating review of program capability, we would expect more positive results. And if the acceptance of delegation were conditioned in some respects on the federal granting of program funds, we would expect even more positive results. I should think any administrator with the ability to wield such sharp weapons would stand a very good chance of being "relatively successful in handing over program authority."

Let us look a little more closely at emissions trading and generic regulations. To paraphrase Fix again: "While emissions trading originated as far back as 1972, over time a strong constituency formed supporting the innovation—first among EPA professional staff and among key government officials outside of the agency and finally, with the development of a generic rule principle, among state and local officials."

This generalization is questionable. Many states took exception to EPA's first emissions-trading policy. EPA revised the policy and published a proposed rule in April 1982. This second effort was better, but still had problems. Emissions trading provides many opportunities for gamesmanship and, unfortunately, industry is better equipped to play the game than the state and local agencies who are responsible for environmental protection. Yet emissions trading can be effective.

In Pennsylvania we have developed a number of "bubble" applications, but they have all been resource-intensive, technically demanding, and time-consuming. They will also be as resource-intensive to administer as they were to implement. Are state and local agencies to anticipate more of these efforts in an era of declining state and federal resources for generic bubbles?

After some industrial pressure, Pennsylvania recently drafted a generic bubble regulation for sources of particulate matter and sulfur dioxide. The state has had the authority to bubble volatile organic compounds for some time, having developed those regulations after assuring us that this was a practical bubble application that could be readily enforced. We developed a generic bubble to conform as closely as possible to EPA's draft emissions trading policy of April 1982. After the industry sector that had requested the generic regulations reviewed the draft regulation, they asked us to withdraw the draft regulation and to stop our efforts to develop a generic regulation. Confronted with a realistic generic bubble regulation, industry expressed a preference for a revised case-by-case implementation plan to accomplish its aim of modifying the regulations.

Trades involving hydrocarbons and sulfur dioxide are difficult, but practical and enforceable. Trades involving particulates are difficult, frequently impractical and nonquantifiable, and frequently unenforceable. This statement does not mean that particulate trades are completely impossible, but that they must be much more carefully thought out and controlled.

It is always easier to criticize a paper than it is to offer constructive suggestions. I would suggest, however, that based on over twenty-five years' experience in this field, I have several ideas that I believe would help promote the devolution of regulatory authority.

First, EPA has always had a definition of partnership different from that of the states. The states want to be equal partners with EPA and believe that as equal partners they will individually and jointly be more successful in administering federal, state, and local programs.

Second, EPA needs to have a strong advocacy for state and local programs in its central office. The group needs to have the responsibility and the authority to work closely with the state and local agencies to resolve differences between those agencies and EPA in Washington and Research Triangle Park in North Carolina and the regional offices.

Third, state and local agencies need much more direct involvement in EPA policymaking and rule making. This involvement must be at the development stage—not after the concrete has been poured and is beginning to harden. Few agencies want to assume responsibility for rules and regulations that they have had relatively little part in formulating. These three suggestions, if implemented, will go far toward promoting state, local, and federal program relations and would enhance the probability of successful devolution of federal regulatory authority.

COMMENTS

Jeffrey H. Joseph

I will frame my comments around the three goals that are set forth at the beginning of Michael Fix's paper. But first, let me say that I assume I was invited to respond because of my business affiliations. I want to point out exactly what my involvement is with the subject matter. The U.S. Chamber of Commerce, with which I am associated, works on national issues. My experience with the real dynamics of federal and state relationships is somewhat vicarious. I only know what we hear from our national membership of the various kinds of problems that show up. It is from that perspective I am going to respond to Fix's paper.

Fix stated that his first goal was to evaluate Reagan's transfer of regulatory authority to states in the context of the regulatory relief program, which has been one of the four cornerstones of the Reagan promise along with cutting taxes, cutting spending, and cutting regulations to stabilize monetary policy.

The business community is concerned about regulations and about all four of these cornerstones of the Reagan program. In fact, the Chamber of Commerce adopted a platform in 1979 called "Let's Rebuild, America" that named the same four cornerstones as its objectives for the 1980s. Obviously, there is much business (and philosophical) support for cutting regulations. But at the same time we want to cut back on the federal regulations, we also want to make sure that state and local governments handle their responsibilities.

During the regulatory explosion from the late 1960s through the late 1970s, when business was grumbling about the growth of regulations, I am sure that state and local governments were grumbling too about the regulations that affected what they could or couldn't do. State and local government people toss around the same complaints as business people—the federal regulations are expensive, inflexible, inefficient, inconsistent, intrusive, ineffective, and unaccountable.

The Reagan administration has properly focused the debate on the four issues I mentioned and is moving in the right direction in giving back more programs to the states.

In previous years, states were often willing to take over some of the federal programs even if they weren't given the money to do so. But now states are finding themselves more financially squeezed than they have been in a long, long time. State legislatures collectively are looking to raise close to $12 billion this year, whereas they have never asked for more than $6 billion in any previous year. They usually get only about half of what they ask for. This money squeeze implies that their regulatory policies from here on are going to depend on two things: what they have the money to accomplish and what they think the politicians will be rewarded for doing. Politics and money will play major roles from here on.

The second major goal of Fix's paper was to examine some transfer techniques. There are many innovative transfer techniques, some of which have been tried and some that just make sense in terms of clearing out layers of bureaucracy.

Fix's third goal was to address the question of where we go from here. I don't think that improving transfer techniques and taking care of the various procedural things are going to solve the serious problems that remain in the underlying statutes. If the statutes are misconceived at the national level and the states are forced to implement them, either directly or indirectly, a transfer from one end to the other is not going to achieve real reform. The faulty assumption concerning the mechanisms that can be achieved or the cost-benefit ratios that no longer make sense will remain. Revising the Clean Air Act would be a good place for the Reagan administration to begin focusing on statutory reform. Thus far, procedural reforms have taken precedence. Begun in the Ford administration, they picked up force in the Carter administration and picked up even more momentum in the Reagan administration. But the federal-state regulatory nexus cannot be much improved—and will remain expensive, inflexible, inefficient, inconsistent, intrusive, ineffective, and unaccountable—until the underlying statutes themselves are revamped.

CONGRESS AND SOCIAL REGULATION IN THE REAGAN ERA

Christopher H. Foreman, Jr.

This paper examines the prospects for improved congressional management of social regulation. It suggests that a variety of institutional and political realities have impeded the Reagan administration's regulatory relief effort and that such realities are likely to confront any attempt to substantially change the existing regulatory regime. Unlike some recent critiques of the regulatory process that emphasize the economic inefficiency wrought by "political" considerations, this paper portrays such factors as inevitable and even beneficial.

Since this paper aims to set the discussion of regulatory reform (and of the Reagan effort in particular) against the larger background of institutional capabilities, it begins by assessing the tools available to Congress for supervising regulatory bureaucracies and examining some frequent criticisms of congressional oversight. Next, it offers a brief analysis of the fate of the Reagan program in Congress. Since Congress has been unwilling to accede to much of what the administration wants, the paper goes on to ask what kind of action Congress *is* likely to take—and to what effect? Finally, the paper summarizes the general guidance to be derived from the previous discussion. The discussion draws freely upon two decades of scholarship by serious students of public institutions, especially political scientists. Although the Reagan program provides its immediate impetus, this discussion is intended to contribute to the ongoing debate over regulation that is certain to outlive the current administration.

The Limits of Congressional Power

Clearly, Congress must play a vital role in creating and maintaining effective social regulation. But disagreement continues regarding how Congress can and should approach this responsibility. Nearly everyone recognizes that congressional judgment cannot routinely substitute for agency expertise; elected officials (including the president) cannot "micromanage" the national bureaucracy. However, neither the Constitution nor the Congress as a whole offers much help in specifying where and how to draw the line between reasonable and excessive control. Congress's vaunted "power of the purse," a useful tool for agency control, is set forth explicitly in Article One of the Constitution but, otherwise, the Constitution provides little guidance. Legal and historical analysis can establish each branch's constitutionally authorized regulatory powers, but such analyses skirt the hard question of institutional capacity.[1]

Congress itself is uncertain regarding the appropriate scope and mechanisms of congressional control. That ambivalence is reflected in congressional attitudes toward the legislative veto—the controversial device that Congress could rely on to rescind administrative actions before they became effective. Before its recent invalidation by the Supreme Court, the legislative veto enjoyed substantial congressional support, with its proponents claiming that such fine tuning was essential to meaningful agency action.

Others in Congress disagreed. The Senate Government Operations Committee argued that congressional involvement in rule making should "focus . . . on the broad direction of regulatory policy" and recommended that Congress abstain from across-the-board or routine use of the veto mechanism.[2]

Before speculating about what Congress ought to do, it may be helpful to review what it *can* do. This essay's approach to Congress's oversight activities is not limited to congressional information-gathering about implementation of agency policies. Rather, it addresses the full array of mechanisms available to influence policy administration. Such a broad discussion is essential to a realistic and comprehensive assessment of oversight's potential.

We begin with the five areas of administration over which Congress may exercise *some* measure of control. They include power over the following:

1. Personnel, including appointments to an agency's political leadership

2. Agency structure and location within the executive branch

3. Agency appropriations

---

1. For a good example of this kind of analysis, see Morton Rosenberg, "Beyond the Limits of Executive Power: Presidential Control of Agency Rulemaking Under Executive Order 12,291," *Michigan Law Review*, vol. 80 (December 1981), pp. 193–247.

2. U.S. Congress, Senate Committee on Government Operations, *Study on Federal Regulation: Congressional Oversight of Regulatory Agencies—Volume II*, 95th Cong., 1st sess., February 1977, pp. 11 and 122. (Cited hereafter as *Senate Study*.)

4. Agency objectives and tasks

5. Agency and congressional procedures

We will consider the first four areas of control immediately below. Since so much attention has focused upon procedural reform, we will take up some proposals falling into that category in a later section.

Congress influences each of these administrative elements through several means. Congress may legally compel agencies to report to it regularly. One important reporting tool is the public hearing, usually conducted at the subcommittee level. The quality, scope, tone, and intent of such hearings vary widely. Some are routine sessions dealing with noncontroversial items, while others are investigative hearings that can be quite contentious. Some originate in periodic program reauthorization and appropriation, while others result from individual member or staff initiative.

Constituency problems often prompt efforts by individual members to seek redress. Some observers suggest that this informal and largely invisible "casework" function may play a substantial role in oversight.[3] Indeed, some have argued that a kind of "casework mentality" consumes Congress.

Committee reports and informal contacts between congressional and agency staff offer additional nonstatutory methods for congressional oversight. Such reports and contacts are generally accepted as an important means by which Congress may flesh out its intent to a degree not reflected in the statute. Some critics have noted that the reports process is vulnerable to abuse because the biases of subcommittee chairmen or attentive interest groups dominate the text and findings of committee reports.[4] A recent critique of Congress's approach to the problem of sulfur dioxide emissions (i.e., acid rain) suggests that the staff of the House Subcommittee on Health and the Environment deliberately avoided requiring expensive flue-gas-desulfurization (scrubbing) technology in the text of the proposed 1977 amendments to the Clean Air Act. Instead, the requirement was placed in the less visible, but extremely influential, committee report in order to slant the legislative history in favor of mandatory scrubbing.[5]

---

3. John R. Johannes, "Casework as a Technique of Congressional Oversight of the Executive," paper delivered at the 1978 meeting of the American Political Science Association in New York.

4. Michael W. Kirst, *Government Without Passing Laws: Congress' Nonstatutory Techniques for Appropriations Control* (Chapel Hill: University of North Carolina Press, 1969), p. 138. On this point see also Joseph P. Harris, *Congressional Control of Administration* (Washington, D.C.: The Brookings Institution, 1964), p. 214.

5. Bruce A. Ackerman and William T. Hassler, *Clean Coal/Dirty Air* (New Haven: Yale University Press, 1981), pp. 29–30.

Congress's use of each of these five powers is subject to some important limiting conditions. First, each is shared with other actors, principally the president. In the areas of appointments and agency structure, Congress has largely confined itself to ratifying or invalidating White House initiatives. In the case of appointments, this limitation is enforced by the Constitution and subsequent judicial interpretation.[6] Although the Senate must approve many presidential appointments—and can express strong policy preferences during confirmation hearings—it remains powerless to fire agency officials.[7] And while retaining a strong role in executive branch organization, Congress has typically allowed the president to make the first move. Indeed, prior to the 1970s, Congress largely limited its use of the legislative veto to reorganization matters.[8] Likewise, Congress's constitutionally explicit preeminence in tax and spending matters is substantial, but hardly unchallenged. And although Congress can initiate statutory change, presidential leadership is often needed to goad Congress into action. In fact, many observers blame the Ninety-seventh Congress's failure to reform the Clean Air Act partly on the Reagan administration's failure to submit its own proposed legislation.

James Sundquist notes another problem of congressional power: the controls on agency action "are normally applied either *before the fact* or *after the fact*, not *during*—which is usually when they count the most."[9] Even assuming Congress agrees on the need for a specific change in agency behavior, it generally relies on exhortation rather than compulsion—and only before or after an agency takes action. Considerable congressional frustration (and continuing interest in a veto mechanism) stems from the generally blunt nature of the instruments Congress has at its disposal.

Furthermore, important components of regulatory administration may simply lie beyond any political control—shared or not. The public administration literature often cites the difficulty departmental and bureau-level executives face in controlling their subordinates. Administrative implementation routinely takes place out of sight of agency heads in environments that impose

---

6. James Sundquist notes: "The one limit on congressional control over administration that had been enforced by the Supreme Court is the prohibition against the legislators' laying formal claim to the appointive and removal powers that inhere in the executive. In 1974 the Congress tried again to invade that sphere when it established the Federal Elections Commission. Of the six members, two were to be appointed by the speaker of the House and two by the president pro tempore of the Senate. The Supreme Court ruled that provision unconstitutional in *Buckley v. Valeo*, 424 U.S. 1 (1976)." See idem, *The Decline and Resurgence of Congress* (Washington, D.C.: The Brookings Institution, 1982), p. 317.

7. G. Calvin Mackenzie, *The Politics of Presidential Appointments* (New York: Free Press, 1981), ch. 7.

8. Sundquist, *Decline of Congress*, ch. XII.

9. Ibid., p. 316.

their own "situational imperatives"—and at the hands of persons whose behavioral cues derive from peer group and professional norms. Lawmakers cannot possibly know everything so as to be able to intervene accordingly. A recent collection of studies demonstrates the profound impact of professional incentives and training in major areas of regulation including antitrust, environmental and consumer protection, and worker safety.[10] Indeed, some observers express concern that professional norms distort the priorities of the agencies affected by them.[11] In particular, such norms may make agencies reluctant to adopt less stringent or more economically efficient policies.

The congressional posture on agency control differs according to the circumstances of particular cases. Such factors as issue visibility, constituency pressures, and the play of bureaucratic politics can generate varying responses in what appear to be similar situations.

Congress's shifting inclinations regarding agency structure offers perhaps the clearest example of this variability. Between 1966 and 1972, when Congress was very active in social regulation, it frequently consolidated new government functions into single agencies with broad mandates. The effort was designed as a "response to the piecemeal approach that had previously marked much of Federal health and safety action."[12] But Congress gave these new agencies quite varied structures.

To regulate worker health and safety, it created the Occupational Safety and Health Administration (OSHA). OSHA was to be headed by a single administrator and located within an executive branch department, the same structure previously used to set up the National Highway Traffic Safety Administration (NHTSA). However, to regulate general product safety, Congress created a five-member independent agency, the Consumer Product Safety Commission (CPSC). And for environmental protection, Congress approved President Nixon's plan to establish the Environmental Protection Agency (EPA) with a single administrator located in the executive branch (and hence subject to considerable formal presidential control), but outside the confines of any cabinet department.

In evaluating agency structure, members of Congress often expect more from structural reform than it can deliver. While the existing structural hodgepodge understandably strikes many congressmen and quite a few presidents as confusing and wasteful, placing too much faith in the benefits of reorganization is probably naive.

---

10. James Q. Wilson, ed., *The Politics of Regulation* (New York: Basic Books, 1980).
11. K. Robert Keiser, "The New Regulation of Health and Safety," *Political Science Quarterly*, vol. 95 (Fall 1980), p. 486.
12. *Senate Study*, vol. V, p. 314.

Two general lessons can be drawn from the experience with diverse organizational forms. One is that Congress seems more inclined than the executive branch to create independent agencies. Indeed, EPA's recent political problems led to many appeals on Capitol Hill to restructure the agency along these lines.

The other lesson is that tinkering with agency structure tends to direct attention away from questions of policy rationality and effectiveness. Reorganization may have some symbolic payoff or encourage streamlined paper flow. However, it cannot get to the core of agency tasks or values. Nor does it much affect the array of private interests that surround an agency. For example, it is hard to see what a shift in the location or the structure of the CPSC would, by itself, achieve in the way of consumer protection. The agency's mandate would remain expansive and vague and its essential tasks unchanged. The political incentives of firms and interest groups would remain much the same—as would the environment in which policy questions are resolved. Similar considerations limit the usefulness of this strategy in other areas of social regulation as well.

The appropriations process is a far more potent oversight tool than structural change, and it presents several advantages for Congress. First, Congress's budgetary power is constitutionally derived, providing appropriations oversight a special legitimacy. Second, agencies must respond to priorities that have dollar amounts attached to them; the old dictum that "to budget is to govern" is as true in the regulatory arena as for other policy areas. Third, the appropriations process occurs yearly, thus compelling congressional attention on a more or less regular basis. Further, the appropriations committees that play the lead role are, in the opinion of some, more critical of agency claims than the typical authorizing committee, making them more effective overseers.[13] A recent Senate study stated flatly that "the appropriations process is currently the most potent form of congressional oversight," an observation echoed by congressional scholars.[14]

However, agencies are capable of resisting even this powerful oversight mechanism. The relatively small budgets of most regulatory agencies have probably undermined Congress's inclination to examine them carefully. One

---

13. Richard Fenno, *Congressmen in Committees* (Boston: Little, Brown, 1973), pp. 47–51. A considerably less sanguine view of appropriations committees emerges in Paul J. Quirk, *Industry Influence in Federal Regulatory Agencies* (Princeton: Princeton University Press, 1981), chapter 4. Quirk portrays appropriations oversight of the Civil Aeronautics Board as perfunctory and uncritical.

14. *Senate Study*, vol. V, p. 91. The same point is made in Leroy N. Rieselbach, *Congressional Politics* (New York: McGraw-Hill, 1973), p. 299, and in Joseph P. Harris, *Congressional Control of Administration*, pp. 286–87.

cannot, after all, balance the federal budget on the backs of the Federal Trade Commission (FTC) and the CPSC.[15] In addition, the strategy of incremental budgeting—examining only the requested increase in an agency's budget rather than all annual allocations—trades off rare oversight opportunities for a streamlining of the budget process.[16] Finally, Congress must ultimately rely on each agency to monitor spending for its programs. Where an agency falls short, both Congress and the General Accounting Office may be hard-pressed to set matters right. In sum, reliance on the appropriations process to accomplish regulatory oversight is bedeviled by two problems: (1) congressional incentives (or lack thereof) and (2) the inherent scale and complexity of the effort.

Since agency objectives—the fourth area where Congress can exercise control—lie at the hub of regulatory administration, proposals for changing particular statutes have understandably been the subject of considerable disagreement. The most common criticisms of regulatory laws are (1) that Congress's delegations of regulatory authority are unduly broad or vague and (2) that federal regulators are permitted an insensitivity to social costs.

The questions of breadth and vagueness are not easy to settle because agencies need room to maneuver. Broad mandates are understandably worrisome but, in creating an agency, Congress cannot anticipate every contingency that may challenge agency regulators. Statutory vagueness is often condemned as the unwholesome result of congressional indecision—the inability to forge a consensus around explicit, meaningful language. A result of such breadth and imprecision, say some, is diminished accountability, even "runaway bureaucracy." Yet language that is too confining can undermine essential administrative flexibility. Because Congress lacks the resources and the incentive to regularly oversee agency performance, it must delegate responsibilities. The issue remains one of degree.

Prescriptiveness can exacerbate the problem of costs. Congress feared that the environmental regulatory process would be subverted by corporate power or by bureaucratic inertia. The merits of Congress's promulgation of precise and, some claim, unreasonable standards in the Clean Air Act have been repeatedly debated over the past decade.[17] As statutory deadlines were inevitably and repeatedly extended, their legitimacy was undermined. Impracticably stringent standards may encourage regulated firms to assume that

---

15. *Senate Study*, vol. V, p. 42.
16. The standard reference on this point is Aaron Wildavsky, *The Politics of the Budgetary Process* (Boston: Little, Brown, 1964).
17. Alfred A. Marcus, *Promise and Performance: Choosing and Implementing an Environmental Policy* (Westport, Conn.: Greenwood Press, 1980).

an escape hatch will always be provided. It may also lead regulated parties to take a noncooperative posture—making enforcement difficult.[18]

The Delaney Amendment, which compels the Food and Drug Administration to ban substances found carcinogenic in laboratory tests, is frequently cited as an example of legislation that is overly strict and overly specific. Both industry and economists have repeatedly attacked it as being cost-insensitive and unrealistic.

These examples suggest that Congress is quite capable of legislative specificity, but that precision alone does not necessarily lead to better regulations. In fact, they suggest the inherent tension that exists between the goals of accountability and cost-effectiveness. A Congress inclined towards specificity may "overshoot" from the economist's point of view. It may be difficult for Congress to be specific without also being tough. Precision highlights the boundaries of policy coverage, leaving Congress vulnerable to the charge that it has ignored or downgraded interests deserving of inclusion or greater emphasis. In short, critics of statutory vagueness must confront the prospect that clarity may be costly.

Economists also complain that some regulatory statutes serve redistributive goals at the expense of economic efficiency. They charge, for example, that the Clean Air Act has been designed to benefit certain regions of the country that are economically dependent upon coal mining or to slow industry migration from the Northeast and Midwest to the West.[19]

While the frustration of market-oriented economists is understandable, it must not obscure reality. *Most* legislation embodies multiple values. The tax code hardly reflects the sole objective of raising a set amount of revenue, nor is the shape of defense policy dictated only by considerations of military strategy. Both sets of policies are, from a purely economic point of view, "tainted" by distributive or redistributive impulses. Social regulation is no exception. Furthermore, the impact of environmental protection upon local employment patterns, for example, is an entirely legitimate concern of Congress. In any case, it is unrealistic to suppose that such matters will not be addressed by the representatives of affected constituencies.

---

18. Eugene Bardach and Robert A. Kagan, *Going by the Book: The Problem of Regulatory Unreasonableness* (Philadelphia: Temple University Press, 1982), p. 111.

19. Lawrence J. White, *Reforming Regulation: Processes and Problems* (Englewood Cliffs, N.J.: Prentice-Hall, 1981); and Robert W. Crandall, "Has Reagan Dropped the Ball?" *Regulation* 5 (September/October 1981), pp. 15–18. See also Peter Navarro, "The Politics of Air Pollution," *The Public Interest*, no. 59 (Spring 1980), pp. 36–44.

Christopher H. Foreman, Jr.

Congress As Monitor of Agency Performance

Besides the limited nature of Congress's power to influence regulatory administration, one can identify at least three dimensions of congressional oversight that have been repeatedly criticized by scholars, journalists, political activists, and congressmen themselves. They are, in brief, (1) that congressional oversight is fragmented and dispersed, (2) that it is ill-informed, and (3) that it commands insufficient (overly constituent-oriented) attention from members of Congress.[20] These problems are not attributable to constitutional constraints or to the internal dynamics of regulatory agencies. Rather, they arise principally from the technical and complex nature of the subject matter with which Congress must often deal and from the basic stance that members take regarding the oversight task. If valid, these three lines of criticism suggest that considerable responsibility for Congress's problems must rest at its own doorstep. We now move to a discussion of these concerns, with specific reference to regulatory oversight activity undertaken in the House of Representatives during the Ninety-seventh Congress that was elected with Ronald Reagan in November 1980.[21]

Fragmented Oversight

Two frequently repeated truisms are that Congress operates via committees—recall Woodrow Wilson's statement that "Congress in its committee-rooms is Congress at work"—and that committee expertise is essential to institutional effectiveness. David Price has written, "The committee system is a means of bringing expertise and attention to bear on congressional tasks in a more concerted fashion than the free enterprise of scattered members could be expected to accomplish."[22] Yet, committee-based government has also bred frequent claims that insufficient coordination and relatively autonomous "subsystem politics" damage the democratic process.

Congressional scholars agree that the accelerated dispersal of power to committees and subcomittees is the most significant institutional development

---

20. For a single source that discusses all three problems, see *Senate Study*, vol. II, chapter 9. See also Lawrence C. Dodd and Richard L. Schott, *Congress and the Administrative State* (New York: John Wiley and Sons, 1979).

21. The House of Representatives is the focus here due to considerations of space and time. In addition, one might argue that it was considerably more aggressive in oversight during the Ninety-seventh Congress than was the Senate.

22. David E. Price, "Congressional Committees in the Policy Process," in Lawrence C. Dodd and Bruce I. Oppenheimer, eds., *Congress Reconsidered*, 2d ed., (Washington, D.C.: Congressional Quarterly Press, 1981), p. 165.

of recent years.[23] Select committees dominated by reform-minded House Democrats spurred this process during the 1970s. The reforms ultimately adopted included a requirement that the larger committees create a minimum of four subcommittees. In addition, the power of committee chairmen was sharply curtailed by removing their power to select subcommittee chairs and by limiting committee chairmen to one subcommittee chairmanship. The process of committee chair selection was considerably democratized. Along with this power dispersal, the House required committees with more than fifteen members to increase their oversight capacity, generally by establishing separate oversight subcommittees.[24] By the mid-1970s, these changes had produced a substantially more decentralized House with increased subcommittee autonomy.[25]

The rise of subcommittee government has led to enormous frustration both within Congress and among regulators. Many see it as a principal villain in Congress's slow, complicated, and widely criticized response to the energy problem.[26] Jurisdictional overlap provides interested parties with multiple points of access that can be used to retard the legislative process. But, as discussed below, overlap can also offer important oversight benefits. Whether the benefits outweigh the difficulties is an open question.

For example, during the Ninety-seventh Congress, the fragmented subcommittee process led the House of Representatives to respond to the air pollution issue with the following public hearings:[27]

1. Thirty days of hearings devoted almost entirely to the provisions of the Clean Air Act by the Subcommittee on Health and Environment of the House Committee on Energy and Commerce

2. Three days of joint hearings on the Clean Air Act by the Subcommittee on Natural Resources, Agriculture Research, and Environment

---

23. Dodd and Schott, *Congress and the Administrative State*, pp. 112–18.
24. *Senate Study*, vol. II, p. 110.
25. Good short summaries of these changes can be found in Dodd and Schott, *Congress and the Administrative State*, pp. 112–18 and in David E. Price, "The Impact of Reform: The House Commerce Subcommittee on Oversight and Investigations," in Leroy N. Rieselbach, ed., *Legislative Reform: The Policy Impact* (Lexington, Mass.: Lexington Books, 1978), pp. 137–40. See also Roger H. Davidson and Walter J. Oleszak, *Congress Against Itself* (Bloomington: Indiana University Press, 1977).
26. Roger H. Davidson, "Two Avenues of Change: House and Senate Committee Reorganization," in Dodd and Oppenheimer, eds., *Congress Reconsidered*, pp. 120–23.
27. The following list is compiled from committee legislative calendars and includes only public hearings, not closed hearings or mark-up sessions. It omits two days of joint hearings on overall EPA performance that brought together an unusual combination of four subcommittees on July 21 and 22, 1982.

and the Subcommittee on Energy Development and Applications of the House Committee on Science and Technology

3. Two days of joint exploratory hearings on the problem of atmospheric carbon dioxide by the Subcommittee on Natural Resources, Agriculture Research, and Environment and the Subcommittee on Investigations and Oversight of the House Committee on Science and Technology

4. Seven days of EPA authorization hearings looking mainly at agency research and development capacity by the Subcommittee on Natural Resources, Agriculture Research, and Environment of the House Committee on Science and Technology

5. Three days of hearings by the same subcommittee on acid precipitation

6. A one-day hearing on the impact of EPA programs on Connecticut air quality by the Subcommittee on Environment, Energy, and Natural Resources of the House Committee on Government Operations

7. A one-day hearing by the same subcommittee on the public-health dangers of leaded gasoline

8. A one-day hearing on direct combustion of coal by the Subcommittee on Energy Development and Applications of the House Committee on Science and Technology

Obviously, the lead subcommittee on air pollution matters was the Health and Environment Subcommittee of the Committee on Energy and Commerce, chaired by Representative Henry A. Waxman of California. But a substantial number of other subcommittees also demonstrated an active interest in air pollution control. Many more subcommittees (including Senate subcommittees) were active in numerous other environmental matters. Douglas Costle, the former administrator of the Environmental Protection Agency under President Carter, has written of the problems he faced and that his successors must face as they "answer to at least 44 Senate and House committees and subcommittees, each exercising jurisdiction over some piece of the agency."[28]

While some formal collaboration exists among subcommittees, poor coordination is widely acknowledged to be a continuing problem. Indeed, political scientists Lawrence Dodd and Richard Schott argue that power dispersal

---

28. Douglas M. Costle, "A Regulator's Path Isn't a Rose Garden," *New York Times*, April 24, 1983, p. E-21.

"threatens the ability of Congress to conduct serious rational control of administration," leading to what they label an "oversight paradox"—more frequent hearings and greater member activity leading to weakened control. They assert that this results from a decline in congressional bargaining power with the agencies and from overdependence on interest group or agency information and analysis.[29] A Senate Government Operations Committee study stated the problem as follows:

> Committees do have frequent contact with one another. And occasionally, committees do review findings of other committees. They may even hold joint hearings. But there is little active coordination. Rarely is there a division of labor between committees, where one committee indicates to another, "We'll conduct a thorough review of program X and you look at program Y." Still rarer is it for committees to marshal their resources for joint oversight of a single agency or program.[30]

But despite a need for greater coordination, some degree of intercommittee competition is inevitable and even desirable.[31] A committee or subcommittee oversight monopoly could encourage just the sort of intimacy between committee and agency that has been frequently criticized. The dispersal of oversight functions allows "backstopping" of a kind that otherwise would not occur. Indeed, in some instances deliberate overlap might constitute an intelligent approach to policies based on uncertain scientific and technical assumptions, despite the risk of confusion and the resulting demands upon congressional staff and agency bureaucrats.[32]

Committee fragmentation may constitute a more profound burden in lawmaking than in oversight. There is the danger that proposals referred to multiple committees and subcommittees may emerge a confusing and inconsistent mass of proposals.[33]

However, the importance of fragmentation ultimately recedes before other concerns: What kinds of questions get asked at hearings? Do the persons conducting them remain open to the variety of ways that a problem may be approached? Are complex questions of public risk posed in terms of realistic alternatives? Can partisan or narrow aims, at least occasionally, be made to serve broader interests? These are the kinds of tough questions one must ask of an oversight process, and a focus on fragmentation alone may direct attention away from them.

---

29. Dodd and Schott, *Congress and the Administrative State*, pp. 173–84.
30. *Senate Study*, vol. II, p. 95.
31. Ibid., p. 98.
32. For a provocative argument along precisely these lines see Martin Landau, "Redundancy, Rationality, and the Problem of Duplication and Overlap," *Public Administration Review*, vol. 29 (July/August 1969), pp. 346–58.
33. I am indebted to Paul J. Quirk for suggesting this distinction.

Staffing and Information

Besides its fragmentation, another common criticism of congressional oversight is that it is ill-informed. Congress faces two important issues regarding information and its oversight responsibilities. First, is adequate information available upon which to base policy decisions? And second, to what use can Congress put the information it has? Key to both issues is staffing.

Congressional staff grew dramatically in the 1970s. For example, the 1971 *Congressional Staff Directory* lists no separate staff for the Health and Environment Subcommittee of the House Committee on Interstate and Foreign Commerce. The 1981 edition of that volume lists twenty staff persons.[34] During the same period, the staff of the Environment Subcommittee of Interior and Insular Affairs grew from a lone staff consultant to seven members. While not every subcommittee has shown so dramatic an increase—and recent institutional reorganization makes extended comparison a tricky exercise—the general tendency is clear.

The trend has been a mixed blessing. It is clearly defensible as a response to the expanded scope of executive branch activity. When the Ninety-second Congress convened in January 1971, aggressive federal involvement in environmental protection was a recent development. The previous year had witnessed the passage of the first major amendments to the Clean Air Act, the signing of the National Environmental Policy Act (creating—with a little help from the courts—the now-familiar environmental impact statement process), and the creation, by presidential executive order, of EPA. The "energy crisis" of the 1970s lay just ahead. These new responsibilities would clearly require increased congressional capacity to make and monitor policy.

But staff growth has also provoked controversy. Some believe that popular accountability has been jeopardized by the increased legislative role played by unelected staff. One critique portrays legislative aides as "entrepreneurs" who distort the congressional agenda in their search for issues that will enhance their bosses' visibility and advance their own careers.[35] To some limited degree, staffs may be capable of doing things their bosses do not want done. Members of Congress must oversee both personal and committee staff in addition to meeting all their other commitments, so some staff discretion is inevitable. I doubt, however, that a member of Congress would allow a

---

34. By 1981, as a result of reorganization, the parent committee had been redesignated as Energy and Commerce.
35. Michael Malbin, *Unelected Representatives: Congressional Staff and the Future of Representative Government* (New York: Basic Books, 1980).

staff to commit scarce investigative resources, create the opportunity for major newsbreaks, or attend to important corporate or bureaucratic interests without the member's consent and guidance. Any staff person who exhibited such independent behavior would be quickly disciplined, if not dismissed. Furthermore, since all political activity is in some sense strategically self-serving, we must look beyond entrepreneurship to evaluate the merits of the substantive policy choices Congress makes.

A related issue concerns the quality of knowledge Congress brings to the oversight process. Uncertainty plagues all fields of social regulation. Inadequate knowledge regarding the risks associated with various products and industrial processes may be the most vexing difficulty we face in the domestic policy arena. Two brief examples may help illustrate:

The FDA relies upon premarket testing of new drugs, yet such testing is at best an unsure enterprise. As one study notes:

> Testing in humans prior to marketing is limited by the number of patients who can be included in controlled clinical trials within feasible limits of time and cost. Typically a drug will be used in no more than a few thousand patients in clinical trials. This limits the precision with which a drug's efficacy can be evaluated and the frequency of its relatively common side effects can be estimated. And it almost totally undermines the expeditious assessment of side effects that are rare.[36]

Given the massive scope of the regulatory task, it stands to reason that, no matter how great the care taken, problems such as statistically rare (but politically conspicuous) drug side effects are bound to arise. The FDA estimates that between 200,000 and 300,000 over-the-counter drugs are now sold, each subject to agency scrutiny regarding both safety and effectiveness.[37]

Similar problems face EPA under the 1976 Toxic Substances Control Act, which directs the agency to establish the degree of hazard, the magnitude of exposure, and the attendant risks and benefits for chemicals—regulating those that pose an "unreasonable risk" to health or environment. But if, as the legislative history of the statute indicates, one thousand new chemical compounds reach the market each year, the task of evaluating them properly will require enormous energy and ingenuity. Even if EPA continues to follow its 1982 decision to limit recordkeeping and reporting requirements to the

---

36. Paul J. Quirk, "Food and Drug Administration," in Wilson, ed., *The Politics of Regulation*, p. 203.
37. Comptroller General, Report to Congress, "FDA's Approach to Reviewing Over-the-Counter Drugs Is Reasonable But Progress Is Slow," April 26, 1982 (Washington, D.C.: General Accounting Office), p. 1.

250 chemicals judged to pose the greatest risk potential, the agency will still face a considerable regulatory challenge.[38]

The Reagan administration, aware of these difficulties, claims to have adopted a less interventionist approach that emphasizes the careful assessment of available data along with the weighing of costs and benefits.[39] The administration's opponents hotly dispute that claim, however, charging it with not wanting to act and with deferring to corporate interests. Some critics suggest that occasional regulatory overkill is preferable to "allowing situations in which people are not protected because a test showing no hazard was wrong."[40]

Congress's past approach to regulatory risk assessment has been repeatedly attacked as unrealistic. Critics view the Delaney Amendment and similar "no risk" legislation as a politically appealing "straw man unworthy of serious consideration."[41] Some critics suggest that there is no absolutely safe threshold level for many pollutants or toxic substances, asserting that it is economic (if not political) folly to behave as if there were. Society must, according to this view, find more reasonable decision frameworks through which to assess risk and agency performance.[42]

Although it can amass an enormous quantity of data about policies and the challenges they pose, Congress seems to require a strong political impetus to tamper with social regulation. For example, despite strong criticism from both industry and the academic community, there has been little congressional interest in reassessing the Delaney Amendment. During the Ninety-seventh Congress, the various subcommittees of the House Energy and Commerce Committee examined a number of fairly narrow subjects in the food and drug area such as "orphan drugs," infant formula, soft contact lenses, and—in the wake of the Tylenol scare—tamper-resistant packaging for over-the-counter drugs. However, it made no effort to reexamine the basic food and drug law.[43]

This reluctance should not be surprising. It derives partly from the obvious controversy such reassessment would provoke, partly from the permanent status of the Food, Drug and Cosmetic Act that makes routine committee reauthorization unnecessary, and partly from Congress's desire to give needed

---

38. General Accounting Office, "Implementation of Selected Aspects of the Toxic Substances Control Act," December 7, 1982, p. 8.
39. Felicity Barringer, "Chemicals That Cause Cancer Getting 'Benefit of the Doubt,'" *Washington Post*, January 26, 1983, p. A-4.
40. Ibid.
41. Lester Lave, *The Strategy of Social Regulation: Decision Frameworks for Policy* (Washington, D.C.: The Brookings Institution, 1981), p. 13.
42. Ibid., chapter 2, and White, *Reforming Regulation*, esp. chapter 16.
43. U.S. Congress, House of Representatives, Committee on Energy and Commerce, *Legislative Calendar* 97th Cong., 2d sess., 1983.

focus and depth to its oversight efforts. To be sure, the committee's docket was crowded—the Clean Air Act, which is *not* permanently authorized, got plenty of attention. Congress should be capable, however, of arranging its affairs to do rather more than race against expiration deadlines or seize whatever regulatory issue is politically opportune at a given moment. Not surprisingly, the most recent statutory actions in the drug field came when Congress (1) passed the Orphan Drug Act to facilitate the development of drugs for rare diseases and conditions and (2) extended the prohibition on actions by the Secretary of Health and Human Services relating to saccharin, the popular sugar substitute that the FDA had moved to ban on the basis of the Delaney Amendment.[44]

Political Incentives

We turn now to a third major criticism of congressional oversight—that it commands insufficient attention from members of Congress. As the branch of the federal government arguably most sensitive to electoral concerns and the play of group interests, Congress is bound to confront a tough challenge when it acts in highly controversial areas such as social regulation. Major statutory change in the field has been understandably hard to produce.

But why has Congress also tended in the past to shy away from oversight in the narrow and conventional sense contemplated by the Legislative Reorganization Act of 1946? That law reaffirmed a traditional division of labor among legislative (or authorization), appropriations, and investigative committees and mandated that the standing committees of both houses should "exercise *continuous watchfulness* of the execution by the administrative agencies concerned, of any laws, the subject of which is in such committee."[45]

During the 1960s and early 1970s, scholars and journalists tended to point to a single factor that undermined the intent of the 1946 Act: the limited political incentives for congressmen to engage in serious, sustained oversight. Twenty years ago, Seymour Scher studied committee oversight of seven independent regulatory commissions between 1938 and 1961. He found a general congressional distaste for oversight except when members could obtain a direct political advantage from scrutinizing agency activity.[46] Subsequent

---

44. The Orphan Drug Act carries the designation P.L. 97-414. The Saccharin Study and Labelling Act Amendment of 1981 is P.L. 97-42.
45. Quoted in *Senate Study*, vol. II, p. 16. Emphasis added.
46. Seymour Scher, "Conditions for Legislative Control," *Journal of Politics*, vol. 25 (August 1963), pp. 526–51.

research yielded much the same conclusion for other policy areas.[47] Members of Congress were not interested in oversight because it offered little political payoff; they were far more attracted to the visibility provided by enacting new programs. One scholar, describing a key House subcommittee with regulatory oversight responsibilities, noted that "members describe subcommittee inquiries as often tedious and complex, difficult for them and the public to muster much interest in. Legislative work is seen as more tangible, more understandable, and hence likely to crowd out oversight responsibilities."[48]

Whatever the situation may have been in the 1960s, oversight is far more appealing today. Joel Aberbach has speculated that this may be, in part, a legacy of Vietnam and Watergate and disillusionment with the social programs of the 1960s.[49] Indeed, the proliferation of oversight subcommittees may reflect its enhanced appeal. Today, with the Reagan administration's efforts to radically recast the role of social regulation, oversight has come to command great congressional interest.

Some would still argue that casework, the servicing of constituent requests, is more tangible and politically rewarding than oversight. Such activity provides a direct political payoff to individual members when their intervention produces benefits for a particular individual or group. Morris Fiorina has argued that Congress is perversely dependent upon public frustration with bureaucracy. Casework and "pork-barrel" programs, says Fiorina, allow congressmen to claim credit among voters for problems Congress itself has largely created.[50]

Some commentators see a disturbing tendency for Congress to manufacture policy crises and, in so doing, make it more difficult to forge a consensus on reasonable, realistic policies than would otherwise be the case. One can, however, defend such activism as a legitimate means of updating the national policy agenda and safeguarding programs such as the Clean Air Act about which the public cares deeply.

---

47. Morris S. Ogul, *Congress Oversees the Bureaucracy* (Pittsburgh: University of Pittsburgh Press, 1976). See also Morris P. Fiorina, "Congressional Control of the Bureaucracy: A Mismatch of Incentives and Capabilities," in Dodd and Oppenheimer, *Congress Reconsidered*, pp. 332–48, and Donald Lambro, "Congressional Oversights," *Policy Review*, vol. 16 (Spring 1981), pp. 115–28. For speculation that political incentives operate similarly in the appropriations realm, see Ira Sharkansky, "An Appropriations Committee and Its Client Agencies: A Comparative Study of Supervision and Control," *American Political Science Review*, vol. 59 (1965), p. 627.
48. David E. Price, "The Impact of Reform . . ." in Rieselbach, ed., *Legislative Reform*, p. 141.
49. Joel D. Aberbach, "Changes in Congressional Oversight," *American Behavioral Scientist*, vol. 22 (May/June 1979), p. 512.
50. Morris P. Fiorina, *Congress: Keystone of the Washington Establishment* (New Haven: Yale University Press, 1977).

Congress And Reagan's Regulatory Relief Program

The Reagan administration, following a succession of White House initiatives dating back to the Nixon presidency, has attempted to provide regulatory relief in part through review procedures administered by the Office of Management and Budget.[51] Although many observers applaud these efforts for encouraging agencies to deal seriously with hard questions of uncertainty and cost, others question the underlying political intent and ultimate effectiveness of OMB's review procedures. Many critics, noting that businesses have been the most ardent supporters of regulatory relief, have suggested that the White House program is a mere payoff to corporations. This would, of course, undermine the program's ostensible goal of developing regulations with greater economic rationality.[52] Other observers have questioned the validity of indicators used by the White House to claim success in the battle against excessive regulation. They question, for example, whether a decline in the number of pages in the *Federal Register* constitutes an appropriate measure of White House performance in providing regulatory relief.[53]

Reagan's regulatory relief program has gotten a mixed reception on Capitol Hill. To a considerable extent, the support and the opposition it has generated have taken on the partisan and ideological dimensions one would anticipate. Conservative House Republicans have generally encouraged the administration's efforts, even urging that sterner measures be taken.[54] The response from Democrats and moderate Republicans has run the gamut from bemused skepticism to outright hostility.

To date, the Reagan administration has been unable to build a congressional consensus for its policies in social regulation. The administration's most notable successes came early and were in areas where Congress could be expected to show deference: OMB's review powers and appointments to

---

51. For a review of these efforts in successive administrations, see George C. Eads and Michael Fix, "Regulatory Policy," in John L. Palmer and Isabel V. Sawhill, eds., *The Reagan Experiment: An Examination of Economic and Social Policies Under the Reagan Administration* (Washington, D.C.: The Urban Institute Press, 1982), pp. 129–53.

52. Ibid. See also George Eads, "Harnessing Regulation: The Evolving Role of White House Oversight," *Regulation*, vol. 5 (May/June 1981), pp. 19–26.

53. The vice-president's press office issued a fact sheet at the end of 1981 that emphasized the quantity of regulations reviewed and the shrinking number of pages in the *Federal Register* along with cost savings as measures of improvement. The fact sheet noted, among other things, that "the number of *Federal Register* pages has fallen by one-third during the first ten months of the Reagan Administration compared to the same period in 1980."

54. Thomas W. Lippman, "GOP Panel Urges Congress to Sweep Regulations Out," *Washington Post*, January 18, 1983, pp. C-1, C-8.

agency leadership.[55] President Reagan had little trouble installing his own team at the regulatory agencies. Most of his agency heads were firmly committed to redirecting their agencies and their authorizing statutes. With their assistance, the administration obtained substantial agency budget cuts, slowed or rescinded proposed and pending rules, and introduced a more voluntary enforcement approach.

But Congress has been unyielding on certain items. Clearly, major statutory change is the most significant of these, but there have been other areas of resistance. When FTC Chairman James Miller proposed to close some of his agency's regional offices, Congress declined to go along.[56] Administration proposals for the abolition of the Consumer Product Safety Commission (or its reconstitution within an executive department) drew little support.[57] Any change in that agency's status seems more likely to emerge from Congress's concern over its recently limited legislative veto powers than from White House efforts.[58]

Whether the subject has been clean air, toxic waste disposal, worker safety and health, or consumer protection, many in Congress (especially House Democrats) have perceived the Reagan initiatives as overly probusiness. So pervasive is this belief that it has conditioned Congress's efforts in both oversight and lawmaking, choking off support for the president's legislative objectives even though Congress has proven unable to advance reform packages of its own.

It appears that the Reagan administration did not push very hard for the legislation it wanted. When its proposed revisions of the Clean Air Act found their way prematurely into the hands of antagonistic members of Congress, the administration simply backed down, offering only a set of broad statements of principle.[59] Nor, apparently, did FTC Chairman Miller receive much White House help in his bid to limit agency discretion in advertising regulation. The president's regulatory relief campaign has followed an administrative, rather

---

55. Congress was not utterly unconcerned with the OMB procedures. Indeed, the legality, constitutionality, and analytical approach of the OMB process was sharply challenged by members of an important oversight subcommittee chaired by Congressman John Dingell. See U.S. Congress, House of Representatives, Subcommittee on Oversight and Investigations of the House Committee on Energy and Commerce, *Role of OMB in Regulation*, 97th Cong., 1st sess., 1981.
56. Mark Potts, "4 FTC Commissioners In Dispute Over Staff, Delegation of Powers," *Washington Post*, March 3, 1983, p. A-13.
57. Merrill Brown, "Reagan Wants to Ax Product Safety Agency," *Washington Post*, May 10, 1981, p. A-4.
58. Molly Sinclair, "Inside: The Consumer Product Safety Commission," *Washington Post*, July 4, 1983, p. A-13.
59. Joanne Omang, "EPA Revision of Clean Air Act Leaves a 'Shell,' Waxman Says," *Washington Post*, June 20, 1981, p. A-3.

than a legislative strategy—perhaps because other matters took precedence in its dealings with Congress. By mid-1983, according to some accounts, a bipartisan erosion of support for the Reagan program was firmly underway in both houses.[60]

Prospects And Proposals for Procedural Reform

Earlier, we listed five areas of administration over which Congress may exercise some measure of control. We discussed four of the areas in some detail, but put off our discussion of the fifth: Congress's power over agency and congressional procedures. Let us broach that subject herewith.

A respected administrative law expert recently remarked that Congress, "which has ordinarily been sublimely uninterested in . . . the utterly sexless subject of administrative procedure, has in the past few years acquired a burning passion for the field."[61] This newfound appeal may reflect rising dissatisfaction with regulation's imperfections: excessive stringency and intrusiveness, economic inefficiency, impracticability, and general ineffectiveness. In large measure, these criticisms have been more sophisticated and substantive than mere resentment of government red tape. At the same time, however, the goals of regulatory programs are broadly popular; even its most vociferous critics usually dispute regulation's means rather than its ends.

Two important questions present themselves. First, why has Congress shown a fondness for procedural remedies, but been unable to pass a procedural statute? And second, what are the implications for Congress of the proposals currently being considered that would strengthen its control over rule making?

Congressional involvement in procedural reform exhibits four significant attributes. First, Congress has consistently displayed more interest in sweeping procedural reform than in recasting the standards or methods embedded in individual regulatory statutes. Second, the strategies favored by Congress for reinforcing regulatory accountability rely on strengthening the hand of other institutions (the courts, Congress itself) in agency decision-making pro-

---

60. "A Bipartisan Swing Back to More Regulation," *Business Week*, May 30, 1983, pp. 74–75.
61. Antonin Scalia, "Regulatory Review and Management," *Regulation*, vol. 6 (January/February 1982), pp. 19.

cesses.[62] Third, congressional reform proposals are extremely diverse, each attracting its own special constituency. And, finally, despite many years of debate, the high profile of regulatory matters, and strong moves toward economic deregulation, regulatory reform in Congress is moving very slowly.

At least in part, Congress's preoccupation with procedure over standards reflects the institution's political incentives. The Paperwork Reduction Act of 1980 and the pending regulatory reform legislation do not arouse competing interest groups as strongly as specific proposals on carcinogens or ambient air quality do. A broad procedural statute may affect a range of agencies and programs but is harder to interpret as a politically motivated "attack" on a particular interest. Procedural reform allows Congress to respond to demands that it "do something" about the federal bureaucracy without offending important constituencies.

Congress has responded to the challenges of regulation by emphasizing greater accountability. Hence, one sees an inclination to reform regulation by enhancing Congress's oversight role through such devices as the now-prohibited legislative veto and "sunset" (under which programs would terminate automatically unless Congress voted periodic renewal). Perhaps surprisingly, some have sought to enlist the judiciary—itself a relatively unaccountable mechanism—to assist in the control of agencies. For example, the so-called Bumpers Amendment aims "to reduce (or eliminate) the deference which courts accord to agencies' interpretations of their governing statutes, and to require clear statutory authority for agency actions."[63] The judiciary may find it difficult to live up to the expectations of Bumpers Amendment supporters. With its enhanced power, it could find *itself* blamed with contributing to the problem it was supposed to solve.

Different constituencies, each with its own spokesman, have rallied around each proposal. Georgia Representative Elliott Levitas was the most conspicuous advocate of the legislative veto in the House. Prior to his 1982 defeat, Harrison Schmidt of New Mexico was its major patron in the Senate. Similarly, former Senator Edmund Muskie became strongly identified with the push for a sunset bill during the late 1970s.[64]

Since so much complex, controversial legislation is enacted by giving credit and concessions to the various interests having a stake in it, one could read the "omnibus" character of the pending regulatory reform legislation

---

62. Christopher C. DeMuth, "A Strong Beginning," *Regulation* 6 (January/February 1982), pp. 16–17. See also President's Commission for a National Agenda for the Eighties, *Government and the Regulation of Corporate and Individual Decisions in the Eighties* (Washington, D.C.: Government Printing Office, 1980), chapter 6.
63. Scalia, "Regulatory Review," p. 21.
64. Malbin, *Unelected Representatives*, chapter 4.

as a piling up of constituencies for the various components of the regulatory reform effort. That is, one could conceivably produce a winning coalition by gathering the proponents of cost-benefit analysis, the legislative veto, the Bumpers Amendment, and so on under one statutory roof without giving careful thought to their cumulative effect on regulatory programs or congressional control. Staff familiar with the progress of the regulatory reform legislation on Capitol Hill confirm that an essential feature of the congressional politics of regulatory reform has been precisely this sort of "pile-on" dynamic.

Even in the realm of procedural reform, however, Congress has been slow to produce results, despite instances in each chamber of majority support for various bills.[65] During the Ninety-seventh Congress, the Senate voted 69 to 25 to attach a legislative veto provision to the regulatory reform bill that passed the following day 94 to 0.[66] However, predictions that Congress would finally enact a major rewrite of the Administrative Procedure Act fairly early in the Reagan administration were not borne out.

Despite its discomfort with the legislative veto provision, the administration supported the reform bill, but could not muster sufficient votes for passage. Furthermore, other matters such as the deficit and defense spending took up an enormous amount of the time, energy, and political capital the Reagan administration might have expended on regulatory reform legislation. President Reagan's Executive Order 12291 (which strengthens Office of Management and Budget involvement in rule making and mandates cost-effective decision making in agencies) offered a vehicle for at least some of the policy shifts the administration sought. Perhaps, then, the president had diminished incentive to push as hard as possible for procedural reform legislation.

If the currently debated reform package, or something very much like it, is ultimately adopted, how would these reforms affect Congress's ability to influence the administration? Now that the legislative veto is unavailable, other devices, such as joint resolutions requiring a presidential signature (what FTC Chairman Miller has dubbed a "regulatory veto"), regulatory (or cost-benefit) analysis, sunset, and the regulatory budget, seem especially pertinent in this regard.

In its 1983 decision *Immigration and Naturalization Service* v. *Chadha et al.*, the Supreme Court struck down the legislative veto as an unconsti-

---

65. *Government Regulation: Proposals for Procedural Reform—1979—96th Congress, 1st Session* (Washington, D.C.: American Enterprise Institute for Public Policy Research, October 1979). (Cited hereafter as AEI, *Government Regulation*).

66. William Chapman, "Republican Senate, Rebuffing Reagan, Supports Curb on Federal Regulators," *Washington Post*, March 24, 1982, p. A-4; and Caroline E. Mayer, "Senate Votes Controls on Regulators," *Washington Post*, March 25, 1982, pp. D-1 and D-12.

tutional infringement by Congress upon executive power. To circumvent this objection, proponents of the legislative veto have embraced versions of the joint resolution veto as a substitute. Like the legislative veto, the purpose of the joint resolution veto is to provide Congress with an effective means of enforcing its institutional will on bureaucratic decisions. Under one version, rules would become effective unless Congress or the president vetoed them. An alternative approach would prevent agency rules from becoming effective unless the Congress and the president affirmatively *endorsed* them.

Many see the fundamental issue in stark terms. Congressman Levitas states: "Administrative rules and regulations are laws. We must not forget that fact. The question becomes then: Are we going to let unelected bureaucrats continue to pass laws without effective Congressional control?"[67]

Many of the familiar arguments against the legislative veto will now be turned upon the joint resolution veto. Might it disrupt the operation of carefully crafted rules and increase an already staggering congressional workload?[68] Is it a further invitation to statutory vagueness or an opening for narrow, but well-organized, interests?[69] Like the legislative veto, the joint resolution might be open to the charge that the additional workload would make Congress *itself* less accountable. Forced to rely more than ever upon its staff to keep up with a torrent of agency rule making, the Congress's work might reflect less than ever the considered opinion of elected members.[70]

Of the two versions advocated, the one requiring affirmative joint action before regulations become law is clearly the more problematic. If it were made applicable to many regulatory programs, congressional scrutiny of each regulation would be cursory at best. It would also confer greater political leverage upon interests that are well organized, widely distributed among congressional districts, and intensely committed to blocking a rule. It is one thing for members of Congress tacitly to approve a regulation by inaction. It may be quite another to require them to take a stand openly, for the record. If the more stringent version of the veto prevails, clashes will inevitably develop between and among agencies, the Congress, and the president. Indeed, Congress might be chagrined to discover that the independent regulatory

---

67. Testimony of Congressman Elliott N. Levitas in U.S. Congress, Senate Subcommittee on Administrative Practice and Procedure of the Committee on the Judiciary, *Hearings on Regulatory Reform—Part 2*, 96th Cong., 1st sess., 1979, p. 121.
68. *Senate Study*, vol. II, p. 115.
69. Mark Green and Frances Zwening, "The Legislative Veto is Bad Law," in U.S. Congress, Senate Committee on Governmental Affairs, *Hearings on Regulatory Reform—Part 1*, 96th Cong. 1st sess., 1979, p. 1060.
70. Prepared statement by Antonin Scalia, ibid., pt. 2, p. 149.

commissions, often thought of on Capitol Hill as "arms of Congress," have become considerably more subject to White House control.

Critics concerned about the social costs imposed by regulatory programs have long urged that such programs be subjected to some kind of cost-benefit analysis. Economists have found much regulation to be inefficient and have urged such analysis as at least a partial solution. President Reagan's Executive Order 12291 was a significant step in this direction, although the compliance of some independent regulatory commissions has been purely voluntary. In debate about the regulatory reform legislation, Congress is weighing proposals to extend such cost-benefit analysis to all agencies, including the commissions.

Reservations about cost-benefit analysis abound. Such analysis, some say, may impart to decisions an unwarranted gloss of scientific neutrality. Furthermore, it may understate intangible or long-term benefits resulting from the "dynamic adjustment" of an industry to regulation.[71] The political uses of analysis are widely recognized. A recent GAO study, for example, charged that the Office of Management and Budget, influenced by the administration's desire for regulatory relief, had waived a requirement for regulatory impact analysis (under the executive order).[72]

Congress's role in any wide-ranging scheme of regulatory analysis will, like its use of the joint resolution veto, be vulnerable to political pressures. Congress would be unlikely to abide by the findings of a regulatory analysis in the face of intense political pressure to do otherwise. As a recent assessment of congressional subcommittee dynamics puts it: "Congressmen on a particular subcommittee know whether an agency is making 'appropriate' decisions by the decibel meter: committee members know something is amiss when they hear their constituents clamoring."[73] In sum, then, cost-benefit analysis, while a valuable tool, must not be oversold. It does not show promise as a strategy by which Congress might avoid contentious policy making and difficult value choices.

Sunset bills have been introduced in each of the last several Congresses.[74] The concept's appeal lies in its "action-forcing" character; Congress has to

---

71. Robert Pear, "Fiscal Plans Bear the Telltale Signs of Cost-Benefit Analysis," *New York Times*, February 14, 1982, p. E-2. A critique of cost-benefit analysis is contained in Aaron Wildavsky, "The Political Economy of Efficiency: Cost-Benefit Analysis, Systems Analysis, and Program Budgeting," *Public Administration Review* (December 1966), pp. 292–310.

72. Felicity Barringer, "Study Faults Regulatory Analyses," *Washington Post*, November 5, 1982, p. A-13.

73. Clifford M. Hardin, Kenneth A. Shepsle, and Barry R. Weingast, *Public Policy Excesses: Government by Congressional Subcommittee*, Formal Publication no. 50 (St. Louis: Center for the Study of American Business, Washington University, September 1982), p. 10.

74. The House Government Operations Committee's *Legislative Calendar* lists several bills that embody versions of the sunset concept.

act affirmatively to continue programs. While a legislative veto does not necessarily require any affirmative action and regulatory analysis falls mainly to the agencies, sunset laws give Congress no choice but to make a clear statement of its intent. Or do they? Standing alone, sunset clauses merely extend a program's life without intruding upon priorities or methods. Some sunset proposals have also provided for executive branch reports to Congress that would evaluate programs slated for renewal.[75] This requirement hardly seems significant in light of the burden of reports and testimony Congress already bears. But the most obvious weakness of sunset is that, in the long run, it would not make much substantive difference; most regulatory programs (or, at least, their objectives) enjoy either broad public support or the backing of a vocal constituency that would vigorously protest program termination. Only the most obscure or politically defenseless regulatory program would be vulnerable to shutdown. Furthermore, recent history suggests that Congress can end programs once a consensus for doing so emerges; the Civil Aeronautics Board is slated for elimination in 1985 because economists and consumer advocates succeeded in changing the political environment in which such regulation was evaluated.

An oversight mechanism that has generated considerable enthusiasm in some quarters, but whose enactment does not appear imminent, is the regulatory budget. This device would, in theory, allow Congress to apportion regulatory social costs among agencies in much the same way that it parcels out dollar expenditures from the federal treasury. Thus, in any single year, a regulatory agency could impose costs on businesses and consumers only up to a ceiling designated by Congress.

In theory, such a budget could produce substantial benefits. It would force Congress to be regularly attentive to the total level of social costs imposed by the entire range of regulatory health, safety, environmental, and economic objectives.[76] Hence, a regulatory budget shows promise as a strategy for attacking the dual problems of cost and accountability. It might supplement and help enforce a comprehensive program of regulatory analysis by giving agencies a strong incentive to embrace the least costly means for achieving regulatory goals.[77] In sum, a regulatory budget could give Congress a way

---

75. AEI, *Government Regulation*, p. 38.
76. Christopher C. DeMuth, "The Regulatory Budget," *Regulation* 4 (March/April 1980), p. 37. For details of Senator Lloyd Bentsen's regulatory budget proposal see AEI, *Government Regulation*, pp. 36–37.
77. Lester M. Salamon, "Federal Regulation: A New Arena for Presidential Power," in Hugh Heclo and Lester M. Salamon, eds., *The Illusion of Presidential Government* (Boulder, Colo.: Westview Press, 1981), p. 166.

to coordinate and limit the vast category of private expenditures made pursuant to agency decisions.

Like cost-benefit analysis, the regulatory budget device can be criticized for weighting costs too heavily and being insensitive to long-term benefits. Once in place, it could present substantial difficulties—including the added workload and increased drain on the already thinly stretched resources of congressmen and their staffs. A related, though less evident, problem involves evaluation; even those who applaud the concept of regulatory budgeting acknowledge that precise cost estimates and cost sources would be difficult to obtain.[78] And one would have to find some means to reduce the incentive for agencies to underestimate costs and for businesses to overstate them.[79]

Furthermore, flexibility in a regulatory budget could, if taken too far, create perverse incentives for agencies. If regulators were allowed to borrow against future budget allocations, they could wind up dependent upon "carry-forwards." Were this to happen, regulatory budget allocations might become rather like play money, trivializing and undermining the process.[80]

Finally, one must consider where the regulatory budget process would fit in Congress's structure. Given authorization committee and subcommittee interest in *expanding* the programs they oversee, regulatory budgeting would have to take place elsewhere, perhaps in Appropriations, Budget, or some new committee. Committee decisions would almost certainly have to be exempted from floor amendments in order to protect the integrity of the committee's annual budget product. Thus, such a committee would ideally function much like the House Ways and Means Committee.[81]

Congress And Social Regulation: Institutional Realities

The politics and policy choices that now challenge Congress in social regulation have changed dramatically from what prevailed a dozen years ago. Then, reflecting both mass concern and the commitment of activist elites, Congress seemed anxious to expand the scope and vigor of social regulation, identifying new regulatory targets such as worker safety and health and reviving old programs such as the FTC's consumer protection effort. The debate

---

78. DeMuth, "Regulatory Budget," pp. 38–39.
79. One proposal for tackling this problem under certain circumstances is set forth in Lawrence J. White, "Truth in Regulatory Budgeting," *Regulation* 4 (March/April 1980), pp. 44–46.
80. DeMuth, "Regulatory Budget," p. 42.
81. On Ways and Means Committee characteristics see Fenno, *Congressmen in Committees*.

inside and outside Congress today, however, has little to do with expanding regulation's reach. Instead, the question is how to manage an existing regulatory agenda, elements of which are considered ineffective or irrational.

A number of institutional considerations condition congressional involvement. First, Congress, as the most representative branch of the federal government, is acutely sensitive to constituency demands—a state of affairs that can lead to its immobilization. One way of confronting this problem in the area of social regulation would be to arrange for the most controversial regulatory statutes to come up for reauthorization soon after each new Congress is sworn in. This modest proposal might help avoid the problem of election-year paralysis. But like more sweeping reforms, this proposal would likely meet stiff resistance.

Another factor is the unavoidable (and often productive) phenomenon of policy entrepreneurship. Many members, especially those with a strong activist bent, not only seek identification with an emergent policy area but cast about for new concerns to add to the policy agenda. If, as currently seems the case, that agenda is not substantially expanding, one might expect the entrepreneurial inclination to find expression in "defense of the faith," that is, a public posture of vehement opposition to perceived challenges to a program's domain or methods. Obviously, whether one likes or dislikes this depends upon one's personal policy agenda.

Third, Congress as a whole will generally challenge agency behavior only under very limited circumstances. These include situations where: (1) some narrow interest (but one distributed among many congressional districts, such as used-car dealers or banks) objects aggressively to an agency proposal; (2) some particular decision (such as the FDA's proposed ban on saccharin or the NHTSA's proposed seatbelt-interlock ignition system on new cars) triggers massive public protest; (3) there is strong evidence of indisputably pernicious behavior that directly endangers the public health or safety; or (4) a widely publicized disaster or near-disaster provokes a call for action. These situations can produce fairly prompt consensual intrusions into agency decision processes. Otherwise, Congress's attention to administrative detail is more limited to the far smaller cohort of members with a routine interest in a policy area. It is instructive that while the last four presidencies have experimented with progressively more elaborate regulatory review mechanisms, one Congress after another has failed to pass a variety of oversight schemes.

Fourth, Congress has long been committee-centered; descriptions of the resulting "policy subsystems" are common in the political science literature. The movement toward decentralization during the 1970s has enhanced subcommittee autonomy and, along with it, both the opportunity for entrepreneurship and the difficulty of party leadership. The Speaker of the House, once a virtual monarch, is today a cajoler of largely autonomous subcommittee princes. In the Senate, a body historically less bound by considerations of hierarchy than the House, independent activism is traditional. A conspicuous recent example is Senator Robert Stafford of Vermont, chairman of the Committee on Environment and Public Works, who is anything but a "president's man" on environmental policy, despite a Republican-controlled White House and Senate.

Fifth, the question of incentives aside, the ability of Congress to control regulatory administration is undermined by obvious resource constraints. "The plain but seldom acknowledged fact," wrote Morris Ogul, "is that systematic, all-inclusive oversight is impossible to perform."[82] Selectivity is unavoidable under any conceivable oversight framework. The best one can hope for is a Congress that exercises considerable care in the selection of oversight targets.

Sixth, since no oversight regime or statutory delegation can entirely substitute for self-control on the part of regulators, some delegation of discretion is both inevitable and desirable. Congress's past inclination to overspecificity risks bottlenecks and needless stringency that could be hard to alter in a sensible fashion.

Seventh, economists are unlikely to persuade Congress to address regulatory policy solely on the basis of efficiency. Congress is, and ought to be, concerned with the allocative impact of regulatory policy choices. Therefore, those who oppose having economic regional protection embedded in laws like the Clean Air Act will have to adopt legislative strategies that directly address the inevitable distributive effects without compromising the statute's primary objectives. One might be compelled to tackle such concerns in separate legislation.

---

82. Morris Ogul, "Congressional Oversight: Structure and Incentives," in Dodd and Oppenheimer, *Congress Reconsidered*, p. 318.

COMMENTS

Patrick McLain

As somebody who has engaged in oversight daily for eight and one-half years, I found Christopher Foreman's paper particularly interesting. I agree with many of his observations and, while he points to many apparent weaknesses in the oversight process, I think he would agree with me that, overall, the process works adequately.

In making that observation, we may need to clarify what oversight is—and what it is not. Foreman, in a couple of instances, gives an erroneous impression of what oversight entails. Oversight is not Congress assessing the safety and effectiveness of some 200,000 over-the-counter drugs. Oversight is not Congress assessing the risks of different hazardous substances. Although Foreman mentions different kinds of oversight, my definition of oversight is very simple: Oversight is an examination of whether laws and programs are being implemented and carried out in accordance with congressional intent. Congress's job is not to enforce the law, as a reading of the Constitution makes clear.

I question whether some of the weaknesses that Foreman attributes to the oversight process are weaknesses. He correctly observes that Congress is slow, but is a deliberate and slow Congress necessarily a bad thing? The deliberative nature of the oversight process allows Congress to avoid taking some regrettable actions. If Congress were less deliberative, the omnibus regulatory reform legislation would now be law. Instead, Congress is still deliberating over it.

Another apparent weakness that Foreman discusses in his paper is the many overlapping jurisdictions that exist within Congress. But overlapping jurisdiction brings with it several benefits. First, it elicits more input, more debate, and more perspectives from those who would be affected by a particular congressional action. One of the greatest benefits of overlapping jurisdiction is that it largely disperses the impact of what Foreman calls the crisis of participation. Overlapping jurisdiction insures that no particular congressional committee becomes the captive of a special interest, be it an affected industry or a public interest group.

All in all, the existing oversight process—not only within Congress, but within the entire federal regulatory apparatus allows for a responsible balancing of the crises, as Foreman rightly points out. Those crises are of technology, accountability, and participation. That observation brings us to something that has been of particular interest to Congressman Dingell's committee: the proper role of the Office of Management and Budget in regulatory review. In the context of the different crises, OMB represents the worst of all worlds. First, it is susceptible to the crisis of accountability; OMB does not see itself as accountable to anyone. OMB is also susceptible, through the White House, to the crisis of participation. And, finally, I question OMB's ability to deal with the crisis of technology.

In Foreman's discussion of the various congressional oversight powers, he emphasizes the power of appropriation. This power has had considerably less impact in the current administration than it may have had in years past. If Congress wanted to achieve a desired result by reducing funds, I don't think that many of the agencies or departments would resist. Jim Miller, for instance, is not complaining about reductions in the budget of the Federal Trade Commission. At the same time, increasing an agency's budget will not necessarily get results if that agency is not of a mind to faithfully carry out the law. So I question the current validity of the power of appropriations as a tool for congressional oversight.

One power Foreman did not mention, one which I believe to be an effective tool in getting results, is the power of accountability through exposure. Many agency heads would concede that they fear having their failures exposed in the forum of a congressional hearing and the subsequent media attention. The case of the Environmental Protection Agency provides a graphic example of this. I think that most of the agencies, although they have not been focused on in the manner that EPA has, share that concern.

The corollary to this point is Foreman's statement that members of Congress are not attracted to oversight because it offers little political payoff. Again, that may have been true eight or ten years ago, but since about 1975, oversight has proven attractive to many members of Congress. I don't think it is fair to suggest that members of Congress are only interested in enacting new laws. Many members take great interest in overseeing the implementation of the laws that they have passed.

I will now make some observations about the omnibus regulatory reform legislation. I agree with many of Foreman's observations about the weaknesses of various elements in that legislation, including his notion that those elements represent a piling up of entrepreneurial constituencies. I wish I shared his belief that Elliott Levitas was the only driving force behind the legislative veto. Right now, he is not. I think that legislative veto is the driving force behind the omnibus regulatory reform legislation, but I think unfortunately Mr. Levitas is not the only driving force behind legislative veto.

I also disagree with Foreman's assessment that the failure of the Ninety-seventh Congress to pass the omnibus regulatory reform legislation was a result of White House ambivalence. I don't believe the White House was ambivalent. The administration wanted that legislation, and I saw their efforts to push it through. It was not adopted because enough influential members of Congress began to look at it and they concluded that it represented, not reform, but relief from the regulatory process for those seeking its passage. Somebody said that any legislation that passed the Senate 94 to 0 meant that nobody had read it. I think that is probably a fair assessment.

Although it wasn't mentioned in great detail in Foreman's paper, one area in which Congress can be faulted (although the Oversight Subcommittee of the House Energy and Commerce Committee might be one exception) is that it has done an inadequate job of responding to and overseeing the Reagan administration's regulatory relief program. That is something that Congress ought to be putting more emphasis on.

COMMENTS

Paul J. Quirk

The idea of congressional oversight often appeals to commentators and participants a good deal more than the actual practice of it. In principle, supervision by Congress has seemed an important means to discipline administrators and ensure that congressional intentions are faithfully executed. But the performance of oversight—criticized as episodic, superficial, or excessively partisan and political—has often been found wanting. One can doubt whether either side of this ambivalent attitude is well founded. Some of the complaints seem to result from a failure to define what oversight is expected to accomplish or an absence of defensible criteria for assessing performance. Nor is there an extensive empirical literature describing how members of Congress or committees engaged in oversight actually behave.

More work on congressional oversight, both analytic and empirical, is clearly needed, and the Reagan administration's regulatory relief program is a potentially revealing context for such research. Christopher Foreman's essay is a useful, and in some ways impressive, contribution that serves well the purposes of this volume. It also has some limitations, including some of the usual vagueness about the functions of oversight.

The main virtues of the essay are Foreman's thoroughness in reviewing the literature bearing directly or indirectly on regulatory oversight and his balanced, and often perceptive, commentary. He discusses thoughtfully the advantages and problems of using specific language in regulatory statutes, the strengths and limitations of various techniques available to Congress for controlling the bureaucracy, and the often insurmountable political obstacles encountered by Congress when it attempts to reform social regulation by amending the substantive statutes. Because of the difficulty of substantive amendments, he notes, Congress is biased toward procedural legislation as the main vehicle for regulatory reform; but, as he also shows, all the major procedural proposals are severely limited as to their likely efficacy.

Among his other observations, two in particular are worth noting. Research and commentary on congressional oversight, Foreman points out, often

Paul J. Quirk

have been preoccupied with questions of staffing, procedure, and organization. As a result the actual conduct and effects of oversight have been seriously neglected.[1] Still, with regard to the influence on congressional oversight of the Reagan administration's regulatory policies and political style, the casual evidence is fairly clear. Because the administration, in its rhetoric and some of its actions, has been openly and crudely pro-business, cavalierly dismissing regulatory goals, Congress has been deeply skeptical of the relief program even in areas where many would concede the need for reform.

In certain respects, the paper could have gone further. In discussing each of the several forms of congressional control, the essay does not develop or sustain a well-defined overall argument. He might, for example, have described the circumstances under which each of the methods of control (investigations, appropriations, procedural requirements, and so on) are most effective, or he could perhaps have defined the main consequences of oversight for administrative performance. Even if only suggestive, some such integrating argument would have been useful.

Foreman's treatment of regulatory oversight under Reagan is exceedingly brief. Besides the sheer amount of actual and attempted policy change, the relief program was a revealing occasion for oversight because of the character of the affected issues (some of which were highly salient, technically complex, or both), the wide variation in the quality of the administration's policy formulation and analysis, and the difference in party control between the Senate and House. On what kinds of issues did Congress intervene, and with what effect? Did oversight force the administration to conduct more careful analysis and adopt more discriminating solutions? Or did it, by simplistic rhetoric and sensationalism, tend to prevent even cautious and moderate reforms? How did the Democratic House differ in the volume and character of oversight from the Republican-controlled Senate? Foreman does not examine such questions, although useful answers could result with a modest amount of research. Nevertheless, Foreman's task of reviewing and commenting on the literature, besides being well executed, is ambitious enough, and the limitations cited do not seriously undermine the value of the essay.

In the remainder of my comments, I will make several points that elaborate upon and in some respects modify Foreman's treatment. As a basis for analysis, we must recognize that congressional oversight is neither directly nor primarily a form of decision making. Its distinctive contribution to the political system is to expand the scope of conflict and debate—that is, to facilitate the participation of more groups, broader constituencies, and their

---

1. An important addition to the literature is in progress: Joel D. Aberbach, *Congressional Oversight* (Washington, D.C.: The Brookings Institution, forthcoming).

political representatives on a larger number of administrative issues. When a committee engaged in oversight makes policy demands, the agency still must decide whether to comply; and in important matters, compliance will often depend on the degree of broader support for the committee's position. The actual impact, in other words, depends on the political results, actual or expected, as conflict expands. If not for this tendency, administrative oversight performed by Congress might not serve any useful purpose. The executive branch itself has methods of supervision and review, but will often restrict the scope of conflict if permitted to do so. To recognize this conflict-expanding function affects how one evaluates Congress's organization, procedures, and staffing for oversight and the manner of its performance. Simply put, practices and arrangements that would be unsuitable for decision making, which is to say resolving conflicts, may serve ideally for creating them.

It may not matter, then, if congressional oversight lacks coordination, is unsystematic, or occurs either in rather large or small amounts. The function of expanding conflict has alternative mechanisms and is subject to wide tolerances. Even in the complete absence of legislative oversight, most of the political conflict over administrative policy might still occur, expressing itself through other channels; in fact, most democratic political systems operate without formal oversight. In the United States, administrators must worry about congressional investigations before they happen, and the effects of oversight spread, by anticipation, beyond the programs Congress actually explores.

Moreover, the combination of overlapping jurisdictions, weak coordination, and entrepreneurial orientations among the committees—all well described by Foreman—seems to produce something like a competitive political market that, to a considerable extent, regulates itself. A committee's expectation of political support for an investigation bears some relation, even though imperfect, to the public's desires and interests. Since committees will seek to differentiate their products, central coordination is not needed in order to avoid wasteful duplication. Sometimes one finds several committees or subcommittees attending to the same general subject, but this indicates an extraordinary demand and each committee attempts to offer a distinctive response. This differentiation was apparent in the numerous investigations of the Environmental Protection Agency's performance under Administrator Anne Gorsuch, which Foreman cited as showing lack of coordination. The duplication and rivalry were by no means wasteful. Only because the committees tried to outdo each other in pursuing the investigation did Congress finally insist on having direct access to the pertinent documents.

In one very significant respect, though, congressional oversight is not self-regulating: The committees have little incentive and, as Foreman notes, show little inclination to limit their demands on the time of department and agency officials. Frequent congressional hearings become burdensome to senior officials not because of the time spent testifying, but because of the much greater amount of time they spend preparing to appear. An official is likely to devote several hours to reading and being briefed before each appearance—not only reviewing, but committing to memory, a vast amount of information, much of it marginally related to the topic of the hearing.[2] This enables the official to answer more of the questions that may arise unexpectedly, including those asked by members of Congress to test the official's competence. But it has little to do with the information actually needed to run an agency. Repeatedly forced to go through this exercise, heads of agencies find they lack adequate time to manage and make policy.

Because of this problem, some argue that the volume of congressional oversight should be reduced—for example, by restricting authority for oversight to the full committees. But before contemplating such drastic measures, we should try to reduce the burden of oversight on senior officials by encouraging more of the testimony to be given by subordinates. This, clearly, is more easily said than done. Frequently it is only the appearance of a high-level official that makes a hearing salient to the press and successful for the committee. The officials, needing to maintain good will, cannot often disappoint committees by refusing to appear.

Still, if the problem is indeed serious, there may be a solution short of reducing the number of hearings. Perhaps Congress and the executive branch could negotiate overall limits on the demands to be made of major officials—permitting Congress to allocate the time in its own way. Failing that, the Office of Management and Budget might control appearances unilaterally, much as it now controls the content of testimony. Over the long run, Congress might even be persuaded that an official who attempts to know everything that is going on in an agency, rather than concentrating on key tasks, in all likelihood will not be effective. In the end, no such limited solution may be possible. But if so, two important values—accountability to Congress and effective leadership—will remain in serious conflict.

Finally, I want to amplify Foreman's call for more research on the actual performance of the oversight function and its effects on agency behavior. To what groups, values, and interests does Congress strongly respond in conducting oversight? For example, do members of Congress look out for "diffuse" interests that are widely shared among the general public, or is their focus generally particularistic and narrow? How does oversight affect the

---

2. See Herbert Kaufman, *The Administrative Behavior of Federal Bureau Chiefs* (Washington, D.C.: The Brookings Institution, 1981).

quality of policy deliberations? Does it usually introduce pertinent perspectives and information, or does it more often undermine the chances for balanced decisions? In addressing these questions, one must take care to treat the actual administrative and policy effects of oversight as a separate issue—since however the members of Congress behave, the administrative process will filter their demands. On all the questions, of course, the findings will vary. Ultimately, therefore, we wish to know the frequency of each pattern and the circumstances that produce them. As of now, unfortunately, little serious research on these questions exists.

ABOUT THE AUTHORS

Martin Neil Baily is a senior fellow in the Economic Studies Program at the Brookings Institution. He specializes in labor markets, macroeconomic policy, and productivity. For the past five years, he has been analyzing the reasons for the slow growth of U.S. productivity in the 1970s. He is the author of numerous articles and edited *Workers, Jobs and Inflation* (1982).

Gregory B. Christainsen is associate professor of economics at California State University–Hayward. He is a coauthor of articles on the sources of productivity growth for the *American Economic Review*, the *Natural Resources Journal*, the *Journal of Environmental Economics and Management*, and the *Quarterly Review of Economics and Business*.

Robert W. Crandall is a senior fellow at the Brookings Institution, where he specializes in the economics of regulation, industrial organization, and antitrust policy. His publications include *The Steel Industry in Recurrent Crisis*, *Controlling Industrial Pollution*, and *The Scientific Basis of Health and Safety Regulation* (with L. Lave).

George C. Eads is a professor in the School of Public Affairs at the University of Maryland, College Park, and a consultant to The Urban Institute. Between June 1979 and January 1981, he served as a member of President Carter's Council of Economic Advisers (CEA), where he was especially active in regulatory reform issues and, on behalf of CEA, chaired the Regulatory Analysis Review Group. He has written extensively on regulatory matters and is the author of *The Local Service Airline Experiment* and the coauthor of *Designing Safer Products: Corporate Responses to Products Liability and Product Safety Regulation*.

E. Woodrow Eckard is manager of regulatory economics for the economics staff of General Motors Corporation. Dr. Eckard specializes in economic policy analysis, including government regulation of the auto industry. He is the author of several journal articles on industrial economics and regulation.

Michael Fix is an attorney and a senior research associate at The Urban Institute. His work at the Institute has concentrated on legal and institutional issues relating to regulation. His writings on regulatory issues have been published by, among others, the Joint Economic Committee of the U.S. Congress, the Urban Law Annual, and the American Enterprise Institute. He is currently completing a study of the impact of shifts in federal regulatory requirements on the provision of transportation to the disabled.

Christopher H. Foreman, Jr., is assistant professor of government and politics at the University of Maryland, College Park. His interests include the politics of regulation, government reorganization, and problems of organizational leadership. He has served on the senior staff of the President's Commission for a National Agenda for the Eighties.

James K. Hambright is director of the Commonwealth of Pennsylvania's air quality control program. Mr. Hambright is a past president of the State and Territorial Air Program Administrators and has worked closely with that group and with the Environmental Protection Agency.

David Harrison, Jr., is an associate professor at the John F. Kennedy School of Government at Harvard University. Dr. Harrison specializes in regulation and environmental policy and issues related to the auto industry.

Robert H. Haveman is professor of economics at the University of Wisconsin–Madison, and research associate of the Institute for Research on Poverty. He specializes in public economics and human resources economics. His books include *The Economic Impacts of Tax-Transfer Policy* (with F. Golladay) and *Earnings Capacity, Poverty and Inequality* (with I. Garfinkel).

Jerry J. Jasinowski is executive vice-president and chief economist of the National Association of Manufacturers. He has been assistant secretary for policy at the U.S. Department of Commerce, senior research economist for the Joint Economic Committee of Congress, and assistant professor of economics at the U.S. Air Force Academy.

Jeffery H. Joseph is vice-president of domestic policy for the Chamber of Commerce of the United States. He is also an associate professor at George Washington University's Graduate School of Business Administration, as well as a daily television commentator on business news.

Robert A. Leone is a lecturer in public policy at the Kennedy School of Government, Harvard University. Dr. Leone specializes in the study of industrial policy and business regulation. He has written numerous articles on the competitive effects of government policy, including several on the impact of energy, environmental, and trade policy on the auto industry.

Patrick McLain is counsel to the Subcommittee on Oversight and Investigations of the Committee on Energy and Commerce of the House of Representatives. He is responsible for oversight of the laws, programs and agencies within the jurisdiction of the committee.

Jerry L. Mashaw is William Nelson Cromwell Professor of Law at Yale University, where he specializes in administrative law. He is the author of *Bureaucratic Justice: Managing Social Security Disability Claims*; *Introduction to the American Public Law System* (with Richard Merrill); and numerous journal articles on regulatory and social welfare topics. His most recent book is *Due Process and Its Discontents*.

Paul J. Quirk is an assistant professor of political science at the University of Pennsylvania and staff associate in government studies at The Brookings Institution. Dr. Quirk specializes in administrative behavior, the presidency, and regulatory politics. He has written *Industry Influence in Federal Regulatory Agencies* and is working on a collaborative, book-length study of the politics of deregulation.

Susan Rose-Ackerman is professor of law and political economy at Columbia University and director of Columbia Law School's Center for Law and Economic Studies. A professional economist, Professor Rose-Ackerman is currently researching and teaching on law, economics, and administrative law and public policy. Professor Rose-Ackerman is the author of *Corruption: A Study in Political Economy*, coauthor of *The Uncertain Search for Environ-*

mental Quality, and editor of a forthcoming volume entitled *The Non-Profit Sector: Economic Theory and Public Policy*.

Isabel V. Sawhill is codirector of The Urban Institute's Changing Domestic Priorities project. Dr. Sawhill's areas of research include human resources and economic policy. She has directed several of the Institute's research programs and held a number of government positions, including that of director of the National Commission for Employment Policy.

Murray L. Weidenbaum is Mallinkrodt Distinguished University Professor at Washington University in St. Louis, where he is also director of the Center for the Study of American Business. He has written widely on the burdens of regulation and on prospects for reform. He is also author of *The Future of Business Regulation* and *Business, Government, and the Public*. In 1981-1982, he served as President Reagan's first chairman of the Council of Economic Advisers.

PARTICIPANTS

Martin Neil Baily
The Brookings Institution

David Beam
Advisory Commission on Intergovernmental Relations

Warren Buhler
The Regulatory Eye

Gregory B. Christainsen
Colby College

Timothy Conlan
Advisory Commission on Intergovernmental Relations

Robert W. Crandall
The Brookings Institution

George C. Eads
University of Maryland

E. Woodrow Eckard
General Motors Corporation

Allen Ferguson
Public Interest Economics

Michael Fix
The Urban Institute

Christopher H. Foreman, Jr.
University of Maryland

William Gorham
The Urban Institute

James K. Hambright
Pennsylvania Department of Environmental Resources

David Harrison, Jr.
Harvard University

Robert H. Haveman
University of Wisconsin

Jerry J. Jasinowski
National Association of Manufacturers

Jeffrey H. Joseph
U.S. Chamber of Commerce

Robert A. Leone
Harvard University

Patrick McLain
House Subcommittee on Oversight and Investigations

Jerry L. Mashaw
Yale Law School

Paul J. Quirk
Ohio State University

Robert D. Reischauer
The Urban Institute

Susan Rose-Ackerman
Columbia Law School

Laurence Rosenberg
National Science Foundation

Isabel V. Sawhill
The Urban Institute

Murray L. Weidenbaum
Washington University, St. Louis

HD
3616
U47
R135
1984